SLOUCHING 1
BLUBBERHOUSES

SLOUCHING TOWARDS BLUBBERHOUSES

A (right grand)
Tour de Yorkshireness

Tony Hannan

Scratching Shed Publishing Ltd

For Robyn, Lauren and Louis.

Acknowledgements

This book would not be so factually extensive without the explanatory texts and video commentaries on public display at the various museums, galleries and other venues visited in its pages. My sincere appreciation goes to their unknown writers, historians and producers, unsung trojans all.

I am grateful, too, to everyone who agreed to be interviewed along the way and, of course, the beautiful and beguiling county of Yorkshire itself.

The Author

Tony Hannan is a Yorkshire-born journalist and author. Among his other books are *Being Eddie Waring*, an acclaimed biography of the BBC sport commentator; *Tries and Prejudice*, a co-authored autobiography of England's first muslim rugby international Ikram Butt; and *On Behalf of the Committee*, a history of northern comedy, from music hall to internet.

God's Own Contents

Such was that happy garden-state,
While man there walked without a mate:
After a place so pure and sweet,
What other help could yet be meet!
But 'twas beyond a mortal's share
To wander solitary there:
Two paradises 'twere in one
To live in Paradise alone.

The Garden, Andrew Marvell
(born 1621, East Riding of Yorkshire)

Yawkshire! Yawkshire!

Prologue

DO you know, had Yorkshire been an independent nation it would have won more medals in the 2012 London Olympics than Australia, South Africa and 2016 hosts Brazil?

Yes, of course you do. The buggers just would not stop going on about it, would they?

As the flame in Stratford fluttered its last, a county noted for a certain degree of self-satisfaction had finished 'twelfth in the table', as confirmed on a map especially produced by agency Welcome to Yorkshire. 'Olympic Heroes' was its name; if you're a Lancastrian you doubtless have it pinned to your bedroom wall. Seven golds, two silvers and three bronzes to be precise, with the birthplace of each white-rose athlete and its must-see attractions detailed faithfully.

First to hit the medal trail - for Yorkshire *and* Team GB - was Otley cyclist Lizzie Armitstead who, in the women's road race, took silver. As did rider Nicola Wilson, from Morton-on-Swale, in the team eventing.

Slouching towards Blubberhouses

Huddersfield cyclist Ed Clancy went one better in the men's pursuit. Nicola Adams of Leeds made history as the first ever Olympic gold medallist in women's boxing. The Brownlee brothers of Bramhope - Alistair and Jonathan - crossed the line first and third in the triathlon. North Yorks pair Kat Copeland and Andy Triggs-Hodge took top prizes in the women's lightweight double sculls and coxless fours. And who will ever forget poster-girl Jessica Ennis, Sheffield's then still single-barrelled sweetheart, bringing it all home in the heptathlon on that truly amazing Saturday night in the Olympic stadium? York men's eight rower Tom Ransley and Clancy added to the haul with bronzes, before Hull boxer Luke Campbell completed the treasure trove with gold.

Never mind that - as the spoilsport *Daily Mail* later pointed out - three of those athletes were 'shamelessly poached'. According to the *Mail*, Triggs-Hodge, Copeland and Ransley may have spent: '...varying amounts of time training within Yorkshire's borders, but the county's claims upon them as honorary Tykes conveniently ignores how they were born in Buckinghamshire, Northumberland and Kent.'

And these things matter deeply to the *Daily Mail*, who also reckoned - with tongue in cheek one hopes - that Mo Farah and Bradley Wiggins should have represented Somalia and Belgium respectively, for the very same reason.

London, the *Mail* continued, its dander well and truly up, had delivered twice as many medals as Yorkshire in total. While Glasgow, with but a seventh of Yorkshire's population (60,000, as against four million), had contributed golds in rowing and tennis, silvers in swimming and tennis, and bronzes in hockey. Furthermore: '...the good folk of Yorkshire can't even agree on whether [Alistair] Brownlee belongs to Dewsbury, where he was born, Horsforth, where he grew up, or Bramhope, where he lives. The Royal Mail painted a postbox in Horsforth gold in Brownlee's honour, much to the annoyance of a Bramhope resident who did the same to a postbox in his village only for the Royal Mail to repaint it red.'

No matter. Whatever your method of calculation, in terms of actual gold medals won, Yorkshire still finished top of Team GB's 'County Championship'. And as the wins piled high, so did the levels of hubris.

Lancashire - once you've stripped Greater Manchester and Merseyside out of the equation - finished third.

How to explain these almost nationalistic outbursts of pride? From where do they originate? The UK's biggest county by far until 1974, when its 6,000 square miles were controversially sliced up in boundary changes that still left North Yorkshire as the largest with over 3,212, can it really just be about size? Well, that's what we are here to find out.

The clichés about Yorkshire are ubiquitous and many.

This is God's county, isn't it? Why would anyone want to live anywhere else?

You can always tell a Yorkshireman, but you can't tell him much.

Yorkshirefolk are blunt and bluff. We take as we find and speak our mind, in rhyme if that's at all possible.

A spade is a spade, a shovel a shovel and a doilum a doilum except, of course, when are singing the praises of the broad green acres which swell beneath us chilblained feet.

Primping and preening is frowned upon - 'She's all fur coat and no knickers' - no one likes a show-off. Unless, again, there's a whole countyful of us at it, sharing our magnificence with the rest of the world. Come take a look for thee senn, if tha dun't believe us? We're right friendly an' all.

To the outsider - or 'offcumden' (aye, we have a word for it) - Yorkshire might inspire thoughts of sweeping picture-postcard dales, oily cobbled streets, grumpy old bores, sheep, brass bands, pints of ale (not just any ale - *real* ale), dry stone walls, more sheep, rugby league, beef dripping, dark Satanic mills, dour football teams, whippets, clogs, flat caps, striking miners, cricket, Hovis butties, race riots, *Wuthering Heights*, Ilkley Moor bah't flat cap, *Billy Liar* and puddings flooded with gravy that never quite rise like they did on *Farmhouse Kitchen*. And Yorkshire is - or has been - those things too.

In other words, it's a fascinating, infuriating, amusing, mysterious and even exotic region that simultaneously feels part of the UK and yet one step removed. Yorkshire has contributed much to the cultural and financial wealth of these islands, yet it is also a place where independence campaigns aren't seen as being entirely ridiculous, as they no doubt would be in Oxfordshire, Leicestershire or Sussex. The same might be claimed for Cornwall, Devon and to an extent Cumbria, admittedly, but they don't have Yorkshire's sheer scale and range of influence.

So, let us slouch towards Blubberhouses. Let's explore all of the above and, while we are at it, enjoy a right grand tour of a county that boasts - and boasts is the right word - sights, sounds, people and places like no other. As the world once again turns its eyes to Yorkshire with the capture of the opening stages of the 2014 Tour de France, now is as good a time as any.

As the bard himself, William Shakespeare, might have put it if only he'd come from where he was supposed to: Some are born Yorkshire, some achieve Yorkshire and some - like yourself - have Yorkshireness thrust upon them.

◇ *Friendly warning: this book contains occasional 'industrial' language, used entirely in context*

Tyke (*noun*) :-
1. A small child, especially a cheeky or mischievous one.
2. An unpleasant or coarse man.
3. A dog, especially a mongrel.
4. A person from Yorkshire.

Origin: late Middle English, from Old Norse tík - i.e. 'bitch'.

1. Baa Baa Black Sheep

◇

The Great Yorkshire Show

WELCOME to the Great Yorkshire Show. Not just Yorkshire Show, mind, but 'Great' Yorkshire Show - as organised by the Yorkshire Agricultural Society every year and staged at the Great Yorkshire Showground, Harrogate.

Tuesday, 9 July 2013: hottest day of the summer so far according to BBC *Look North* weatherman, Paul Hudson. Ever-chipper Paul is on site not only to present his forecast live in around four hours' time, but to announce - and pump the hands of - the winners of Yorkshire's Pub of the Year.

The venue for that will be The Pride of Yorkshire, a mock public house in and among several other such displays in a not-so quiet corner of the Show's two hundred and fifty acres that henceforth will forever be Welcome to Yorkshire, official name and slogan of the county's tourism agency.

Those displays include a sandy beach ('A Coast to Boast About'), with donkey rides on William and Bob for the toddlers; an exhibition on a giant wave simulator by the UK's 'top young surf star Josh Braddock'; a Yorkshire Water beach hut '...where you can tell us all about why you love the Yorkshire Coast'; a play-zone in which to test your rugby league skills with Leeds Rhinos; a chocolate making machine; and le world's first Official Grand Départ 2014 merchandise.

On sale: T-shirts (£20), caps (£15), tote bags (£8) and Official Yorkshire Grand Départ Hoodies at a princely £45 each. Also, Official Yorkshire Grand Départ mugs (£10).

The sun beats down.

In The Pride of Yorkshire - '...where you'll learn more about what makes Yorkshire ales better than the rest...' - we await the late arrival of charismatic Welcome to Yorkshire chief executive Gary Verity. When he arrives, dressed smart but casual, open collar, regulation black, yellow and white wraparound cycling sunglasses pushed back, he doesn't so much walk as bound into the place.

'We are so proud to reveal the Yorkshire public's pub of the year,' he says, taking up the microphone. 'We are very proud of all our pubs in Yorkshire. It's one of our great distinctive features. They are very often the hub, the lifeblood and beating heart, particularly of our rural communities. We are blessed in Yorkshire with more independent breweries than anywhere else in the UK.' Two hundred of them, in fact. 'That, as I told our friends from France, makes Yorkshire the European capital of beer and I am pleased to say nobody has debated it with me yet.'

Then, 'without further ado', he passes his audience - a large number of whom, you suspect, are simply sheltering in the shade - to '...Yorkshire's weatherman of choice, the great Paul Hudson of the BBC, who has arranged the weather for us this week. Last year we had the chap from ITV and it rained for three days. So we changed jockeys and have had a much better result. We've also employed Paul for the Tour de France, to make sure the weather for that is perfect too.'

***

IT is a hell of a re-invention. Yorkshire has long admired its own reflection in the mirror, but in the past nobody else much noticed or cared, certainly not to this extent. Nowadays, just about everyone has the county's name on their lips; just about every product manufactured here or associated organisation comes with white rose attached as standard. Yorkshire sells.

And nowhere is that transformation from dour and - on a good day - scenic stereotype to outright sexiness more apparent than at 'England's premier agricultural event'.

Well, it's as sexy as any restricted space with 8,000 sweaty animals in it and a corresponding mountain of sheep, cow, horse and pig dung can be.

Since the demise of the Royal Show in 2009, only the Royal Welsh Show and Royal Highland Show are now bigger. Buckingham Palace can't feel too put out; His Royal Highness The Prince of Wales is the Yorkshire Agricultural Society patron and the Queen herself opened the 150th show in 2008.

This particular opening day, held as ever on the first Tuesday in July, twelve months on from 2012's day two and three washouts owing to rainfall of Noah's ark proportions, is the 155th. Until last year, bad weather had never prevailed, the only other cancellations coming as a result of the First and Second World Wars and an outbreak of foot and mouth in 2001. It's a stubborn old beast, right enough.

Founded in 1837, the GYS's initial brief was '...to hold an annual meeting for the exhibition of farming stock, implements etc, and for the general promotion of agriculture.' With one or two added bells and whistles, it still is.

The first show was held in the Barrack Yard at Fulford, near York, in 1838, before the event hit the road and eventually settled in Harrogate - via such places as Leeds, Northallerton, Hull and Malton - in 1951.

Despite bearing the appellation 'Great' from as early as 1843 - '...by popular acclamation rather than in any official sense...' - early attendance figures were relatively small. In 1842, a reported 6,044 people turned up at York, rising to around 54,000 one hundred years later.

Now into its third century, the Show's mood is once again transformed, not least as a result of the sheer volume of humans, livestock and motor vehicles involved. In 2006, an all-time high attendance of 135,111 was recorded and it hasn't dipped much, if at all, in the meantime.

Those cars - or more accurately the surrounding fields co-opted as temporary car parks - were chief culprit in 2012, deemed unsafe due to the extreme conditions. This year, we are in more danger of melting into sticky parched gravel.

It's quite a panorama, stretched out over the line of trees ahead, as you dip over the brow of the hilltop entrance and negotiate your place on the grass. Every so often a tractor hauling a passenger trailer goes by - sponsored by Land Rover of Ripon - a shuttle for those who lack either the ability or inclination to do the remaining 800 or so metres on foot.

In the distance, one of those giant 'Skyview' wheels glints in the sun, standing sentinel over a hazy vista of tents and ant-like figures as if in some anachronistic mediaeval battlefield painting.

The gates have been open since 7.30am, the day's events commencing around an hour and a half ago with morning prayers in the bandstand on the President's Lawn. The car radio plays Lou Reed's 'Perfect Day' and thus does it appear to be, full of folk who reap just what they sow.

It's glorious out, so I opt for a five-minute stroll under an overhead viaduct and enter the arena through shady trees and one of ten colour-coded gates, in this instance gold. Birds tweet, caw and hoot. Flowers - or are they weeds - release pleasing scents into a warming atmosphere. Raised as a cast-iron townie, I couldn't name any of them if I tried, but there is one unmistakable pong as the appropriately named 'brown gate' cleaves into view.

Let me come clean. Were it not for the fact that I am researching this book, the chances of my being anywhere near the Great Yorkshire Show are remote. If pushed, I could think of lots of ways to spend a nice summer's day, most likely, though not exclusively, involving alcohol. Watching cows flick flies off their arse with their tail for eight hours, or applauding a chap in a bowler hat pinning a rosette on a hen - especially in this heat - would not be among them.

As a child, an aunt and uncle owned a farmyard up Haworth Road. In the field opposite, they kept a horse, Domino, so named because he delivered pizza. Or maybe because he had a white spot on the end of his nose, I don't know. Anyway, giving Domino a sugar lump was torture; if he didn't slaver snotty horse juice all over my flattened palm he might bite off my fingers. They could try it at Guantánamo Bay. And as an adult, contact with any cat or dog will reliably turn my eyeballs into a couple of liquefied lychees.

It's not that I hate animals, far from it. Some of my best friends belong in a zoo. Unless it is chasing me up a tree or chewing my leg off I would not wish any critter harm and, on an intellectual level, reckon they are better off free range - just so long as that means downfield, which makes today's first four-legged encounter doubly disconcerting.

It comes at the entry point in 'hounds and terriers', where what sounds like hundreds of beagles are packed into individual kennels, yelping pathetically and barking for all their worth. The noise is ear-splitting.

It all looks rather uncomfortable and certainly makes me feel that way, but what do I know? Maybe they are having fun; dogs will be dogs and all that.

It takes a visitor time to acclimatise at any theme park, get the lie of the land, so to speak. Here, that is helped by clear zones - country pursuits; pigeons, poultry and rabbits; livestock; forestry and so on - all linked by concrete avenues that encircle an impressive show-jumping ring at the centre.

Over the rest of the year the site is largely grassland, dotted here and there with permanent facilities that attract around one million people annually on their own. Today, it buzzes with refugees in sun hats, a hive of activity not only due to the presence of the Yorkshire Beekeepers' Association.

Running along these avenues are rows of stalls, tents and trade stands, touting everything from handmade crafts to Yorkshire Dales ice cream to Gucci handbags to state of the art kitchens to the very latest speedboats (a snip at £29,995). Mohair socks? Not a problem. And here is a tumble dryer to lose them in. Cottage industry to corporate brands.

The Retired Greyhound and Royal Pigeon Racing Associations flank a shop selling Puffa jackets, tweed coats and shooting trousers (£49.99 a pair). There's a family history tent - yorkshireancestors.com - where visitors can discover if they are lucky enough to have a white rose descendant. There are tents and banners for such publications as *Country Living* magazine, *The Farmers' Guardian* and *The Yorkshire Post*.

Big name high street sponsors like Sainsbury's, ASDA and Marks and Spencer have set up camp. It is their backing, along with a £24 adult entry fee, that helps to allay a cost to the organisers of around £3million.

Which is another reason why I should hate it. The Napoleonic line about Britain being a nation of shopkeepers has never felt truer than in our post-Thatcherite car boot sale culture, where spending money on stuff - or dreaming about doing so - is preferable to a pint and pleasant stroll.

Shopping, for me, is punishment.

Yet I must admit that it isn't long before I'm right in the swing of it - wondering how that classic MG would look in the garage I haven't got; pondering if I'd suit a polka dot deerstalker; contemplating which bag of Yorkshire Crisps '...deliciously moreish and convivial...' sounds most enticing. Chardonnay Vinegar flavour or Cheddar and Caramelised Onion Chutney? Neither, I'll stick with ready salted.

Partly, that's down to a drift in aroma - animal muck usurped by candyfloss, fresh fruit and roast venison, among other olfactory delights. 'Four quid for a bacon sandwich?' howls someone, with incredulity.

Partly, it's about how, especially up among the JCBs, feeders, mobile livestock handlers, bale stackers, milkers, tractors gleaming red as dogs' knobs, huge yellow lorries '...standard rear tip, hydraulic front suspension', heavy duty lawn mowers, combine harvesters, diggers and crop sprayers, there appear to be farmer-types here who might actually find some of this gear useful.

But mainly it's *ai no corrida*, a realm of the senses. Everywhere, people and things to gawp at. At the Great Yorkshire Show, human beings too are herded in and then conform, by and large, to type. Look at us, it seems to confirm, we're just another species of animal really, aren't we? Albeit one that is second-in-command to Mother Nature.

Not that anyone seems to have caught on.

***

NAVIGATING off-duty squaddies and on-duty pushchairs, the day really gets going in country pursuits, where an upper-middle-aged bloke named Les is explaining, between gulps for air, how best to train a spaniel puppy. He does this via a microphone attached to his ear, in a gently sloping and verdant part of the site that also houses a couple of small lakes - into one of which a group is being shown how to cast fishing lines - plus a well-attended picnic area.

'It's learning how to turn on a whistle,' Les tells his audience, roasting gently behind a white picket fence. 'What I do every now and then is drop a ball into cover for the dog to find and bring back. Anybody who knows spaniels would know that this is a very spectacular dog.'

He brings on Loxie, a retriever deliberately kept untrained as an aid to empirical education. 'This is the bit people get bored with, the kingpin to all good training - the sit and stay, the steadiness. As you can see, if I throw this dummy, the dog's off. Right. I'll show you how to stop that.'

Whispered aside to Loxie: 'Don't forget, I've got a gun.'

This gets a laugh and her owner is off again, stressing the dog's role in helping him to bag pheasant, partridge and rabbit. 'Stay,' he barks. 'So what you do - stay! - is drop the dummy behind. Stay! Stay! And it's very important - stay! - that you pick it up by hand. Stay! This teaches the dog - stay! - that when it sees a bird down - stay! - it doesn't go until it's told to go. Stay! So we are now teaching the dog that what it sees down - stay! - is not necessarily hers to retrieve. Stay! If I were to throw this over the dog's head now - stay! - it would be off - stay! - as I'm not in a position to stop it. Stay! Stay!'

Another important thing, Les says, is to walk back to the dog and make contact. 'Don't be fussing on, though. Stay! There's no need for all this fussing and praising every time it does something right. Load of codswallop. Unless it's a nervous dog, you don't need all that sort of stuff. Stay!'

Then comes a trained dog that successfully resists the

temptation to give chase when a homing pigeon, brought in especially for the purpose, is suddenly released from a box beneath some cunningly disguised branches. After which, Les shows us how to take our dogs for a walk, not in a muzzle - 'you don't need them, a good simple collar and lead will do' - without yanking their chain should they get a little ahead of themselves. Nor are little treats allowed.

'It's like you parents, with your kids,' says Les. 'You don't say: "Do as you're told and I'll give you a sweetie." At least, I hope you don't. You want them to do as they are told because they respect you. Not because they're frightened or because you bribe them. Respect. It's the same with dogs.

'And remember. I do have that gun. Only kidding.'

Treat your dogs like children and your children like dogs. Such 'no-nonsense common sense' values are prevalent at the Great Yorkshire Show. Behind us, for example, is a recruiting tent for the Countryside Alliance, set up in 1997 - the organisation, not the tent - to 'promote rural interests' with its headline-grabbing support of fox hunting. A poster staked in the ground says: 'Stunning view? Thanks to grouse shooting, heather moorland [is] thriving!', as confirmed by a giant photographic blanket of purple propaganda.

If this were America, many of the people here would be devotees of tea party politics, you suspect, toting rifles and their right to bear arms. A while later, I spot a strawberry-haired bloke in a 'No Surrender' T-shirt bearing the logos of Help for Heroes, Leeds United and the English Defence League, at which no one else appears to bat an eyelid; just one more red neck among many?

That sight brings home another fact. It is only towards the end of the afternoon, walking down this very same hill in fact, that I spot my first non-white (not counting pink) faces. They belong to a line of Asian schoolchildren being led

9

like ducklings behind their teacher, each clad in an unnecessary orange tunic - unnecessary because no one could miss them anyway.

And yet, for all that, there is no doubting the show's diversity. It might say Yorkshire on the tin, but the visitors and exhibits do hail from far and wide. Cowpokes from Cumbria, coach parties from Cornwall. An American couple gape in wonder at a captive bald eagle - '...they would never allow that in the USA...' - part of a birds of prey collection that also includes a Russian vulture.

'It's too warm to send it up there,' says the handler, matter-of-factly. 'It would fly worried you see, circling around, looking at everything. Either that or be off at 90mph and not come back.'

***

SHEEP. Weird creatures, aren't they?

A fact never more obvious than when there are a few gathered together in a judging ring.

We are on Fifth Avenue, staring at an array of straw-filled pens in barns that hold such breeds as Beltex, Bleu du Maine and Berrichon, along with an outdoor shearing theatre and a tent containing Angora goats. Sunburnt shoulders lean over metal railings, as men and women in white coats from farms the length and breadth of the UK cajole their woolly exhibits. Ice creams are licked. Shearing? No, get your own.

Sheep. They don't mind running around in groups, do they, but aren't at all comfortable performing alone.

The poor beasts are wrestled about for a bit while a chap in a butcher's hat from time to time points and prods at them with a walking stick. The sort of activity a community might invent having got bored of chewing grass.

But what it definitely confirms is that I'll contentedly watch anything when there are winners and losers involved. Mere seconds pass before I'm rooting for one particular sheep, number 488, a cantankerous little bugger leading its handler a right merry dance. Neither of their moods is improved when the judge shunts the duo to the end of the line without a further glance, leaving them to dally there in last place.

By the end, the discontented bleats and baas are truly deafening, ovine tongues vibrating like football rattles.

At least the official then thanks my pair for coming, mentioning something - I can't quite make out what - about colouring. The winning sheep looks a bit orangey to my untrained eye but, in any case, sheep and handlers are then urged offstage, though it is unclear who is doing the pushing and who is doing the pulling.

For what it's worth, *my* best in show is a Whitefaced Woodland. It has very cool wraparound horns; like Satan.

Just up the track, past something called a 'carcase competition' - yikes - it's a similar story with the pigs.

These beasts too are unruly. Guided around in circles, nudged with sticks and diverted by vision-blocking boards if they get too near the perimeter or a rival portly swine, they cut a more comical sight.

I am rapidly turning rural, hazarding an opinion - inside my own head - that a) these are sows and b) a breed of Old Spot. For a start, there are nipples, lots and lots of nipples, big floppy ears and, well, spots, black with grey edges. With their skin of purest pink and wispy bleached hair, they resemble so many naked Boris Johnsons, down on all fours, absorbed in a game of farmyard dodgems.

I might also put forward the view, were anyone interested, that the black pinstripe suits and bowler hats worn by these judges are far from ideal attire in such a heatwave.

Questions, though, remain. Is that a whiff of crackling in the air? And if so, to whom - or what - does it belong? How is one pig 'better' than another? In what manner of sophistry are these judges engaged?

Wandering off toward the cattle enclosure, the tannoy causes a flutter of excitement with news that a Yorkshire-born Saddleback pig has been made champion of champions for the third year in a row. 'I suppose that's what they're looking for, isn't it?' says one man in a string vest that is struggling to contain its own cargo of belly pork, to a female companion, presumably his wife. 'The ... the ... they're looking for...' and the point tails off, exhausted.

If sheep are weird and pigs funny, cows up close are astonishing creatures; a contradictory mix of power and grace on a fearful skeletal frame, the most expensive ones anyway. They are also a little better behaved, while horses take all this showing off palaver completely in their stride. Along with trotting around in rings of their own, these snooty nags, of course, are also the stars of the main Showground.

Ignoring various jumps set up in the middle, a number of horses are being ridden around the circuit at a leisurely pace when I take a seat. They look very impressive and immaculately groomed to me until, thankfully, a woman who plonks her flanks at my side cures me of any such notion. Hopeless and out of control, she brays, and she may be correct. At least one tail is swishing. Can that be allowed?

***

TWO days later, on day three, an inquiry is launched after the detection of an illegal - though unspecified - substance.

Responding to the first such cheating allegation in the history of the Great Yorkshire Show, honorary director Bill

Cowling says: 'It is something that would give the exhibitors an advantage by falsifying the appearance of the animal.'

Lipstick? Mascara? Pancake? Fake tan?

I just knew there was something dodgy about that orangey sheep.

***

I AM on safer - if not steadier - ground with beer.

The Pride of Yorkshire awaits, in the Welcome to Yorkshire tent. And the route takes us around the back of the main ring, behind the Grandstand and President's Box. Outside the latter stands a uniformed guard - hands off the President's box!

Across the way, just up the avenue from the Isfaha Carpet Palace ('direct importers and specialists in Persian and Oriental carpets and rugs') and 'United Colors of Benetton' is The Yorkshire Church. Well, it figures. This being God's own county and all. Bound to have His Own Tent.

'Free bad jokes - step this way,' says a sign, trying to lure wayfarers in with a riddle. 'What do you get if you cross an elephant with a worm?'*

A little further to the right is the President's Lawn, which I am betting he doesn't mow himself. It's the perfect spot for a lunchtime burger and it's there where I overhear a TV news reporter telling his viewers, that along with 8,000 animals, this year's show will also boast 125 tonnes of straw.

Even hay fever is bigger in Yorkshire.

After which the 'pub' beckons, where they are giving away free thimblefuls of ale, or 'the new European pint' as national sales manager Brian Smith, about to give a talk on

---

* *Large holes in the garden.*

13

the history of the Black Sheep brewery, quips. The advertised speaker, owner Paul Theakston, is unavailable so Smith, wearing a promotional green T-shirt - '...most don't have this bulge in the front, mine does for some reason...' - is brought off the bench. 'Are you over eighteen?' he teases one elderly lady, who has stepped forward to try a sample.

He also promises a competition at the culmination of his talk in which you can 'win free beer for a year'. If there's a better way to get an audience to stay put, I've yet to hear it.

And so the lesson begins. Theakston it was who set up the Black Sheep brewery in 1992, having been the sixth-generation chairman of family business T & R Theakston Ltd, still located just around the corner from the Black Sheep premises in the village of Masham, nine miles from Ripon.

Following acrimonious attempts to sell the family inheritance through the 1970s, a tale that would make a hell of an historical drama, Theakstons was eventually bought, against Paul's wishes, by Matthew Brown, a company from Blackburn. The preferred option was Grandstand Whisky, who would most likely have gone on distilling their malts, while Paul was left to go on tending his casks.

Passionate about beer making and brand identity, this particular member of the Theakston family's great worry was that Matthew Brown might one day be taken over by a corporate giant - which is exactly how matters progressed. The first takeover was by Courage, who in 1987 became part of Scottish & Newcastle. Scottish & Newcastle has since become an acquisition of Dutch group Heineken.

'Not that I would call [insult] them, because I did twenty-two years with Bulmers, who were also taken over by Heineken,' Brian Smith interjects in his own tale. 'So they're looking after my pension, which I hope to draw fairly soon.'

Last orders for Paul Theakston were called when he

was asked to live and work in Edinburgh. It was then that he decided to go it alone, from scratch in the old maltings in Masham, '...there aren't so many breweries available for sale in the Yorkshire Dales.' Two years later, the money had been raised that allowed him to finance the operation and proceed.

'It would have been much easier to acquire a new factory unit, install some shiny stainless steel brewing plant and produce perfectly acceptable beer,' is how Black Sheep's imaginatively put-together website puts it, 'but that was a million miles away from what Paul had in mind.'

'He was going to call this new brewery Lightfoot's,' Brian tells us, explaining how, in 1919 - '...which is about the time I started in the trade...' - that was the name of a much earlier company taken over by T & R Theakston Ltd. 'Then right at the death [Scottish & Newcastle] said: "Sorry, Paul. You can't call it Lightfoot's. We own that name." "What the hell are we going to call this brewery?" he asked his wife, Sue, who replied: "Well, you're the black sheep of the family..."'

Black Sheep's first brew was '...bloody horrible. I tried it. Too heavy.' The second, Black Sheep Special, now Black Sheep Ale, was 'magnificent'. Since when, what began as the archetypal microbrewery has become a brewing figurehead in a county blessed with more independents than anywhere.

The company supplies over 300 pubs in the North Yorkshire region alone, a function that Welcome to Yorkshire's Gary Verity later calls integral. 'Our public houses are under attack from all sides, whether in terms of alcohol duty or the medical fraternity,' he points out, getting vaguely political. 'Yet they are a vital part of the community.'

And how many pubs do Black Sheep own? None.

'All we've got,' says Brian Smith, 'is the Black Sheep visitors' centre in Masham. That's our flag sheep, if you like.'

They are not averse to the odd pun, Black Sheep, as

further exemplified by the Black Sheep Baa...r tent, currently doing stellar business down by country pursuits.

'We sell our beer direct to the trade and can honestly say you can get a good pint of Black Sheep from Lands End to John o' Groats,' Brian continues. 'Things have changed immensely since the good old days of the 1960s and '70s, when people queued outside pubs to get in. We have to find other ways. We do a lot of trade now in supermarkets, with our range of bottled beers. All Creatures is a beer we did at 3.5 per cent ABV [alcohol by volume] in cask, which we also do now in bottles. Export is very important to us. Obviously, we can't export cask beer because it's a living product. It needs to settle. Stick it on a ship and it will go cloudy. It just won't work. So we send a lot of bottled beers all over the world. We are looking for innovations all the time.'

Brian points to a quirky illuminated Black Sheep hand pump that, instead of being under the bar in the traditional way when drawing cask ale, ensures pints are pulled into the glass at eye level. Theatre is important if you are going to challenge lager brands aimed at a younger customer. 'You'll remember those dirty old barmaids in the pubs,' he winces, 'when beer used to slop all over their fingers and back into the beer via the autovac..?'

The British Isles' pub market, says Brian, is shrinking. 'We are seeing a number of pubs closing and that's very sad, it makes me well up. At a rate of eight or nine a week they are shutting, or becoming fashion or charity shops. But the pubs left are cracking places, we've got to keep supporting them. We're very fortunate in Yorkshire to have some of the best pubs about.'

More contentious, among real ale buffs anyway, is Black Sheep's decision to bring out a keg version of their famous ale. 'There's a big market for it,' Brian insists. 'We know we can brew something much better than the products out there and sell it as quality keg beer. Not at the expense of Black Sheep cask, but at the expense of other keg beers. With cask beer being a living product, it's difficult to sell it into some of the sports clubs, because they don't do the turnover, same with hotel bars... we believe there is a good opportunity. We also now sell a range of other people's products, just to keep our wagons full when we're delivering.'

To wrap up, Smith goes through a Black Sheep range that, in bottles, includes Holy Grail, specially commissioned to commemorate the 30th anniversary of *Monty Python's Flying Circus* in 1999 and still going strong (well, 4.7 ABV). With 'more hops than a killer rabbit' it is '...dangerously fruity against a biscuity malty background. You can always taste it when an ale has been tempered over burning witches.'

And as for those cask ales: 'Best Bitter at 3.8 we class as a good session beer, not too strong, three or four pints and you're fine. Golden Sheep at 3.9 is beautiful, just right on a hot day like this. It has a citrus-y fruit taste to it. Black Sheep Ale is 4.4 per cent. And right at the top end of the Richter Scale is Riggwelter, a full-bodied dark beer at 5.9 per cent.'

A riggwelter, incidentally, is a Dales and therefore old Nordic term for a sheep that fell over. As fates go, it's not uncommon, usually due to the weight of a fleece getting too heavy with rainwater. A sheep in that predicament is 'rigged'.

'It can't get back up again and just dies,' says Brian. 'If you have four or five pints of Riggwelter, you too will fall over, get very wet and die.'

***

THE Yorkshire Pub of the Year, by the way, is The Carpenters Arms, Felixkirk. It is on the outskirts of the market town of

Thirsk, should you wish to pop in. Around ten thousand Yorkshirefolk voted.

In third place is The Foresters Arms, Carlton-in-Coverdale. Silver goes to the Woolly Sheep Inn, Skipton, '...where I used to go on a Friday night, when I'd had enough of Keighley,' jokes Paul Hudson.

***

SINCE it's inception in 2009, Welcome to Yorkshire has done - and continues to do - astonishing work.

The paradigm shift from downbeat to upbeat is a marketing triumph. Spin, yes. But spin at least based upon reality. And nowhere is their bright and shiny vision more blatant than when the sun is cracking the flags at the Great Yorkshire Show.

It is almost time to go, but there is still a fair bit to see on a late afternoon amble to the exit gates. Stalls pushing wind turbines and solar panelling confirm that cultural mores - even in agricultural Yorkshire - are fluid as time.

On the other hand, a *Top Gear* ride from the popular BBC series of that name and propaganda stands from such establishment machines as the RAF, RFU and ECB - the latter sponsored by Yorkshire Tea, 'let's have a proper brew' - show middle England standing its ground, tethered not so much by geography as the instincts of class.

Here at the top end of the site, the livestock - if that is the correct term - are smaller. Today, it's rabbits. Tomorrow, pigeons. On Thursday, it will be poultry.

The barn wherein the rabbits are housed (hutched?) is full of pens, one per animal. This, I assume, is a matter of necessity, or by the time the judges completed a circuit there would presumably be a few more entrants than if the contest were held in an open ring, as with the rest of the farmyard. A real painting the Humber Bridge job. Some of the rabbit pens already have ribbons attached - red for first, blue second and yellow for third place. Today's main prize will be awarded at 4.10pm says a sign pinned to the wall.

As thrilling a prospect as that is, I opt against hanging around and, on the way out, pass a trestle table on which are being sold free range eggs. This strikes me as odd. Even I know that rabbits don't lay eggs.

'Mum, are these real?' asks one inquisitive toddler.

'Yes, they're real,' his mother replies. 'Put it back!'

Next door is a fashion pavilion and next to that a working forge, full of fire, sparks and hardy looking blokes who hammer out horseshoes and the like, while the sweat sprays off their backs like Wain Wath falls. Hard enough graft in the mildest temperatures this, but with the thermometer pushing upwards of 30 such activity seems like masochism.

As indeed does the exhibition of forestry skills, further along Sixth Avenue. Before two nosebleed-inducing wooden poles, up which Cumbrian lumberjacks raced earlier in the day, a collection of buzz saw-wielding carpenters conjure perfectly proportioned planks from tree trunks.

Turns out there *is* something worse than a paper cut.

And from there it's back down through myriad garden displays (sheds, fences, 'outdoor rooms', hot tubs...'), the Discovery zone, picnic area and bee pavilion - outside which a bearded Bruce Springsteen lookalike makes 'skeps', old fashioned wicker hives - to complete the circle.

There's even a dry stone walling course from a firm based in Otley, whose piles of material are scattered in front of a gang of blokes, hands sunken in flesh where hips used to be, pondering their own intended victory over mortality.

And at the foot of this greenery, in the spot where this

morning we were welcomed by Les and his hunting dogs, another lecture is underway, given by a chap who holds aloft a large cut-out picture of a 'sea bass'.

'All these restaurateurs and idiot chefs on the TV,' he says, presumably unaware that, in the cookery theatre just around the corner, Rosemary Shrager, is just now explaining how to make a rabbit terrine, 'the people who call this a sea bass... well, in this country we don't have a sea bass. You wouldn't say a sky bird or a field cow, would you? It's a bass! There's no namby-pamby nancy world underwater.'

Furthermore: 'You see that Canada goose over there? They don't even come from Canada!' And, while he is at it, something should be done about: '..them flaming Spanish - fishing in our waters.' In short, he seems rather grumpy. Well, it has been a long and hot day, I suppose.

Everyone, it seems, has an opinion around here. At just about every stall, someone is happy to put you right, sometimes gently, sometimes not so gently.

Hardly surprising, then, that the walk to the brown gate should be past a tent rallying support for hunting - 'Vote-OK: Every time you see the word HUNT remember what it stands for... Help Us Next Time.' And then some famous 'supportive' quotes: 'In matters of conscience, the law of the majority has no place,' - Mahatma Gandhi. 'In politics, an organised minority is a political majority,' - Jesse Jackson. 'The only thing necessary for the triumph of evil is for good men to do nothing,' - Edmund Burke. 'There may be times when we are powerless to prevent injustice, but there must never be a time when we fail to protest,' - Elie Wiesel.

Or, as Rosemary Shrager puts it while explaining the appeal of the creature she has just hacked into pieces: 'Because the rabbit goes where it wants, does what it wants and eats what it wants, that is transferred to the meat.'

2. Well, I'll Stand the Drop of York

A History of Yorkshire - Part One

THE county's Archaeological Society reckons that human occupation in Yorkshire can be traced back 125,000 years, with the significant caveat that it is only since the end of the last Ice Age - ie around 10,000 BC, give or take two or three millennia - that walking, grunting and no doubt chelpin' two-legged homo sapiens began to set up shop here continuously.

Prior to that, in the Lower Jurassic period of 180-205 million years ago, say, through the Middle Jurassic era of 152-180 million years back to the Upper Jurassic of 135-152 million years past, your typical Yorkie may well have been a belligerent lump of ocean coral or a sea urchin, possibly even a shark, ammonite or spectacularly rude plesiosaurus.

Indeed, the roar of a dinosaur can still be heard on occasion to this day.

Those interested in such matters (prehistoric lizards, that is, not grumpy old sods with out-of-control eyebrows), or with inquisitive children to entertain, could do worse than visit Scarborough's small-but-perfectly-formed Rotunda

Museum. Designed by so-called 'father of English geology' William Smith and having originally opened in 1829, these days it promises interactive displays and free guided-tours.

The Jurassic was also the period in which Yorkshire's distinctive landscape began to form; its sedimentary rocks - limestone, shale and grainy oolite sandstone - being layers of sand, mud and decomposed marine life, gradually crushed and forced together by sheer weight of water. Yorkshire's swampy mid-Jurassic vista would have been one of flooded riverbanks and lush sub-tropical vegetation. In the Upper Jurassic, the future wide acres bathed beneath warm and shallow seas that were home to our plesiosaur friend, various molluscs, shellfish and other marine creatures.

Later, in the Cretaceous period of about 65 to 135 million years ago, maybe our early Tyke (let's call him Amos, no, on second thoughts let's not) was one of several million swarming micro-organisms that, having popped their clogs, sank to the seabed and helped to form what would one day be the dizzying sea stacks, arches and chalk cliffs of Flamborough Head or, a little further inland, the somewhat less vertiginous rolling Yorkshire Wolds.

Unlike the intrepid 21st-century explorers who hunt their fossilised remains on the North and East Yorkshire 'Dinosaur Coast' of Scarborough, Whitby, Robin Hood's Bay, the quarries of Ravenscar and beyond, however, there is nothing to suggest that they had real butter for tea.

***

SO, that last Ice Age: the one over 10,000 years ago when, like the North Sea itself, Yorkshire was a frozen wasteland.

Even then, it appears, some obstinate locals managed to adapt. We see their 'footprints' in the vast clay deposits and boulder debris of the awesome glaciers that this way flowed from the Lake District, Scotland and as far afield as Scandinavia. When the planet began to heat up again, these ice floes began to melt and thereby retreat. Their luggage was dropped where it often lies still, unless turned into a public attraction like the one clogging the entranceway to Seamer station, near Scarborough.

Cue also the arrival of those first two-legged settlers, venturing north from a warmer southern continent.

Given the vastness of the timescale and lack of written evidence, facts get a little sketchy here. But essentially, with the ice gone, it isn't long - archaeologically speaking - before the Yorkshire landscape is covered in a thick blanket of forest. And within those trees and shrubbery, pursued by Stone Age hunter-gatherers firing bows and arrows and chucking spears, is an abundance of deer, boar and other such edible wildlife. On the forest floor can be found the nuts, berries, vegetables, fruit and other staple foodstuffs that form a more typical part of these extended human family groups' diet.

By and large, this seems to have been a wonderful time in which to be alive. Better even than 1895, when twenty-one leading Yorkshire and Lancashire clubs broke away from Twickenham to form rugby league. True, your mornings were spent hunting and foraging, but after that your time was your own. On the down side, pubs had not yet been invented and nor, in all probability, had any recognisable code of football. But on the up side there was plenty of time for relaxation, hobbies and other recreational activities. As predicted by W.B. Yeats, however, things fell apart. The utopia could not hold.

By 3000 BC (ish), the Mesolithic ancestors of Compo, Clegg and Foggy had gone Neolithic. In other words, they began to put down roots and lay claim to permanent territory. A previously nomadic lifestyle was swapped with that of a hard-working labourer, possibly through human greed or perhaps necessity, as a growing population sought to control an environment drained of natural resources. Either way, forests were flattened, farmsteads established, animals domesticated; it was an epoch-ending agricultural revolution.

Nip ahead another 1,000 or so years into the Bronze Age and, with such developments as flint mining, pottery, far-flung trading in non-native plants and communal construction projects like bank and ditch earthworks, burial mounds and religious monuments, along with that rather useful bronze material itself of course - not to mention copper and gold - a fixed way of life was complete. Its ghost can be traced in the settlements, field systems and other countryside structures we see around us today.

Indeed, the Rotunda Museum plays host to a unique skeleton from that era. Gristhorpe Man, a six-foot warrior chieftain with all his own teeth, found buried in a coffin made of a scooped-out oak tree, left this world around 2200 BC. He has been in his latest place of rest since 1834, when members of the Scarborough Philosophical Society put him there.

Though Gristhorpe Man, wearing fragments of a skin cloak, was most likely a high-status individual going by his grave goods of bronze dagger with polished whalebone handle, a wicker basket that once held food, flint tools etc, he is more general confirmation of a decent Bronze Age diet. Bradford University's Archaeological Dept, who in 2005 gave him a health check while the Rotunda was refurbished, say he lived to a ripe old age. Despite a number of warrior-appropriate healed fractures, he died from natural causes.

For his fellow Bronze Age Yorkshire-folk, life carried on as it always had. When they weren't off hunting upland and, doubtless, quarrelling with the neighbours, they were clearing forests, cooking or tending farms, roundhouses and livestock. Then, around 700 BC, iron arrived and, some five hundred years before the birth of Christ, the Celts, with their new-fangled weaponry and tools, wandered into our tale.

I say 'wandered'. The remains of a burnt-out Iron Age hill fort at Castle Hill, Huddersfield, dated around 430 BC, suggests that 'charged' may have been more like it. Britain was now dominated by tribes and sub-tribes, forever falling out, both with each other and among themselves, usually over territory. Of these, the Yorkshire-based Brigantes were the most populous and influential, although the further east an Iron Age Tyke ventured, the more likely he or she was to bump into a member of the Parisii, thought now to have been based near Bridlington, who buried their dead in chariots.

The kingdom of Brigantia took its name from a Celtic goddess and the word's root meaning, height or elevation, though whether as a literal reference to the upland Pennine geography or implications of nobility is unclear. To the north of Brigantia, above the Tyne, lived the people of the Votadini, around what are now the Scottish Borders. North west, in today's Cumbria and North Lancashire, were the Carvetii, possibly related to the Brigantes. South of the Humber and in what are now the lower Midlands were the Corieltauvi and Cornovii. To a greater or lesser extent, these tribes and others like them were adding an indelible stamp to the future shape of the British Isles, with Yorkshire very much at the forefront.

Yet viewing an historical timeline in absolute terms is to risk missing the point. Cultural tides are complex and fluid; patterns of circumstance, influence and even procreation overlap. Or to put it another way, if a lassie from Lancashire wants to cross the moors and leap into the arms of a lad from Yorkshire, whatever the era, good luck stopping them.

The modern-day village of Aldborough, for example, in the parish of Boroughbridge, near Harrogate, sits atop

Slouching towards Blubberhouses

Isurium Brigantum, a Romano-British town that once marked the crossing of the north-bound Dere Street over the River Ure. An important Brigantine settlement well before the Roman legionaries began their conquest of the region in 70 AD, by the early second century Isurium Brigantum was widely renowned as the tribe's capital and administrative centre, most likely taking over from Stanwick in Richmond.

Even then, though, pragmatic 'Yorkshire'-folk simply got on with the job in hand - living - as a 357-year occupation that was in varying degrees accepted, despised and actively adopted by the populace-at-large bubbled on around them.

***

IT is with the Roman invasion that the true history of Yorkshire begins - for that's when written records first began to be passed down. And if you want to learn more about the development of modern life in the broad acres then there is one place you really do have to visit ... the county town and nowadays city of York.

Not only is York the place where, in 2008, the earliest brain in Britain was found in a mud pit (some bright yellow spongy material rattling about in a skull that ended up being dated circa 300 BC), it contains more museums and areas of historical interest per square mile than anywhere in the UK.

Assuming you aren't in a Parisii chariot or getting a 'backie' from Lizzie Armitstead, the best way in is by train. Rattle past rutted fields with highlights of freshly-fallen mid-March snow, springtime still an unlikely promise, and even the scarecrows that dot an otherwise flat and wide open inter-city hinterland look frozen half to death. From behind glass, as viewed through the steam of a scalding cup of Leeds station's finest green tea, it carries the look of harsh terrain, a mind-blowingly tough environment in which to get by in the days before electricity and central heating. And already, as we stop to pick up passengers in Ulleskelf, around five miles out of Tadcaster, there are hints of the story about to unfold.

Pull into York, though, and the city's event-laden past smacks you straight in the face. Not only does the train station itself have a story to tell - rebuilt after heavy bombing during World War Two and more recently renovated also - before it stand the famous old city walls, with the towers of York Minster on the skyline to the north east. Failing to block the view, another of those big wheels that no self-respecting 21st century mecca of tourism, it seems, can manage without.

At the station, there is a plaque to the memory of railway worker William Milner who, along with a colleague, died in one such bombing raid in 1942. As station foreman, Milner was going back to his burning office for a first aid kit when he met his end, posthumously receiving the King's commendation for gallantry; an act of selflessness fitting in a city where, since the Industrial Revolution, the railways have been a juddering symbol of modernity.

Step back inside and walk along the old footbridge, built in 1938. Traversing platforms and tracks destined for London and Edinburgh, it takes you directly to the National Railway Museum, around 600 yards away. There is another route from the city via an arched tiled tunnel running beneath the East Coast line, but that doesn't have the same frisson.

Admission is free - a donation of £3 recommended - with Station Hall, once York's main goods station, built in the 1870s and still a working building into the 1960s, the centre of attention for adult and school trips alike. Today, it houses engines and carriages spanning - and span is the right word given the sheer size of the place - over one hundred years of railway history with not a fleck of soot in sight.

Slouching towards Blubberhouses

Among the trains on display during this writer's visit are a number of royal vehicles, including the saloon car of Queen Victoria herself, built to the Empress of India's exact home from home specifications and therefore guaranteed to amuse. Aunt Adelaide's saloon from the 1840s, the world's oldest surviving railway carriage we are told, can also be nosed into, as can the carriage of George V, inherited from Edward VII, updated with a bath. Apparently, this particular King George was the first person to take a soak on a train. Alas, with or without a rubber duck has gone unrecorded.

Want to know what a railway chef did if he ran out of ingredients? He stuck a note in a hollowed-out potato and threw it at the next signal box. Once the signaller telegraphed up the line, the supplies were waiting at the next stop. Open in its present guise since 1975 (although collections have been in situ here since the then-Patent Office Museum acquired Stephenson's Rocket in 1862), the National Railway Museum is a treasure trove of such info that would, in less enlightened times, have been called a treat for boys of all ages.

Not that it's only about peering at old trains. Along with a 'Brief Encounter' restaurant that, by the smell of it, still serves authentic boiled beef and cabbage, are red brick walls hung with evocative tin plates advertising Player's Navy Cut cigs, Brooke Bond PG Tips ('tea you can really taste'), Fryco 'aerated waters and beverages' and Colman's mustard. There are ornate iron machines that once dispensed tickets ('1d to be given up to collector') or Nestlé Swiss milk chocolate or the extent to which you had put on or lost a few pounds.

Daily talks and demonstrations ('a short introduction to the Bullet train - the only one outside of Japan') are on the menu, too, along with exhibitions and events. The fiftieth anniversary of Dr Beeching's controversial railway report was in the pipeline on my trip there, along with a look at the stories of early trains (nowadays we have late trains) and a seventy-five-year celebration of Britain's world steam speed record-breaking A4 class locomotive Mallard - resident in the Great Hall. On 3 July 1938, it scorched downhill at Stoke Bank, between Grantham and Peterborough, at 126mph.

For those who find humans more fascinating than valves, smokeboxes and rivets, there are photographic 'blogs' - i.e. quotes - of railway users down the years. 'We were obsessed with trainspotting,' says one, on a picture of a dozen schoolboys in caps scribbling furiously into their notebooks. 'We'd stand for hours collecting locomotive numbers with other boys, whom we did not know, but who enjoyed the same thrill as an express approached at speed.'

'When the train stopped at a station,' says another, 'my father dashed out to get three cups of tea. The whistle blew as he climbed aboard. Our tea was in china cups balanced on top of each other, splashing all over the place.'

'My husband and I had a terrific argument early in our married life,' says a third, somewhat royally. 'He left to go to his parent's house. I missed him so much, I went to York station to get a train. As I was about to get on, he alighted from the train. What a reunion!' There's no photo of that.

In the gallery alongside hang three excellent paintings. The first, a comical 1967 image by Terence Cuneo, is of the busy concourse of Waterloo Station. The other two are a pair by George Earl. In *Going North* (1893), a group of friends - and several of the artist's beloved sporting dogs - prepare for a shooting trip to Scotland at Kings Cross. In *Coming South* (1895), one month later, the same friends get ready to return.

To move away from the crowds to the edge of Station Hall is to descend into an elephants' graveyard of insulated fish vans and unglamorous passenger trains. At the far end of which is a 1970s Pullman. Down below, at trackside, the commanding height of this behemoth startles. Yet step on from an upper-level platform bedecked with ABBA posters imploring us to 'Keep Britain Tidy', and an otherwise familiar memory feels sadder somehow, even a little banal.

It's a lesson that history - when viewed from a single perspective - is seldom to be trusted.

***

FRIENDS, Romans, Yorkshiremen, lend me your ears. I come to praise York, not to bury it. The past brings this place alive. And as you wander from gate to bridge to wall or bar (of both varieties), you are never far from a rattling good yarn.

For a broadbrush history of what came to be known as the White Rose county, the best place to start, as its name suggests, is the Yorkshire Museum. Equidistant on foot twixt station and Minster, set in squirrel and pigeon-filled gardens over Lendal Bridge - upon which even the sandwich shop has turrets - it is most often accessed by the gatehouse on the conveniently named Museum Street, over the River Ouse.

It is here where you can take an interactive - of course - trip from pre-history to medieval mayhem, via bloody royal intrigue, civil war and everything between. Most immediately you are confronted by the people who, in any lasting sense, stuck their flag in the earth here deepest.

Having invaded the south east of England in 43 AD, the Romans' conquest of what was then still a collection of tribal kingdoms had gone along in stages. Until, in 71 AD, it was the turn of the Brigantes to face and then fall beneath the might of the Ninth Legion, who then built a fortress. In time, that construction evolved into an important city, Eboracum, destined to be capital of England's north and second city of an increasingly colonised land. A similar fort, incidentally, was erected in Doncaster, destined - as the birthplace of Louis Tomlinson - to be the capital of the One Direction fan club.

'What have the Romans ever done for us?' asks the opening Yorkshire Museum display, above a floor map of the Roman Empire, guarded by a statue of Mars, the God of War.

Inspired by many aspects of Greek culture, the Romans brought learning, philosophy, theatre, sports and art. 'Physical and musical competition, training and performance in Olympic-inspired games, gladiatorial-styled combats and gymnasia provided educational development and improved discipline,' we are told. 'Theatrical productions, poetry recitals and music entertained the wealthy and the masses alike.'

Who knows, perhaps the poor Brigantes had some of that classy culture stuff of their own, but simply forgot - or weren't egotistical enough - to write it all down.

Still, as Euripedes says, 'action achieves more than words', so on into the bowels of the museum we go, past another motto, this time Seneca's, that might also be culled from a 'Teach Thi' Senn Tyke' phrasebook: 'Economy is too late when you are at the bottom of your purse.'

For the chronologically minded, a swift diversion to the gallery *Extinct* is in order. Here is found the eyebrow-raising revelation that 'ninety-nine per cent of the rich and vast diversity of species ever to have lived on Earth' - since the first organisms appeared some 3.8 billion years ago - have now vanished. Forever. The five episodes of mass extinction that took place during the past 500 million years are outlined, the most recent and famous of which being the one 66 million years ago that ended the Cretaceous period, on account of the random asteroid that most likely zapped the dinosaurs.

Prior to that, in the mid-Jurassic, when Yorkshire was warm and subtropical, 'dinosaurs roamed everywhere'. And thanks to some fossilised tracks discovered on the coast, preserved for the ages in a glass case, you can walk in their footsteps and 'see how *their* feet compare with your own', unless, it warns, you are wearing stilettos. Happily, I'm not.

By my dodgy maths, these extinction events seem to happen every 50 to 150 million years, which would mean we're due another any minute. Best crack on then.

If the demise of the dinosaurs had an upside, it's in the fact that it created the opportunity for mammals - i.e. you and me - to flourish. And thus we did, although that, as the next natural history section is keen to remind us, did not mean an end to extinctions. One local example of an absent furry friend is the wildcat, formerly resident right across Britain. The loss of its natural habitat and targeting by the fur trade saw these animals vanish from England half a century ago, although there are still around four hundred 'Heinz 57 variety' types roaming the wilds of Scotland, having in the meantime mated with varying breeds of domestic pussy.

A wildcat can get lonely.

Specifically in Yorkshire, six species of bumblebee are extinct, part of a potentially disastrous picture worldwide. With no bees buzzing from flower to flower, crops cannot be pollinated and, if that continues, we won't be needing any asteroid. Firmly on the side of environmentalism, however, the museum does not ignore the odd ethical ambiguity. Take those charming grey squirrels leaping about merrily on the lawns and in the champion beech, lime and ash trees outside, over-running the native reds. One way of attempting to deal with that issue is to trap and kill the 'interlopers', but is that the right thing to do? And what about the bigger and stronger black squirrel that has been here for the last 90 years? Those blighters are now out-competing the greys. Should they be culled also?

Whether in the animal or human kingdom, you are seldom far from a row about who has a right to be where.

***

TIME, like your average legionary, marches on. And so must we. *The History of York* takes us back to AD 71, when York was still a garrison town.

Aside from the delights of empire and conquest, one thing that really appealed to the Romans about Yorkshire was its ready supply of lead, a metal for which the invaders found many uses. In the east of the region especially, lead mining and miners proliferated. Otherwise, for your ordinary Joe in the hills, moors and dales, romanisation was a distant rumour impacting little - if at all - on day-to-day existence.

In York, as elsewhere, organised local communities drawing on thousands of years of hunting and gathering had lives dominated by the demands and rewards of agriculture. But here, once the Romans finally did reach the north, they very definitely brought a far-reaching new era with them.

There is a tendency in 20th century history books to frame Rome's influence on a rough and ready population as 'civilising'. And so, to a large extent it was, although such portrayals do risk minimising the intrinsic worth of those existing cultures trampled beneath no doubt chilblained feet. Similarly, the Romans' departure, some 336 years later, was said to herald the 'Dark Ages', an out of favour term with which few contemporary historians are now comfortable.

What cannot be denied, however, is the impact on future British life of classical philosophies and a pragmatic attitude to warfare, politics, civic infrastructure, architecture, science, public entertainment and much else besides. As Rome's second English city, York - destined one day to be the court of three emperors - was very much at the forefront of the development of the Britain Isles we see around us today, not only in the north, but all points of the compass.

Slouching towards Blubberhouses

Roman pragmatism was there from the get-go. Given how permanent bases tended to be established in areas of greatest discontent, not to mention the time it took to quieten those places down, it seems fair to say that the Romans will have met with curmudgeonliness in Yorkshire, tough to believe, I know. Yet here as elsewhere, with military authority imposed, tribal leaders were thrown a bone. Local power might be retained in exchange for Roman rule. The upshot: a new mongrel culture took root, a blend of imperial ideals with the patterns of behaviour and beliefs that went before, though Greek-like coins and those Gallic-style Parisii carts subsequently dug up in the Wolds also point to the existence of similar - if less prominent - 'foreign' interaction previously.

And in fact, prior to officially annexing Britain some twenty-eight years before the birth of Eboracum, Rome itself traded with the island and its people over several centuries. So while any opposition to Roman occupation was put down ruthlessly, over time it seems that often new exotic goods and products were persuasion enough. Items formerly considered rare or luxurious were increasingly adopted as the welcome trappings of extended Roman society. In much the same way as modern disquiet re an 'American empire' is undermined by a taste for rock 'n' roll, HBO and endless repeats of *Friends*.

Handily positioned atop the marshy flood plains of two rivers, the Ouse and the Foss, with excellent views in all directions, it wasn't long before Eboracum - a key fort along with those in the likes of Chester, Gloucester, Exeter, Lincoln, Wroxeter, Caerleon and Colchester - began to dominate the England's north. The men who built it, Rome's Ninth Legion, were drawn mainly from provinces across Northern Europe, very few originated in Rome itself. They and the Sixth Legion who followed in their hobnailed boot-steps - contrary to popular myth, legionaries did not wear open-toed sandals -

had braved the plains, deserts and forests of Africa, Spain, Germany and ancient Pannonia before arriving in Britain, thereby adding another set of ingredients to the melting pot. Over the decades to come, the fort became a town, then a larger town and then, after 200 years, a Colonia, the highest status of Roman city which, given its position by then as the capital of Britannia Inferior (Upper Britain), one of the country's two provinces, was richly deserved. For all its importance as a strategic and economic centre, though, there is debate as to the depth of Eboracum's wealth. Along with enjoying close trade and exchange links with the rest of the Roman Empire, introducing Yorkshire to such exotic goods as olive oil and wine, the city was largely dependent upon the surrounding countryside for more mundane supplies. And while it had the usual temples, bathhouses and markets, Eboracum seems better described as sizeable than grand.

The best an inquisitive modern visitor can do is take a walking tour complete with free audio download - there are also trails for those interested in Jewish history, the Great War, Viking, Medieval and Georgian times. In *Daily Life in Eboracum*, commencing at the south door of York Minster by the statue of the Emperor Constantine - of whom more anon - the stroll takes you from the site of that first military fortress to two rows of Roman sarcophagi in the Museum Gardens, via roads and lanes above a bathhouse (now The Roman Bath pub in St Sampson's Square), a warehouse complex, a harbour at Fossbridge and vast slave-trade burial ground.

Whatever its eventual size, then, with more and more civilians tempted into its shadow, the town began to flourish. From its origins as a temporary wooden camp, it developed into a hefty stone garrison built to an out-of-the-box Roman street plan, with some 60,000 tonnes of limestone, imported from the quarries of Calcaria - Tadcaster to you and me - for the walls of the fortress alone. Also coming in from Tadcaster was the aqueduct that channelled constant water into the pipes supplying the city's many public fountains and wells. In a room with a beautiful tiled floor mosaic as its centrepiece, the Yorkshire Museum displays coins and other votive offerings from such sources, along with grave goods, altars and fashion items bearing transcriptions to the gods.

Dwarfed by the likes of Rome itself then, and other major cities of the empire, York was important nonetheless. Hadrian (reputed to be a Spaniard) was the first emperor to visit in AD 122, followed by Septimus Severus (a Libyan who died of pneumonia here in AD 211) and Serbian Constantius Chlorus in AD 296. When the latter died suddenly in AD 306 after beating off the Picts, his soon-to-be well-known son, Constantine the Great, a later convert to Christianity who founded Constantinople, held the distinction of being the one and thus far only Roman Emperor to be so 'coronated' in the city. Through it all, an eclectic array of ideas, goods, attitudes and tastes further infiltrated the lives of everyday folk.

Nor was the place made any less cosmopolitan by the 'unofficial families' of around 10,000 rank and file soldiers, unofficial because the legionaries were not allowed to marry. It's here, again, where the museum comes over all interactive. 'Walk in the footsteps of Eboracum's Roman citizens ... take the plunge ... try on a tunic ... slip on some sandals and feel a real Roman floor beneath your feet.'

Tempting. But with folk watching, not *that* tempting.

By the fourth century AD, the once glorious Roman Empire was well and truly in decline. With trouble mounting in the East - ie Middle East, not Filey or Brid - the imperial gaze shifted and Eboracum, like the rest of Britannia, was left to fend for itself. After a brief period of prosperity and only a few short years after Constantine had assumed power on the steps of York's Principia, the attentions of a Rome mired in political, monetary and military crises were inevitably elsewhere. Soon, Yorkshire's fertile fields and navigable rivers were exploited only to service expensive foreign campaigns.

As across the rest of Europe, Germanic tribes saw their opportunity for invasion, fostering alarm and instability. A distracted Rome could no longer afford to care and its last soldiers left Britain in AD 407. Along with the rest of the province, York and by extension Yorkshire lay abandoned, seemingly doomed and drifting toward obscurity.

***

OFTEN, to take one step forward in life you've got to take at least a couple of steps back. At the Yorkshire Museum, you must take several steps, each of them leading downstairs. It's here that we are regaled with the next chapter in York's story, the era of the Anglian kings.

With the Roman Empire having crumbled, York was left to a fate shaped heavily by the Germanic influence, the soon-to-be predominant Angles having originated in Angeln, on the Baltic shore of what is now Schleswig-Holstein. As its grand old buildings began to decay, York's residents made their homes outside the city walls, most often with wood - it took eighteen trees to build your average Anglian residence. Assuming the kingdom of Northumbria, meanwhile, these new rulers saw Eboracum's rich history as a source of their claim to rule, their inheritance, and fought off all further intruders. Thus did the Principia - once slap-bang middle of the Roman military fortress - evolve into the beating heart of the Catholic Church in the North of England. And, in time, stonemasons would use York's Roman-built walls to begin constructing a medieval city.

Slouching towards Blubberhouses

No one knew it then, of course, but York would weather the turbulence of its next 1,000 years with its position as England's second city and the North's centre of influence intact. In hindsight, given its economic, religious and, most crucially, politically strategic position, how could it not be so? Dynasties would rise and fall here. Decades of peace and prosperity would book-end long periods of war and unrest. Yet still its reputation held firm, very much the right county for an argument.

But first, there is Eboracum's more immediate future to worry about, initially in the hands of those Angles. One such, King Edwin, chose the city - re-named Eoforwic - as his seat of power. Baptised in York's original Minster in AD 627, it was Edwin who brought Christianity to York and he is said also to have re-introduced education. The Minster itself, a far more humble structure than today's cathedral of grandeur, was later finished in stone by King Oswald as the centrepiece of his capital city (the building, in its most recent guise, was not begun until 1220 and only completed, give or take the odd improvement, in 1472). In short, over two-and-a-half centuries, Roman Eboracum was reborn as Anglian Eoforwic and that was bound to attract unwanted attention.

This it inevitably did, from the next heroes - or villains - of 21st century York's tourism trade, those pesky Viking raiders. It was they who put paid to the last two Anglian kings - Osbert and Aella - and it was they who, in taking control of northern England under what was then known as the Danelaw, founded the noisy, smelly and never less than lively Jorvik.

For a hint of the type of people we are dealing with here look no further than the names of the men who captured Eoforwic from the Angles: Ivar the Boneless and his Great Heathen Army. Once here, not only did the Vikings - who according to many a historian have had a bit of a bad press, what with their mythical horned hats and tendency to rape first, pillage second and ask questions later - cut a swathe through the top half of the country, they spent much of the rest of their time in power struggles with the Saxon rulers of the south. Result: carnage. They must have been a fearsome beardy sight when they first sailed up the tidal Ouse on the first day of November AD 866, fresh from the North Sea, in their actual kit of iron helmets, chain-mail and leather armour.

On the other hand, the arrival of Ivar and chums also opened up a lucrative commercial network between Britain, Scandinavia and the rest of Europe that outlasted the Vikings' 100-year or so reign by another century. Surrounded by lands that remained overwhelmingly agricultural, wherein most folk still lived in tiny villages tilling the soil, York was able to trade in amber and silk. And going by more unearthed finds, the Vikings were just as keen to claim ownership of the history of the city as their Angle predecessors. Along with the expected swords, knives, jewellery and solid gold arm-bands (awarded to great Viking warriors) - and some perhaps unexpected animal bone ice-skates - are silver coins from Jorvik's own mint, inscribed with the Latin word 'Ebor'.

All of this and more is in the Yorkshire Museum, but for a more hands-on Viking experience it's across town you must go. Hail Coppergate; home of Marks and Spencer, Starbucks, Top Shop and the Jorvik Viking Centre.

Having attracted over 15 million visitors since its creation on the site of actual Viking houses, workshops and backyards excavated between 1976-81, the Jorvik Centre is as hi-tech and child-friendly as these things go. To roll up at its doors is to be met by a 'bouncer' in Viking garb. And having paid a tidy sum to get in, it's downstairs into the glass-floored gloom where, amid a host of video and audio displays, a party of schoolchildren are being lectured in the principles of wattle and daub. Their yawns aren't stifled long for soon we are in a Disney-like realm of rides and animatronics, a seat on a moving carriage of 'time capsules' giving a full sensory overview of life in AD 975.

And the first thing to note - apart from the silky tones of a narrator who sounds very much like the BBC's Dr Alice Roberts in your ear-piece - is the distinct lack of aggro, unless you count a couple arguing over what to have for supper. Here, domestic day-to-day life is stressed, with craftsmanship of leather, bone, antler and wood, unpleasant pongs and the old-Norse tongue in evidence. In Viking times, it was women who kept the keys to the house, the word 'husband' meaning just that, 'house-bound'. And as if to emphasise this, several of the men portrayed are the cheerful dimwits of popular northern comedy tradition.

Among the hustle and bustle is a fisherman gutting fish, a tradesman dealing in amber, the blast of a blacksmith's furnace ... and all of it in the 'gata', the Scandinavian word for street, subsequently anglicised to 'gate', as in Fishergate (street of fishermen), Swinegate (pigs), Monkgate (monks), Spurriergate (spur-makers), Colliergate (coal) and so on. The fisherman's facial features, incidentally, are reconstructed from an actual Viking period skull found in York.

The twelve-minute ride begins on a notional River Foss, with the houses and workshops of the city positioned ahead. Children play a board game with pieces of jet, stone and walrus ivory. Our narrator asks one bloke, in Nordic, about a comb he is making and off we go, twisting and turning past 'new' two-storey buildings rendering damp and cramped one-storey wattle and daub jobs defunct, a cup maker ('Coppergate' relating to cups), the premises of a butcher that reveal a diet similar to our own, the interior of a Viking house complete with its own cellar, and the filthy market streets.

Also filthy, we are told, is the water, drawn from wells that share backyard space with rubbish pits and toilets. 'This is one reason everyone drinks beer,' says Dr Roberts, 'even the children,' alcopops having not yet been invented. Each plot is long and separated from its neighbour by a wattle fence, ideal for a gossip to heave her bosom over. And perfect, too, for that outside loo, where one grunting and trumpeting fellow ends our journey by telling us he is busy. 'We should leave him alone', says Alice, an imaginary peg on her nose.

With the funfair ride over, we are back in a more academically traditional world of human skeletons and glass cabinets that describe and display the five tonnes of animal bone, oyster shells, thousands of Roman and Medieval roof tiles, 250,000 pottery shards and 20,000 'individually interesting' objects unearthed in the original Coppergate dig. Younger archaeologists can wield a trowel of their own in the hunt for pans, fish bones and lumps of Viking-age poo among other such delights at the Jorvik's DIG activity zones, located in a converted church on nearby St Saviourgate. Back in the main museum, there is also a very handy timeline.

From the moment the Vikings sacked the holy island of Lindisfarne in AD 793, through the capture of York 73 years later and on; via the defeat of these invaders from Denmark, Norway and Sweden by England's West Saxon king Ethelred and his brother Alfred at the Battle of Ashdown, Berkshire, in 871; the permanent settling of the Vikings in northern England in 876; Alfred's agreement to accept a boundary between his kingdom and that of the Viking King Guthrun - later known as the Danelaw - in 886; to the murder in an ambush of the last King of Jorvik, Eric the Bloodaxe, by Earl Maccus in 954 ... it's all there in good old-fashioned words.

And even beyond their supposed demise, the Viking hoardes kept coming back for more. Raids on Welsh coastal

41

monasteries by Vikings from Ireland, the Isle of Man and Scottish Hebrides went on unabated. In 994, Olaf of Norway and his pal Sven 'Forkbeard', son of the Danish king, teamed up in an ultimately fruitless raid on London, before wreaking havoc across the rest of the South East.

In 1013-14, King Sven of Denmark and his son Cnut sailed up the Humber and Trent, before Saxon king Ethelred the Unready fled abroad. Sven was named King in Danelaw, and Cnut then became King of England after the deaths of Sven, Ethelred and Ethelred's son, Edmund Ironside. In 1042, Edward the Confessor, Ethelred's other son, returned from exile in Normandy. And then in 1066 ... well ... we know what happened in 1066, don't we?

***

UPON the death of Edward, Harold Godwinson - who always sounds more like an accountant than a king to me - is crowned the last Anglo-Saxon ruler of England. But still, those dogged Scandinavians won't give it a rest.

No sooner is Harold in situ than King Harald (no relation) of Norway again captures York, beating the English at Fulford, south of the city (a scene you can get a look at if you can manage the two hundred and seventy-five steps over seventy metres that take you to the top of the Minster's central tower). This time, however, the Viking stay is shorter than it is sweet. Joined in battle at Stamford Bridge by Harold, the invader - Harald Hardrada to give him his full title - is killed in action and the English King returns south victorious.

The victory, however, costs him dear. Harald's trouble causing has given Duke William of Normandy - aka William the Conqueror - an opportunity to attack England's south coast. And it is during the Battle of Hastings that a more than likely knackered Harold takes one in the eye from a stray arrow - allegedly - having effectively ended one era, that of the Vikings, and launching a new 88-year Norman dynasty.

Remarkably though, three years later, the indomitable Danes were back in York, capturing a castle that is itself a most excellent museum these days, and seizing lots of treasure. The last two such attacks, in 1070 and 1075, also resulted in a loss of local valuables but brought no political change. At last, the Danish Kingdom of Yorkshire belonged to the past. And yet, as a wander through the Jorvik Centre gift shop on the way out confirms - this is modern Britain, there is *always* a gift shop on the way out - the urge to plunder remains intact. Seventy-five quid for a souvenir bearded axe?

Personally, I make do with a fridge magnet.

***

NO sooner was William the Conqueror crowned King of England than the people of Yorkshire rose in rebellion. So he marched north and swiftly stuck up the first motte and bailey fortified-castle on the site of York Castle Museum and what would come to be known as Clifford's Tower, the castle keep.

Then, three years later with William fighting bother-causers elsewhere, the Yorkshiremen and a supportive Viking army were at it again. His response: the Harrying - or Harrowing - of the North. To put these troublesome new subjects in their place, ie under Norman rule for once and for all, his men went on the rampage. They destroyed villages, food-stores and massacred the people they had fed, before burning crops in the fields. They smashed up tools of agriculture, slaughtered animal livestock and salted the land. It was an act of genocide; around 100,000 people starved to death, from the Humber to the Tees.

Slouching towards Blubberhouses

In due course, a region laid waste to and depopulated by scorched earth atrocity not only recovered, it prospered. To the extent that by the 12th and 13th century several new towns had been founded from earlier Yorkshire settlements, including those at Hull, Leeds, Doncaster, Barnsley, Sheffield, Scarborough, Bradford, Northallerton and Richmond. Monasteries and priories at Bridlington, Pontefract, Bolton and Fountains Abbey were also built afresh or re-founded on earlier sites. Yorkshire persevered.

Yet even as old Danish-cum-Anglo-Saxon influences hung on among what remained of the general population and any new settlers, the road to a happier state was blocked by an upper rank of society almost totally French-born. As those monasteries suggest, the church was one crucial agent of control. Lots more Norman castles rose, as across the rest of Britain, any hint of northern rebellion quashed, apparently forever.

Jorvik now became Yorke, a city rebuilt in stone in the shadow of two imposing castles, an awe-inspiring Minster and the beautiful St Mary's Abbey, the ruins of which and its cross-shaped church lie still in the grounds of the Yorkshire Museum where, on rainy days like this, they can be gaped at through glass patio doors. Once again, York had growing influence. Powerful people were drawn here and a succession of English kings would come to adopt the city as their northern base.

Yorke Rediscovered is a gallery that tells the story of this particular Benedictine Abbey and, more specifically, the four life-size statues on display, found by pioneering Enlightenment figure, the Reverend Charles Wellbeloved. Excavated in 1827, the awesome foursome of saints and apostles were face down in the mud when Wellbeloved, one of a number of Georgian antiquarians intent on reviving interest in York's Medieval past, got his hands on them. It was Wellbeloved who rescued these once brightly painted 11th century sculptures from their fate as foundation stones for the later church building. And it was he who first placed the Yorkshire Museum itself on top of the Abbey ruins, also still on view, to protect them for future generations, an act of preservation and presentation that was indeed, as the literature insists, visionary.

Expanding in size and wealth, St Mary's Abbey became the richest and most powerful monastery in the North of England, with its original church rebuilt in the style of the Minster in 1294 to reflect that status. The four statues - who I want to call Fleegle, Bingo, Drooper and Snorky, but probably shouldn't - would once have stood above that new 120m-long building's west entrance. But stride back along the corridor on a trip to the recently refurbished WCs and even this more mundane part of the site has an intriguing story.

'Builders got more than they bargained for when they were installing new toilets earlier this year,' reads a sign outside the gents, dated 2012. 'A skeleton was found less than a metre below the current floor level. The ground directly beneath your feet marks the final resting place of a Roman man. We do not know his name, profession or even what he was like, but evidence suggests he was brutally murdered.' Cripes. York is that sort of place.

***

IN 1154, with the Norman age over after a couple of Williams, a Henry, a Matilda and, lastly, the original William's grandson Stephen, the era of the house of Anjou kicked in, setting the country on its latest path toward war and turmoil.

To begin with, things were bright enough with the Angevins, whose first king, Henry II, son of Matilda and

Slouching towards Blubberhouses

Geoffrey Plantagenet and the first in a long line of fourteen subsequent Plantagenet rulers, was the most powerful monarch in Europe. Our modern judicial system began to be developed, driven by personal greed rather than altruism admittedly, and more efficient modes of government were formulated. Henry's son, Richard, the Lionheart, maintained that reputation for brute strength, but by the time of the last Angevin king, John, only a fragment of Henry II's Angevin Empire remained. After squabbling with the Pope over the appointment of the Archbishop of Canterbury and then backing down, in 1215 John was forced to sign the Magna Carta before dying in ignominy a year later having reneged on the deal. Civil war ensued, leaving his out-and-out Plantagenet successor, Henry III, with a right job on his hands - especially given that he was only nine years old.

By 1227, though, having assumed the throne from his regent, John's now grown up son had restored the Magna Carta and order in the realm with it, securing the throne until 1272. It was then that Henry III's son, Edward I - aka Longshanks and named after Edward the Confessor - determined to create a bona fide British empire once again. In 1298, he tried to expand his Anglo-French kingdom into Scotland, moving his court to - guess where - Yorke, thereby promoting the city's status to royal capital of England.

That's the good news. The bad news is that, thanks to two more controversial Edwards, the start of the Hundred Years War in 1337 and no end of warring royal cousins mean we are soon deep in War of the Roses territory, a period that, along with having far more serious implications, gave rise to a theory re subsequent Yorkshire-Lancashire animosity that, given the facts, turns out to be fatally flawed.

What are those facts, you say. Tell us, tell us, do. Well sadly, the ins and outs of this particular bear pit of British history are so complex that there simply isn't room enough here to do it all justice. To flesh out the detail, you'll have to join a library or eat the internet or something. But in a nutshell, far from being a fight between the lands of Gracie Fields and the Chuckle Brothers, the Wars of the Roses that tore the country apart from 1455 to the start of the 16th century were on the whole about dynastic struggle.

Whose side you were on depended upon the royal house you were in, Lancaster or York. It was not necessary to have any actual allegiance to either of those two counties; in fact it was more of a north-south row than east against west. Think of Prince Andrew, today's Duke of York. When was the last time you saw him shopping for Aunt Bessie's in the Stirling Road branch of Poundstretcher? And, as usual, those who suffered most were the humble folk history forgot.

This, let's remember, was a time when kings enjoyed a good scrap, as the example of Richard the Lionheart among many attests. He spent just ten months of his decade-long reign in England and the rest of the time off crusading. To most, war was the sole reason for existence, the only measure of whether they were any good at the job or not. Battlefields back then were as common as car parks in the here and now - an appropriate metaphor it turns out. And perhaps the most alarming point of all is that contrary to popular myth, Yorkist strongholds were predominantly in the midlands and south, while Lancastrians held sway in a north that contained the geographical county of Yorkshire.

Admittedly, this fixed north-south state of affairs did shift briefly with the Yorkist conquest of the Lancastrians in 1461 and subsequent rise to popularity of a certain Richard III, whose bones were recently discovered in Leicester.

In fact, at the time, the War of the Roses weren't even known as such. They were most widely referred to as the War of the Cousins, with most Yorkist land in the North looted regularly. A large part of the Lancastrian army would have been recruited from Yorkshire, with white rose soldiery largely hailing from the South, Ireland and Wales. And even more confusingly, the actual roses themselves are a more recent invention too. The House of York fought under the symbol of the 'sunne in splendour', an astronomical effect said to have been witnessed by Yorkist Edward IV before the battle of Mortimer's Cross in Herefordshire. The House of Lancaster's sign, meanwhile, was a double S collar, or swan.

So where did the roses come from? They originated with the first Tudor king, Henry VII, who took up a tenuous claim to the throne in 1485. He was linked to the House of Lancaster through the Beaufort family, but that had been an illegitimate relationship legalised later for respectability's sake. To shore up his position, he wed Edward IV's daughter Elizabeth of York, thereby uniting the houses and bringing civil war to an end. To symbolise the moment, his spin-doctors came up with white and red roses intertwined. During the 14th and 13th centuries respectively, roses had been used as emblems by the original Duke of York and Earl of Lancaster. Yet it isn't until Victorian times that the ever-verbose Sir Walter Scott is said to have popularised the term 'Wars of the Roses'. Shakespeare, too, may have played a part with references to the flower, plucked by the warring rivals, in his history plays of the period.

Whatever the reality, like death and taxes, those roses are here to stay. The very idea of Yorkshire Day is based upon them. For it was in Northern Germany on 1 August 1759, the date of the Battle of Minden during the Seven Years War, that the King's Own Yorkshire Light Infantry are said to have picked white roses to commemorate fallen comrades in their victory over France.

3. Pudding on the Ritz

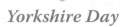

Yorkshire Day

A BOILED ham sandwich after noon, Thursday August 1, 2013. I'm in Skipton, North Yorkshire - 'The Gateway to the Dales', as it says on the road signs - to watch a gaggle of local and visiting dignitaries return from their procession through town, clad in ermine, chains and similar regalia.

Yorkshire Day. Twenty-four hours in which Yorkshire wears its pride on its sleeve. Just like the other three hundred and sixty four, you are no doubt thinking, but with a bit more pomp and circumstance.

These days, thanks to online social media, it's easy to discover what the rest of the country thinks of it all. On Twitter, for example, several of my Lancashire-based chums were already bridling the night before. 'Dear Yorkshire. No one is fussed. Yours, the rest of the UK.' 'It was only invented because a full year of you being miserable bastards got tedious.' 'Tomorrow is Yorkshire Day. Hurrah. Yawksher. Yawksher (in dull monotone voice). Every other day belongs to Lancashire, la la la...' etc.

Slouching towards Blubberhouses

And the best: 'Yorkshire Day is like every other day - only much slower . . .'

At which point, it's worth noting that the organisation Friends of Real Lancashire has staged its own Lancashire Day - 27 November - since 1996, but no one seems to have noticed.

Not that us Yorkies should gloat. In the town charged with hosting this year's festivities, Skipton, the only sign of anything significant is a bit of a traffic tailback. And even that turned out to be the fault of a dodgy traffic light near Tescos.

In fact, other than a few more orange-bibbed police than usual, a possibly related pealing of church bells and the odd flag - white rose, blue background - hanging limply from Eastwood's chippy, various cafés, shops and the town hall up near Skipton Castle, there is little sense of occasion at all.

***

FIRST celebrated in its modern form by the Yorkshire Ridings Society in 1975, a protest at Local Government reorganisation, the Welcome to Yorkshire website describes Yorkshire Day as when: '...the UK's largest county comes together to indulge in vast quantities of regional pride.'

But there is a far longer history, going back to Minden Day, 1 August 1759, as described in chapter two, a battle in the Seven Years War championed thereafter by successors to the King's Own Yorkshire Light Infantry. Coincidentally, August 1, 1834, also saw the culmination of Wilberforce's campaign to abolish slavery in the British Empire.

Nowadays, the Yorkshire Ridings Society invites Lord Mayors, Mayors and an assortment of other civic heads to a march through one of the county's territories, for which the local newspapers unfailingly turn up. Since 1998, that parade has gone through Huddersfield, Hull (twice), Wakefield (twice), Halifax, Leeds, Bradford, Penistone, Redcar, Malton, Hedon, Scarborough and, in 2013, Skipton. On the face of it, it's all just a bit of, ahem, fun, and allows for the harmless propagation of a few favourite stereotypes and myths.

Yet a slight fact checking detour to the Yorkshire Ridings Society website - 'Actively working to preserve the integrity of Yorkshire' - reveals a more territorial undercurrent. 'Did you know? The number of acres covered by Yorkshire is more than the number of letters in the King James Bible,' it helpfully points out, while going on to explain how Yorkshire Day's oldest annual celebration takes place in York.

It is there, once Yorkshire flags have been carried around the city walls, that 'The Declaration of Yorkshire Integrity' is read out, at each of the bars. 'By tradition, the boundaries of the ridings run to the walls of York, so by walking out of three of the bars it is possible to read the declaration in each riding,' the website says. 'At Monk Bar, the reading is inside, for the city.'

In 2013, it will be read at 11:38am, representing 1,138 years since the Ridings were first mentioned in the Anglo-Saxon *Chronicle*. Eccentric much?

The clue is in the name, I suppose. The Yorkshire Ridings Society can get itself in a right old lather about those ancient borders, trumpeting how, only in April, Keighley-born Local Government Secretary Eric Pickles marked St George's Day with a formal acknowledgement of England's traditional counties in the life of the nation.' Leader of the Conservative group on Bradford Council from 1988-1990, Pickles (who, one suspects, must really love hearing from them) is quoted: 'The tapestry of England's counties binds our nation together. This government has binned the arbitrary Government Office euro-regions, and instead, we are championing England's traditional local identities, which continue to run deep.

Slouching towards Blubberhouses

Administrative restructuring by previous governments has sought to suppress and undermine such local identities. Today, on St George's Day, we commemorate our patron saint and formally acknowledge the continuing role of our traditional counties in England's public and cultural life.'

The website has an extended quote from Rupert Barnes, Vice-Chairman of the Association of British Counties, too. Who knew that such a movement exists in a world wherein we are all so pushed for valuable time? 'Counties are the basic tapestry on which countless generations have made their lives. They have shaped our identities and our view of ourselves and have remained a constant throughout centuries of change to become a vital part of British culture, geography and heritage,' he says, admittedly putting it rather elegantly.

'The counties predate any transient lines drawn for convenience or administration and predate the kingdom itself, rooted in history and cultural identity, so that the ancient counties are of the people not of the state. Statutes on administration have respectfully left the ancient counties alone. This pattern of the counties brought down to us through the centuries is the pattern around which the nation has grown and grown great, and worthy of celebration.'

'The Government's timing could not be better for our campaign,' concludes the YRS site. And lo! The campaign in question is revealed as 'A Ring of Roses', aka 'The Yorkshire Ridings Society's biggest and most exciting Yorkshire Day project yet. What better way to mark our [historic] boundary than by flying Yorkshire flags in all the settlements on or very close to [it] on Yorkshire Day?'

Alas, the exact degree of enthusiasm is unknown although, in late July, the Society had requests for '...well over a hundred flags so far. If you have a Yorkshire flag please fly it on Thursday or perhaps for a few days either side. In fact, every day is a special day in Yorkshire, so why not leave it up?'

***

BUT what does Yorkshire Day mean to those of us with little appetite for local government strife, for whom boundaries are predominantly things to bash fours and sixes over?

The signs hadn't been good on Wednesday's *Look North*, when comedy enthusiast Martyn Barrow was studio-interviewed on account of having set up a page on Facebook.

Billed as a 'central repository for Yorkshire humour', its creator was then probed for how that category of comedy might be properly identified beneath a graphic of a road sign: 'Welcome to Leeds. We're right, you're wrong.' Well, yes. That would do it. There was also a map of the UK on which every county but one was marked 'NY' - Not Yorkshire.

By way of illustration, Mr Barrow told of how a chap knocked on a neighbour's door, to be met by the lady of the house. 'I'm awfully sorry,' she says, 'Harry's passed away. He died last night.' 'What a shock,' the visitor replies. 'Before he went, did he say anything about a pot of paint?'

Lazy Yorkshireman tells doctor he is unable to sleep. 'Here's two tablets, take them before you go to bed.' 'No,' says patient, 'I've no trouble sleeping at night,' was another.

A filmed package from Barnsley market didn't fare much better, at least to begin with. 'We're all funny really, aren't we?' said the first interviewee. 'We're from Yorkshire. We're all down to earth.' 'We are quite dry and do take the mickey out of us-selves a bit more,' added a second, with a tad more insight.

'We don't make the jokes, we are the jokes,' said another man in similar vein, while a fourth - 'My brother were that ugly, me mam had to feed him wi' a catapult...' - was surely 'Yorkshire' only in that it was told in Barnsley.

'We've talked about northern humour, but what's so special about Yorkshire?' co-host Charlotte insisted valiantly, finally forced to supply a relevant example of her own.

'Why should you never ask anyone if they come from Yorkshire? If they're not from Yorkshire they'll be insulted. If they are from Yorkshire, they'll have told you already.'

But it was an old boy in Barnsley market who got to the nub of it. Bloke and his son laiking 'I Spy'. 'Something beginning with T,' says the lad. 'Television?' says his dad. 'No.' 'Table?' 'No.' 'What then?' 'T'oven door.'

**

YORKSHIRE Day dawns bright and sunny.

It commences with a display of ambush marketing by England sponsors Yorkshire Tea in Manchester, where Australia are already facing series defeat in the opening day of the third Ashes Test match at Old Trafford.

This leads the Sky Sports commentary team into a discussion about tripe while, on the radio, Geoffrey Boycott tells his BBC *Test Match Special* colleagues that one poor sap could have been '...bowled out with a toffee apple.'

Meanwhile, back in Skipton, with the Lord Mayors' parade done and dusted, the rest of the celebrations can get underway. Rest of the celebrations? Why, yes. Yorkshire Day isn't just a day anymore. It's four days. More, if you count the lead-up. Just over a fortnight ago, promotional banners were strung from the lampposts as Clogfest 2013 rolled into town.

Ah, clog dancing. Now there's an activity as Yorkshire as they come. Except that, as it turns out, it isn't. The genre's only specific annual national festival may be held here in

North Yorkshire, but the old wooden boogie took root in the cotton mills of, yikes, Lancashire, aided by a flood of Irish immigrants in the mid-eighteenth century. Geordies have been partial to it, too, while clogs were a staple ingredient of music hall, clattering on Variety stages the length and breadth of the UK. Nowadays clog dancing is a folk festival staple.

On this particular Saturday afternoon, muggy but with a refreshing breeze, there is an ideal bit of cloud cover for Yorkshire's greatest fast bowler 'Fiery Fred' Trueman, around whose fine bronze statue of the man in full flow one hundred or so onlookers gather, near a temporary raised stage. The event - sponsored by Skipton brewery Copper Dragon - is sited on the small man-made 'island' bounded by Eller Beck and the Leeds-Liverpool Canal, across from which is Pennine Cruisers with its promise of thirty-minute boat trips.

As sandstone dappled waters lap gently against the rubber tyres tied to well-worn towpaths, doubtless by clogs in some deep industrial past, two men hose down *Dalesman*, a red and blue barge. Alongside, stands the Aagrah Indian bar and restaurant, in the under-hang of whose windowed extension a number of tourists sit resting in the shade.

Opposite, and with more moored barges in between, folk mill about licking ice creams. Others line the old stone bridge on Coach Street, above its precarious steps, leaning on the wall and peering out across the canal basin. What they are looking at is four women in pinnies dancing to a chap in a fancy waistcoat who canoodles a fiddle.

When the synchronised bobbing and foot tapping comes to an end, a compere says: '...that's it for this section, but don't go away. In fifteen minutes it will be time for the showcase, when we'll have twenty-four groups for you, including Wallop, the dancing horse.'

It's a charming scene. Traditions are being celebrated

but the past is held at bay, no one seems entirely in its thrall. People are simply out to enjoy themselves.

Creativity, diversity and change are at the heart of Skipton's Clogfest, in which women outnumber men several times over. Long skirts, ribbons and embroidered tearoom pinafores are to the fore for what to the uninitiated looks like colour-co-ordinated line-dancing, but with enough room for personal and group expressions of individuality; a right grand metaphor for the community ideal.

Though the majority of participants are middle-aged, there are children's groups here also - the Dancetastics from Haworth being one - so an active thriving culture is still being passed on to future generations. And far from being just a white rose thing, the dancers braving a black stage accessed by some not very clog-friendly steps, hail from far and wide. Three lads in flat caps and two girls named the Rattlejiggers, for example, have travelled up from Nottinghamshire.

Awaiting her turn is Sue, a member of the Ridgeway Step Clog group from Oxfordshire. Clad in black waistcoat and red dress, she is as good a person as any to ask about the appeal of a pastime with roots in the northern industrial revolution but which now confounds the stereotypes. And straight away, firm but friendly, she puts me right.

'What we do is not straight clog dancing as such, it's stepping, with influences from Ireland, America, Canada, Wales and elsewhere,' she says of a group formed in 1998 and named for their proximity to the more ancient Ridgeway path from Avebury to Ivinghoe Beacon. 'Clog dancing started in the cotton mills. Boredom got to the workers and they began tapping out sounds to the noise of the machines. Then people thought they would earn a bob or two doing it in music hall - usually the men. I suppose, like most things, it has just spread and you start to make it your own.'

Sue puts the attraction of stepping down to intricacy. 'A lot of memory and thought goes into step clogging because the steps are so fast,' she says, of her own participation. 'And you have to make clear sounds - or try. We often get mixed up with morris dancing as that can involve clogs, but step clogging is more precise. For me, it's about being part of a group of people and putting in the hours; it's not something you can just dip into. You've got to work at it. It would take a year's worth of lessons to get up to performance standard, unless you are young and have a brilliant memory.'

And the male to female ratio, is that a problem? 'Yes, there are more women than men. My husband has had a go, for something to do. There's no reason why they shouldn't, men seem to like to show off the flashy steps. But we don't get enough coming along. I think there is a little bit of an element within clog dancing of nit-picking, because it is about nanoseconds in terms of matching the footwork with the music. It can be a little constraining, dancing in a group.'

According to Sue, where the southern-based groups differ from their northern counterparts is in their tendency to 'push the edges of tradition'. And reading up on Ridgeway later, their distinctive choreography includes the use of props like garlands, brooms, percussion and sheep. The latter might have gone down well in a town whose name is derived from the Saxon word for those beasts - 'sheep town'.

Still, there is plenty of innovative movement and rhythm from the other twenty-three teams, next up of which is Inclognito, two ladies dancing on home turf to a jazzy saxophone rendition of the theme to *The Pink Panther*. After which it's the Rattlejiggers, followed by a slow accordion waltz by a group called Richmond Castle and then Strictly Clog from Sheffield, who present their version of a Swedish tune to squeeze box backing.

Slouching towards Blubberhouses

When Cheeky Feet (from Bristol and Newport - doing some nifty Irish and Lancashire steps) and Pennyroyal (from Surrey) have done their bit, it will be the turn of Clogaire, a couple of whose members, I am startled to realise when they drop their woollen shawls, live in the farmhouse behind us.

Although Saltaire-based, they are announced as being 'from Leeds' - don't tell anyone in Bradford - and a chat when they are done expands further on clog dancing's surprising range of influence. 'As with all music, influences come in over time,' says Nicola. 'Sailors might come back from sea and introduce the horn pipe, for instance.'

No prizes for guessing where Hadrian's Clog originate and other well drilled and puntastic 'sides' include Camden Clog, Clogarhythm, Carlisle Cloggies, the Lancs Wallopers, Heage Windmillers and Stony Steppers. Ridgeway are eighteen on the bill. I ask Nicola about the clogs themselves, sturdy like little black whales and thus far free of the insignia of Nike or adidas Predator, or any other such trendy brand.

'Mine have beech soles,' she says, turning them over for confirmation, 'some have sycamore. There's a bloke from Wales here who makes and sells them.'

And where are the segs? Given the racket, they must have metal segs like we used to wear in our 'dealer boots' at school. 'If you are doing Appalachian, maybe, but segs aren't traditional in clog step. There would be too many sparks. Wood can be slippery, though, which is why people are being helped down off the stage.'

Oh and that dancing horse, Wallop, last on the bill. Turns out he's a pantomime job.

'The compere plays the back end,' says Nicola. 'It's really funny, when you haven't seen it fifty times.'

***

WHILE days one, two and three of Yorkshire Day are low key, day four catches the eye because they shut Skipton high street down to traffic for 'The Best of Yorkshire Festival', Among the delights on offer: a 'feast of food' from a farmer's market, flat cap throwing and welly wanging. There's a Yorkshire pudding eating contest too.

They like their festivals and markets in Skipton, a town that is actually just outside the Yorkshire Dales, with Craven's limestone hills to the north, gritstone moors to the south and the pastoral Ribble valley out west. Its highlight stands a quarter of mile east of the canal basin. Skipton castle - which stands next to the town's beautiful fourteenth century Holy Trinity parish church on a cliff at the top end of town - was built in 1090, though the family most closely associated with it, the Cliftons, took ownership in 1310.

It was gifted to them by Edward II and, later, the castle might conceivably have been home to a future king if only King Henry's niece, Lady Eleanor Brandon, had lived long enough to give birth to a son instead of dying aged 26. As it is, she rests next door. As does a memorial to George Clifford, the third Earl of Cumberland, designed by self-styled Queen of the North, Lady Anne Clifford. She it was who restored the castle to pretty much its current state and planted a yew that still resides in an early Tudor courtyard, making it one of the oldest trees in Britain.

Read about all of this and more when you wander around the place, inside and out, under your own steam or courtesy of a guided tour. And be sure not to miss the super grim dungeons - a handy threat for unruly children. There's a nice walk behind the castle too, through Skipton Woods, a favourite promenade in Victorian times.

The main reason folk travel here though, is for those

aforementioned festivals and, especially, markets. The place is not exactly lacking in shopping in any case - John Spencer, one half of Marks and Spencer, was born here - with modern hustle and bustle cheek by jowl with olde worlde yards, gift and tea shops, and converted waterway warehouses.

But it's the high street - with its cobbled lane, Sheep Street, parallel - that is the chief focal point. Every Monday, Wednesday, Friday and Saturday stalls are pitched by traders hoping to attract the multitudes of bargain hunters who flock in by car, train and charabanc. On the first Sunday of every month, there's a farmers' market in the Canal basin, just one in a long list of events that over the course of an average year includes the Skipton Music Festival in March; Beer Festival, Triathlon and St George's Day Parade in April; a Waterway festival in May; Skipton Gala plus an Armed Forces and Veterans Day in June; Sheep Day and the Clogfest in July; Skipton International Puppet Festival in September; and a Yuletide Festival and Christmas Market in December.

In which company, Yorkshire Day week (!) has a job standing out, even with 5,000 bags of the best crisps in the world - Bradford's own Seabrooks (for some reason, nowadays billed as 'lovingly made in Yorkshire') - to give away and a large screen showing of the Dales-based film *Calendar Girls*.

Still, they are throwing themselves into it, having borrowed Welcome to Yorkshire's 'urban beach' with its sand, deckchairs, buckets, spades and donkeys. Also on hand are maritime jugglers, comedy lifeguards and a steel drum band that livens things no end on the Friday, amid heritage trails, talks, craft displays, exhibitions and operatic concerts, few of which actually take place on Yorkshire Day itself.

And the organisation charged with getting local companies involved, Yorkshire Society, does appear to be forward thinking. Under the patronage of HRH The Duke of

York, this organisation - no relation to its Ridings namesake - represents: '...the very best that Yorkshire has to offer for those living, working, visiting or investing in the county, whilst also generating funds to directly plough back into regional and local communities.' Nowt to quibble with there.

But the most innovative thing about Yorkshire Day 2013 has nothing to do with Skipton at all. It originates not on the banks of the Aire, but along the nearby Wharfe Valley. A 'star-studded' version of 'Ilkla Moor Baht 'At,' no less, reworked 'to breathe life into our own national anthem.'

***

A LITMUS test for the wider impact of Yorkshire Day on the county might be found in how its evening news and current affairs magazine programmes deal with it.

On ITV, that means *Calendar*, a long-running teatime show that began in 1968, hosted these days by Christine Talbot and Duncan Wood, but once a journalistic breeding ground for future MPs Jonathan Aitken and Austin Mitchell, Zeinab Badawi and the ferret's favourite, Richard Whiteley.

On the BBC it means *Look North*, anchored as we saw at the Great Yorkshire Show by the equally legendary Harry Gration MBE and - at this point in 2013 - a collection of co-presenters since the departure of Christa Ackroyd in July.

Calendar comes on first at 6.00pm. And though I'm not usually watching telly at that time, I do hold it in affection, having made my first ever TV appearance on the programme in 1977. On a whim, I wrote in to be a 'Calendar Kid', i.e. go on a children's spin-off wherein Yorkshire youngsters were invited to submit unusual hobbies, co-hosted by Whiteley's eventual partner Kathryn Apanowicz, and the annoyingly cheerful *Blue Peter* presenter in waiting, Mark Curry.

Slouching towards Blubberhouses

Anyway, to my great disappointment, writing and drawing my own comics didn't get me on *Calendar Kids*, but would I like to come on *Calendar* itself they asked my 14-year-old self. Stardom beckoned. A taxi was sent for my mum and me - we didn't have a car of our own, by 'eck, but we had it tough - a telly and free pop in the waiting room. Best of all, though, was my fellow guest, a man who went on to become a bit of a hero of mine, the comics-collector-cum-cartoonist-cum-horror-film-enthusiast-cum-all-round-popular-culture-factotum Denis Gifford. I don't recall much else, other than Whiteley was host and Denis was kind about my doodling. My mum was impressed that I used the word 'punchline'.

In contrast, the 50-year-old me found the August 1 2013 edition of *Calendar* an altogether less thrilling affair, with headlines verging on trifling by comparison. A billion pound offshore wind farm, for example, set to transform energy production on the east coast. Margaret Thatcher's secret plans to send in the troops before the miners' strike of 1983... trivial stuff like that. Yeah, yeah, but what about Yorkshire Day?

Thankfully, after a story revealing that Doncaster superstar Louis Tomlinson has been given a number 20 shirt by Donny Rovers we are off. A town crier is on the towpath of the Leeds-Liverpool canal as a 'unique gathering of civic dignitaries from all over Yorkshire' board a flotilla of barges heading for Skipton. Cut to the bus station, where they are met by a chap with a giant mace. 'There are 260 civic heads gathered here today,' says the Mayor of Skipton, Cllr John Kerwin-Davey. 'The biggest gathering of civic heads there's ever been in Yorkshire.'

Hang on, is it the gathering that's big or the heads?

'It's very gratifying that I should be mayor when it happens. How is that even possible?' he muses. There is then a swift televisual diversion to Meadowhall shopping centre

62

by the M1, with its 'celebration of everything that's made Sheffield famous', including a life-size cut-out of Jessica Ennis-Hill and displays marking football's inaugural club and the centenary of Harry Brearley's discovery of stainless steel.

Following which we take a trip up Ilkley Moor, where the Harrogate and Skipton Rock Up And Sing choirs show their pink sweatshirts off for the camera. Singer songwriter Alistair Griffin says: 'A lot of kids don't know what 'Ilkla Moor Baht 'At' is. It was great fun to be involved in. You can't let these things die out.' The video - just released - is a laugh. Thorne-born opera diva Lesley Garrett puts the wind in its sails and a song first published in 1916 that most likely originated in West Yorkshire in the latter half of the nineteenth century gets its promised new treatment.

Bombastic Mexborough-born actor Brian Blessed is in it too with a shall we say distinctive Yorkshire 'rap' providing what producer Eliot Kennedy calls 'a 'modern twist.'

If you come from Yorkshire, you can't not be familiar with 'Ilkla Moor Baht 'At'. It's a morbid and, when you think about it, disconcerting tale about a chap who dares to 'court' his sweetheart, Mary Jane, high on the moor without his hat (other items of clothing may also have been discarded). The upshot? He catches his death of cold, ends up as worm-food and then, via a process of impeccable production line logic, duck fodder and a hearty meal for the singer(s), recompense for them having had to pay to bury the bugger. In other words, a tale of good old-fashioned Yorkie cannibalism and the ideal tune with which to rally all to the white rose cause.

Not that Sheffield-based Kennedy, artistic director on *X Factor* among much else, quite sees it that way. 'When you get down to it, it's actually a beautiful song that you can't help singing along to,' he says, before revealing on *Calendar* that: 'As it progressed, it became this huge arrangement with different sections and tempos and key changes. Yorkshire folk are passionate about being from Yorkshire. Everyone gave it their all, which is a fantastic thing.'

Along with Garrett and Blessed, whose unorthodox contribution bursts in just as it looks like turning into an episode of *Songs of Praise*, complete with sweeping views of rocks and bracken, there is hat-based japery from the choir and the always impressive sound of the Grimethorpe Colliery brass band. *X Factor* singer and soldier Jonjo Kerr is also on a track whose profits will go to charity.

So far so upbeat, but then *Calendar* whisks us south, where someone in London has committed a gaffe. 'For several hours, the Department of Communities and Local Government flew the Yorkshire flag upside down,' it reports, 'traditionally a sign of distress.' And then, back in Skipton, pictures of 'crowds' (what crowds?) lapping up the celebrations. 'There's everything you could wish for in Yorkshire,' says one visitor in a straw hat, with a white rose pinned to his lapel. His wife adds: 'We had to come and enjoy Yorkshire, because it's the finest place in the universe.'

Look North's coverage of Yorkshire Day, meanwhile, is brief. A clip of the 'Ilkla Moor Baht 'At' video and that's your lot. No doubt the Yorkshire Ridings Society went apoplectic.

***

IT's a long way from Ilkley to Manhattan. And not only geographically. For the Winter Gardens read Lincoln Center, for Betty's tea rooms read Starbucks.

It's in the latter of those that Rhiannon Gayle, founder of Rock Up And Sing, sips at a scalding hot cappuccino. We are in New York - no relation to *old* York - ahead of the choir's first concert on Broadway, my wife Jacqui also taking part.

Broadway? That's quite a trajectory for an outfit set up in Harrogate in May 2009, isn't it? Could she ever have imagined her choir performing in the Big Apple?

'No, I didn't think beyond the first six months,' she says, originator of a project that has grown into the biggest and most high-profile of its kind in Yorkshire, hence the appearance in Eliot Kennedy's video. 'I decided there weren't enough choirs in Harrogate that were fun. So I just sent a text to some of my friends. We put one ad in the paper and that was that. About eighty-four people came through the door, that atmosphere was good and it has grown from there.'

With a background in classical music rather than rock, Gayle might seem an unlikely candidate to conduct a choir - actually, make that *five* choirs now - more likely to be heard singing Coldplay's 'Viva la Vida' or Dream Academy's 'Life in a Northern Town' than anything from *Così fan tutte* or *Götterdämmerung*, upcoming productions at the adjoining Met Opera. But actually she is the embodiment of music's eternal resistance to pigeonholes. And along with enjoying the best attributes of joint-endeavour, the Rock Up and Sing choirs are proof that an open-minded and cosmopolitan spirit of drive and imagination will always scupper backward-looking stick-in-the-mud insularity, even in Yorkshire.

In the Lincoln Center's Avery Fisher Hall, a group of those able to make the trip are part of a much larger ensemble performing the New York premiere of composer Christopher Tin's classical crossover album, *Calling All Dawns*. Released in 2009 it won two Grammys, the first time that a composition initially written for a video game has landed such an award.

A charismatic former teacher of Birmingham roots who studied in London and eventually moved to Harrogate via Redditch and Wyndham, Gayle says she discovered while teaching that a lot of students preferred to sing in a crowd rather than learn one-to-one. The lesson stayed with her, first in Harrogate and then in Skipton - '...forty or fifty turned up on the first night of that one. Skipton is probably the most "Yorkshire" of all the choirs, just in the way they are, the warmth and the rest of it. When I first arrived in Yorkshire, I used to pick up the phone and think I was in trouble: "Now then..." Yorkshire people can be abrupt and wary to begin with, they take a while to accept you. But once they have they are very warm and friendly.'

As with clog dancing, a big problem is finding enough men. 'Men don't sing. After a pint of beer they might, or in a rugby club,' she says, as the coffee machines chug and the noise of a busy New York afternoon - is there any other kind - go on unabated. 'That why I started "Just for Girls", so as not to have that problem. We do now have a male section - it isn't very big, but they're good. Boys are told it's not cool to sing, but if they do sing they prefer to be among men. They don't like to be in the minority. Get a group together, though, and they all become very close-knit.'

Days later, *Calling All Dawns*, featuring twelve songs in twelve languages including Swahili, Mandarin, Hebrew, Gaelic, Sanskrit, Portuguese and Farsi, and lyrics based on sources like Japanese haiku, Maori proverbs, the *Torah* and *Bhagavad Gita*, is a triumph. Its three movements, day, night and dawn that invoke the cycle of life, death and rebirth, are brought exhilaratingly to life by the most sublime orchestral music and singers of varying ages and nationalities who deserve every second of their standing ovation. And I'm not just saying that because my wife was next to the cellists.

Quite a high. So what next?

'In terms of size, there are no plans for future growth,' says Rhiannon, her coffee finally at quaffable temperature. 'We've got a kids choir now, around four hundred members in all, and that is enough. But what we will do is more interesting stuff, like coming to America, backing well-known artists, award ceremonies and so on. Hopefully, we'll be doing a lot during the Tour de France.'

And why not, they've already recorded at Abbey Road Studios, risking the traffic on that zebra crossing.

Oh and, of course, this being April, there's still the August release of 'Ilkla Moor Baht 'At' to anticipate. It will be on the back of a campaign by music teacher and director Gordon Eddison of Otley to raise awareness of the song, after a claim that only ten per cent of Yorkshire youngsters were even aware of it. 'That seemed an obvious thing for us to do,' Rhiannon says. 'But while we are very much a Yorkshire choir, we are not specific to Yorkshire at all. We do all sorts... world music, everything. We've been in the studio with Eliott - who's worked with Gary Barlow, the Spice Girls and now us!'

Having so far raised around £20,000 for charity, the benefits of communal participation will continue too.

'Being in a choir improves health, including mental health,' she says. 'Singing helps with depression, improves self-esteem and encourages you to push yourself further. This work we are doing is well beyond what anyone thought they would. So it's continually stretching them and if you achieve it makes you feel good. Choirs are about friendship too, and looking out for one another.'

***

LITTLE sign of any such spirit one week later, when Godfrey Bloom, MEP for Yorkshire and Northern Lincolnshire, is caught telling a meeting of UKIP supporters that British aid should not be sent to 'bongo bongo land'.

Now whatever your views on where charity should

Slouching towards Blubberhouses

and should not begin and end, this is just the sort of talk that can give a county a bad name. If Yorkshire Day is meant to prop up insular attitudes like those from a politician who, in 2010, was ejected from the European Parliament for directing a Nazi slogan at a German colleague, you can keep it.

And yet, that very day in the *Yorkshire Post*, comes news that: 'Whitehall officials [are] engaged in a secret plot with a London-based tourism agency to remove Yorkshire's name from next year's hosting of the Tour de France and rebrand it as an all-England event.' The paper goes on: 'Minutes of a private meeting of senior sports officials ... show how the Department for Culture, Media and Sport has decided to market the event as the "England" Grand Départ, in a clear snub to the Yorkshire tourism bosses who last year beat the Government's own Scottish-based bid to secure the event for the region. The minutes form part of a tranche of documents released to the *Yorkshire Post* under Freedom of Information laws, which reveal the depth of the tension and mistrust between Whitehall and the Yorkshire-based team.'

Apparently, UK Sport reckon Welcome to Yorkshire's hosting of the Tour de France is high risk and expresses 'limited confidence' in its suitability to lead the event. 'Most contentious, however, is the revelation that DCMS and UK Sport sought to bypass Yorkshire altogether in the marketing of the event, via the national tourism agency VisitEngland.'

The report concludes: 'Last month, exactly a year before the Grand Départ takes place in Leeds, VisitEngland sent out its first Tour de France press release from its offices in central London. Tellingly, [it] was titled "England gears up to host Tour de France 2014". It made eleven separate references to "England", and just one to "Yorkshire" - a mention of the Yorkshire Wolds in the final paragraph.'

Perhaps they are out to get us after all.

4. Game of Bones

◇

A History of Yorkshire - Part Two

IT's 26 March, 2013. I am having my tea, watching *Look North*.

'Descendants of King Richard III are to fight in the court for the right to have their ancestor reburied in York,' says presenter Phil Bodmer. 'Papers are due to be lodged at the High Court next week arguing that they should have been consulted over the reburial plans, which will see the King's remains reburied in Leicester where they were found. His descendants say there's evidence that the Yorkist king planned a burial in York where he had many links. Cathy Killick has the story...'

And so she does, the opening shot of a skull and pile of bones that the British public are by now so familiar with described as: '...the find of the decade.' By Cathy's account, 60,000 people have already visited an exhibition in what looks like a hastily thrown-up tent, while plans to re-inter the remains in Leicester Cathedral go on unabated. But they haven't reckoned with the likes of Stephen Nicolay, just one of the royal enigma's so-called 'descendants', campaigning to deny the East Midlands city its moment of glory.

The licence to re-inter, says Nicolay, wrapped in a foppish scarf beneath dark flowing locks and looking every bit one of the family, was granted without wider consultation. So for the council to go ahead blithely with their plans: '...we think is morally wrong.' A shot of a waxy reconstructed face, fleshed out from the skull in the ground, tends to reinforce Nicolay's familial claim - it could be his better looking younger brother - but Peter Soulsby, the Mayor of Leicester, is having none of it.

'I have no doubt at all that the High Court will treat this particular case as being something that is plainly daft,' he says, dismissively. 'After 500 years in the shadow of this cathedral, in accordance with the licence, the bones should be and will be re-interred [here].'

Which is as good a time as any for Cathy to nip back to York and grab a soundbite from the curator of that city's Richard III Museum. 'We now get the chance to have [the matter] properly debated before lawyers,' says the anoraked fellow in question, Paul Toy, with a waxwork of his hero in the background. 'It would be immensely helpful not only for this particular case, but anything similar in future.'

Cue our reporter, strolling along the city walls at Monkgate, home not only to 'perhaps the country's only working portcullis, dating from 1300' but this mini museum itself. 'In resorting to the courts, Richard's descendants are relying on legal principles their ancestor helped establish in 1484,' she says, emerging out of soft focus. 'Could it alter his final resting place? What a turn-up for the books if it does.'

Well, a turn-up for *this* book, that's for sure.

***

SO who actually was Richard III? That hunchback hammed up by Laurence Olivier? 'A horse, a horse, my kingdom for a horse?' The villainous geezer who bumped off his nephews, those poor little mites in the tower? To at least try to get inside the possibly criminal mind of a man for whom psychological profiling arrived several hundred years too late - you need to take a trip, like Cathy Killick, to that self-same Richard III Museum. It isn't big, but it sure as hell is clever.

Located in Monk Bar, the tallest of the four main defensive gateways standing in York - the others being Bootham Bar to the north west, Micklegate Bar to the south west and Walmgate Bar to the south east - it's in a prime spot all right. You enter high up on those city walls, via a flight of narrow stone steps and past a heavy riveted solid oak door. Sign a voluntary petition to bring eponymous Dick back to his roots, hand over £3 to the chap on the counter and voila, you're in. The same chap on the counter, incidentally, who but a few weeks later would pop up on the telly in his anorak. I don't blame him, by the way. It's bloody freezing in here.

This first floor entry level room is a shop, full of the usual souvenirs and books, some tatty others less so. But it's on the second floor where the place really comes alive. Up another narrow staircase and we are in a charming if eccentric 'interactive courtroom', in which the voice of Richard III - or an actor playing him - is cross-examined every five minutes on a loop. 'Now is the winter of our discontent...'

The charge: the callous murder of two young princes during a reign of only 26 months. Did he do it? Was Richard indeed the nasty piece of work as portrayed by the bard? Or is he the victim of Tudor propaganda? There is absolutely no doubt which side of the argument the museum bearing his name comes down upon.

Slouching towards Blubberhouses

Violence, firmness and action were required in the role of a king we are reminded. Richard was only accused of the crime after his death at the Battle of Bosworth, from where his body was taken and thrown unceremoniously into that Leicestershire council car park pit. Furthermore, the princes were very much alive when he rode out on a northern tour of his kingdom.

At which point it would be an idea to recap how Richard, at the time of writing still the only true English king to be born in England and marry an Englishwoman, actually ascended to the throne in the first place.

His story begins with the last of the strictly Plantagenet kings, Richard II, grandson of Edward III. This earlier Richard had first worn the crown as a ten-year-old thanks to the death of Edward's eldest son, the so-called Black Prince. Aged 14, in 1381, he impressed many by meeting Wat Tyler and Co face to face at Smithfield, London, during the Peasants' Revolt, before crushing that uprising in a matter of weeks. Afterwards, though, his biggest fans were in the North, their support to an extent bought by the division of vast confiscated properties of the Duchy of Lancaster that had formerly belonged to John of Gaunt, the father of Richard's cousin, Henry of Bolingbroke. Several such hostile extended family members were banished or bumped off, alienating the authoritarian king further.

Then, in 1399, while Richard was away on one of his expeditions to Ireland, trying to reconcile the Anglo-Irish lords there with the Gaels, Henry, who had been one of those banished, returned to claim his father's 'inheritance'. Soon Richard was captured, deposed and dead in Pontefract Castle, most likely left to starve by constructive neglect. Loyal to Richard, York raised an army in defiance, but the die was cast. Henry IV duly took the crown, the Lancastrian line of

Plantagenets had begun and the city paid a heavy price. Out of favour and lacking royal patronage, York's reputation was about to wane.

The Lancastrians - all imaginatively named Henry, as if this medieval version of *The Sopranos* on horseback wasn't confusing enough - duly kept control, just about, for the next 62 years, through Henrys IV, V and VI. It was an era, though, fraught with even more rebellion and instability than usual. Not only were there contretemps galore with France (including Henry V's famous victory at Agincourt in 1415), towards the end of Henry VI's reign, the Wars of the Roses kicked in. Rival claims to the throne went back almost 80 years to Edward III, from whom the Lancastrian dynasty descended via John of Gaunt, Edward's third son. Yorkist claimants disputed this, asserting their claim through a second son, Lionel, Duke of Clarence, albeit via a now female line, the Mortimers, challenging the idea that the succession should pass down the male line only. The gloves were off.

In 1461, the argument began to swing the Yorkists' way. Edward IV, son of Richard Plantagenet, third Duke of York and great grandson of Edward III - more commonly known as Richard of York (who gave battle in vain) - now took power. And despite a brief return for Henry VI in 1470-71, during which Edward temporarily fled to the continent in exile, he was finally able to restore order of sorts, as the 'Wars of the Cousins' raged on. The new king reduced the Crown's debt, largely through building a private fortune by trading in wool, personally enforced justice and patronised a new invention, printing, before his death in 1483. In line to succeed him was his 12-year-old son Edward V, by his marriage to Elizabeth Woodville.

Enter stage left, boo, hiss, Richard III, youngest of four brothers, Edmund (killed, with his father, in the Battle of

Wakefield in 1460), George and Edward IV being the others. As a minor, young Edward needed a Protector and uncle Richard, Duke of Gloucester, seemed ideal. He had, after all, been loyal to Edward IV through his one-year exile and beyond, even against their rebel brother George, Duke of Clarence, executed for treason in 1478, drowned, or so it was popularly believed, in a barrel of Malmsey wine. Richard was distrustful of the Woodvilles, however, allegedly holding the family responsible for Clarence's sobering demise. He was not about to let the lad's mother and her clan muscle in on power by default.

And so, with Edward V's coronation date fixed for 22 June 1483, Richard himself stole in a few days before, declaring Edward and his ten-year-old brother (Richard, Duke of York) illegitimate. Both children were taken off to the Tower of London, then a royal residence, and never seen again. Until, that is, a couple of skeletons were discovered in 1674 and later buried in Westminster Abbey. Was dastardly Richard responsible? It certainly looked that way.

Whatever the truth behind his rise to power, on becoming king, Richard did attempt reconciliation with the House of Lancaster, moving the body of Henry VI to St George's Chapel at Windsor, for example. Before assuming the throne, like Richard II, he had developed a powerbase in the north already through acts of largesse. But that only served to worsen existing resentment in the south. So much so that, with his kingship barely two years old, on 7 August 1485, Henry Tudor, another descendant of John of Gaunt, set down in Wales at Milford Haven determined to overthrow the murderous upstart. And this the soon-to-be Henry VII did, a fortnight later, at Bosworth field in Leicestershire.

The Tudors were in the house.

***

FOR now, though, let's return to that mock trial at Monk Bar. It's here where York's propaganda machine gets into full obstinate swing. 'Your chance to judge the much-defamed 15th century king,' says a sign outside, setting the tone nicely. And once inside, King Richard III's story is presented with a humourous and imaginative streak, with a waxwork of the accused, crown placed jauntily on head, in the dock.

Plastering the walls are facsimiles of tabloid-style front pages - 'The Shield - England's No.1 Medieval Daily - Another Royal Special' - offering a different aspect to the tale through satirical headlines. In one, Edward IV, with a son supposedly born out of wedlock, is named 'Teddy Tights-Down'. 'Gotcha!' screams another, 'Tricky-Dicky seizes Boy-King'. And pinned to a number of tatty old curtains are cases for the prosecution and defence.

'Hunchbacked, deformed, and with a withered arm, Richard III's physical appearance was an accurate indication of the evil character within,' reads one statement. 'There is no contemporary evidence that Richard was deformed in any way,' is the reply. 'The humpbacked monster was created by Shakespeare - a Tudor - and is a theatrical myth.' A point undermined, you'd think, by the hunch on the back of the skeleton just dug up in Leicester, although the bard's 'lump of foul deformity' does seem a bit OTT. It's certainly fair to note that Shakespeare was writing during the reign of Queen Elizabeth I, granddaughter of Henry Tudor, whom it would have been much safer to portray as the savour of the nation.

If Richard had not intended to murder his two nephews, then why imprison them in the Tower? The Tower was a principal royal residence at the time and it was customary for a king to be housed there before his coronation.

Slouching towards Blubberhouses

The rumours of illegitimacy were trumped up! Nonsense, Edward IV had contractually been married and Parliament unanimously voted to offer Richard the crown.

What of the bones found in 1674? Their examination in 1933 was before carbon 14 dating and thus only proved they were pre-1674; many sets of bones have been found in the Tower over the centuries.

In 1502, Sir James Tyrell confessed to murdering the princes on the orders of Richard III? It was a verbal confession extracted before his execution concocted by Henry VII to justify his dubious claim to the throne.

Assuming King Richard didn't have the boys killed, who did? Henry, Duke of Buckingham, Richard's one-time right-hand man, keen to advance his own career? A rift between the two did open shortly after the coronation. Or how about Henry VII himself? 'His behaviour immediately after his accession appears to indicate that he was uncertain of the fate of the two young princes,' says another hand-written poster. 'They were unquestionably a threat to his stability on the throne. Did Tudor, on discovering that the boys still lived, order them put to death? He was undoubtedly a man capable of such pragmatism.'

And thus does the debate go on. You be the jury, it says on a box. Vote here: guilty or innocent? And let's not get started on the implications of two later 'Pretenders', Lambert Simnel and Perkin Warbeck, who each claimed without success to be the now grown-up Duke of York, back to claim his 'rightful' crown.

The bulk of this four-storey 'bar' is 14th century in origin, while Richard III himself paid for the top floor in 1484, the museum having occupied the middle floors since 1993. It's in the upper room that a television set sits plugged in - I'm guessing Richard didn't buy that - upon which a short documentary made by students, *Richard III - Myth or Monster?* on sale in the shop downstairs, is on permanent rotation.

'Richard III is one of the most infamous characters in English history,' presenter James Carr says, before reheating the arguments above, for those presumably too tired to read. It's a useful little summation, again leaning heavily towards 'not guilty', with one history undergraduate getting right to the nub of it. 'Yes, he was a bit of a bastard,' he says, 'but then they all were. You had to be a bastard back then to be a king.'

The museum isn't just about Richard, mind. Why not step inside 'The World's Smallest Prison Cell', the notorious 'Little Ease' measuring just five feet three inches in diameter, as opposed to a 'de-luxe' one along the way, complete with en-suite facilities? These tiny circular rooms in the turrets are where mutinous apprentices and/or Roman Catholics were imprisoned in the late 16th century for refusing to renounce their faith and accept the new Church of England.

There are fun 'murder holes' here too, in a hanging external gallery, beneath which enemy attackers were forced to dodge dropped stones, boiling water or worse.

Yet there is no doubting the ultimate crowd pleaser. An execution chamber - 'Please mind your head, one villain at a time' - that on my visit is shut. It is here that Richard dispatched many an enemy during an unhappy 1483. 'Please kneel, confess your sins and ascend to the block,' says a sign at the bottom of its short and winding staircase. At the top: 'Apologies. The executioner is on holiday. Your appointment with death has been postponed.'

Having said that, the sign on the garderobe (medieval loo) must be pretty popular too, especially with the public outside. 'Please do not use,' it says.

***

BORN on 2 October 1452 at Fotheringhay Castle in Northamptonshire and from the age of nine the Duke of Gloucester, given his family pedigree, Richard was never likely to be anything but a favourite in what he would come to call 'my fair citie of Yorke'. The special relationship was confirmed in 1476 when, on a visit with his council and by now pretty much in control of the entire north of England, he was presented with gifts of bread, wine and rabbits.

Also by then, his brother Edward IV was well into spell number two on the throne, having survived that second one-year intrusion by Henry VI some five years before. Not so lucky had been their father, Richard, Duke of York, the wealthiest magnate in the land, and brother Edmund, both killed by troops loyal to Henry in the Battle of Wakefield in 1460, as the Wars of the Roses gathered pace. The Duke of York's own ambitions had risen into focus when he was made Protector in 1454 after Henry VI (whose initial reign stretched from 1422-1461) fell ill with one his periodic bouts of 'madness'.

In 1460, the man who should have been Richard III was proclaimed heir, but then inexplicably blew the opportunity with a disastrously rash attack on the strongest surrounding Lancastrian forces while besieged in a castle at Sandal, near Wakefield, after which his head, clad in a paper crown, was impaled on a spike at Micklegate Bar, traditionally the monarch's entrance to York and a favoured spot for the decapitated heads of traitors. Less horrifically, it was here where Queen Elizabeth II arrived during her own Diamond Jubilee of 2012.

Though the people of York appear to have enjoyed that latter celebration, they were not so keen on seeing the head of their favourite Duke and hoped-for future king abused in so savage and public a manner. Nor, it seems reasonable to assume, were Richard's wife and children. It added further psychological fuel to an already volatile fire stoked by anti-Yorkist Lancastrian factions over which a by all accounts feeble-minded Henry VI had little control. Three months later, Henry was deposed in the bloodiest battle fought on British soil at Towton, wherein at least 33,000 people died, and Edward, the first Yorkist king, duly took the crown. That he was able to do so, owed much to the influence of a cousin, Richard Neville, aka 'Warwick the Kingmaker'. It was with Neville that the future actual Richard III had spent a large part of his childhood at Middleham Castle in Wensleydale, just one of several large estates owned by his tutor and benefactor across the North of England.

In 1472, Richard inherited these by marrying Neville's youngest daughter, Anne, most likely in York Minster. The couple's first and as it turned out only legitimate child, a boy, Edward of Middleham, was born the following year. After which, matters went relatively peacefully on the home front until, a decade later, it was Edward IV's turn to fall ill. In so doing, he named his brother Protector. Upon the king's death, aged 40, on 9 April, the duty fell upon Richard to take charge of the two princes and Dick's your nefarious uncle: one coronation abandoned amid accusations of illegitimacy and Richard, on Parliament's invitation, invested at Westminster Abbey in 1483.

Suspended in the Yorkshire Museum's splendid exhibition *Capital of the North*, opened in 2013, is an intricately engraved gold diamond-shaped pendant. Known as 'The Middleham Jewel', it is adorned with a blue sapphire, encrusted in 'the finest piece of medieval gold working ever found in England...' found near to the castle five hundred years later in 1985. An object of huge historical significance, given its value it may well have been a gift from Richard to his childhood sweetheart or belonged to the mother-in-law, also named Anne. Certainly, the inscriptions around the side relate to childbirth, an area in which both women had their difficulties, as does the Nativity scene on the reverse.

Yet any hope of fecundity was short-lived. One year to the day after the death of Edward IV and less than a year since the disappearance of the two princes, ten-year-old Edward of Middleham, Richard's only son and heir, died of unknown causes. Almost a year on again - in March 1485 - Anne Neville was taken by tuberculosis. And on 22 August that year, Richard himself rode out to that ill-fated battle with Henry Tudor's Lancastrian forces at Bosworth Field, before being laid low by treachery within his own forces.

***

AS with so many things these days, it has been possible to follow the debate over Richard III's bones via social media.

Celebrities have had their say. 'Where should Richard III's bones rest? Obviously, Leicester,' tweeted the *League of Gentlemen*'s Mark Gatiss in March. 'York has heritage coming out of its ears. Leicester could do with a leg up.' While in May, the Richard III Museum itself put out a photograph of its new 'interim tomb', named 'The King in the Car Park', sited in its Monk Bar premises.

King Richard III returned to York weeks after his coronation in August 1483. He came in via Micklegate Bar, directly beneath the point upon which his father's head had been spiked 23 years before. He stayed for three weeks, hosted a couple of dinners at the Guildhall (now restored after being virtually destroyed in an air raid in 1942) and saw his son, Edward, invested as Prince of Wales at York Minster on 4 September. He halved the city's taxes to the Crown. A great benefactor to the Minster, it was Richard (helped by a few builders and stonemasons) who completed its construction in 1472 and is said to have had an enormous chantry chapel planned. According to various historians, the King's intention was to be buried at the Minster himself one day.

So popular was Richard III in York that, outraged by his 'murder', its people are reported to have maintained a fierce loathing of Henry VII. Most notably, when in 1489 Tudor sent the Earl of Northumberland to collect taxes, the unfortunate fellow was intercepted, dragged from his lodgings near Thirsk and hanged from an oak tree 'like a common felon'.

On such tales do modern-day campaigns rest. In May 2013, the banner of 'the much-maligned' Richard III was paraded from York's Castle Museum to the Museum Gardens by one hundred supporters and 'descendants'. Among this latter fraternity were fifteen 'family relatives' - presumably the other half a million or so by now otherwise engaged - styling themselves 'The Plantagenet Alliance'.

It is this group who hope that a judicial review will overturn the current scenario. 'This isn't about finders-keepers,' said Sandra Wadley, 69, a mere 'friend' of Richard III in her case. Something else it isn't about, according to Paula Connelly of Bridlington, is tourism. 'It's about the proper and dignified reaction to an anointed king and having a fitting memorial. He was Good King Richard in York.' Child-murderer Richard presumably not having the same ring.

Mustn't be facetious. The academic whose research confirmed that the remains did indeed belong to Richard also pitched in, saying the man himself would have wanted a Roman Catholic burial rather than an Anglican one. Dr John Ashdown-Hill told the BBC that: 'There is a lot of evidence that Richard III had a very serious personal faith. If [he] had not died, maybe the Anglican Church would never have existed.' Leicester was chosen under terms of exhumation, which specified that the bones must be buried in the 'nearest consecrated site'.

To that end, some 7,500 people had signed an online petition to leave the king's remains where they were found, in the Midlands, while nearly 25,000 were of the view that he should be reinterred at York Minster. And yet, don't the 7,500 let-sleeping-kings-lie brigade and the likes of Mark Gatiss have a point?

From the religious perspective, as acting dean of Leicester Cathedral Barry Naylor confirmed: 'I can assure people there will be the finest liturgy and we will be very happy to incorporate elements from the Catholic tradition and perhaps Latin plain chant in the services that take place.' And from the rather more practical and less - given that the era itself ended with Richard - medieval point of view, how many more sites of historical interest does York really need?

***

THE answer, of course, is none. For your average history buff, six months here wouldn't be enough to get to grips with everything on offer.

On this writer's visit, the York Art Gallery was closed, due to major redevelopments and not scheduled to reopen until 2015. The York Dungeon, which looks like fun - 'The ultimate thrill-filled journey through York's murky past' - was shut until July. Among its promised villains, rogues and rascals in an 'even funnier' revamped eleven shows: Eric Bloodaxe, Dick Turpin, Guy Fawkes and a host of torturers, witches, ghosts and corrupt judges. And that's without mentioning the Yorkshire Air Museum at Elvington, the York Mystery Plays, Castle Howard, a Chocolate Museum (about chocolate, not made of it) and no end of buildings, bars (the Micklegate hosting a very good museum itself), halls, walks, boat trips and other attractions besides.

I mean, come on York, aren't you being a tad greedy?

And there is still more to investigate, like the English Civil War. That had rather large repercussions around here, didn't it? Why yes, it most certainly did, though the best place to learn about all that is where our Richard III banner wavers departed: York's Castle Museum. And this being York, it couldn't be easier to go there on foot.

Before leaving the Yorkshire Museum, a reminder that history was lived by ordinary folk too. Though tagged on like an after-thought, the mini exhibition *People of York - 1399-1485* confirms how, in the days of the Houses of Lancaster and York, 'activities of kings never reached the people on the streets, struggling to get by.' Yet a new class of traders and merchants did evolve during this '...15th century peak in York's overall prosperity'. And did you know, barbers were surgeons of sorts, who could '...cut your hair or your arm off.'

Then we're back with the five sovereign Tudors who, from 1485-1603, starting with Henry VII and ending with Elizabeth I, made a lasting impression themselves. Kicking off 118 more years of monumental change, the Wars of the Roses were over but, religiously, England would be twice torn apart and rebuilt in a Protestant and Catholic image at great social cost. A cultural renaissance foregrounded such figures as Edmund Spenser, Cardinal Wolsey and William Shakespeare. And thanks to the conquests of adventurers like Sir Walter Raleigh, England grew into a formidable colonial power, all the while dragging Ireland and Scotland closer into a United Kingdom with both itself and Wales.

The fall-out from that religious schism in particular is right here in those statues from St Mary's Abbey and the ruins outside. The culprit, of course, being Henry VIII, son of Henry VII, whose serial-killing and savage destruction of the monasteries in the 1530s and formation of the Church of England that is bickered about to this day set the country and the monarchs who followed - Edward VI (1547-1533), Mary I (1553-1558) and Elizabeth I (1558-1603), with a nine-day burst of poor doomed Lady Jane Grey from 10-19 July 1553 - on a course of martyrdom, turbulence and mutual distrust.

Initially, his 1536 dissolution of smaller monasteries provoked an uprising in Lincolnshire that spread rapidly north. Eventually, those 'pilgrim of grace' rebels were quieted with broken promises. But with England now Protestant, many Yorkshirefolk, as elsewhere, secretly and on occasion not so secretly, refused to relinquish their Catholicism, as evidenced by those cramped cells in the Richard III Museum.

Here across town, only the north and west walls of St Mary's remain upright, leaning into 21st century sleet and rain, along with a few other stone piles that escaped Henry's wrath in 1539. Thus was York's cityscape altered forever, although this latest king, in power from 1509 to 1547, did at least restore clout by establishing York as headquarters of the Council of the North. But come the end of Tudor period, its status was again low. As other northern cities like Hull grew in status and wealth, York became an unglamorous seat of regional government. Its reputation once more lay dormant, awaiting the attention and protection of enlightened Charles Wellbeloved and friends. Only then would attention return to York's treasure trove of archaeology and art.

***

THE wait, however, was anything but peaceful.

Leaving the Yorkshire Museum on Lendal Bridge and

proceeding, as they used to say on Z-*Cars*, in an easterly direction, a walk to the Castle Museum is also an opportunity to wander through the ancient city streets themselves. You'll want to see The Shambles, of course, perhaps the most famous route in York, albeit more of a chocolate box ginnel these days, with shops packed either side.

So narrow are The Shambles that, at one point, it is said to be possible for two people to lean out and touch fingertips from facing upper storey windows. These days the shops are more likely to be pizzerias with 'early bird specials' or Earl Grey tea rooms than the blood and guts butchers of yore, whose stalls and benches - 'shamel' - give the place its name. But as an imaginative aid memoire there are few spots to match it. As a plaque on a redbrick wall explains, the Shambles meat market appears in the Domesday Book of William the Conqueror and was later rebuilt '...in about 1400, when it assumed its present character.'

Of equal interest, if lower in profile, is the mainly 15th century church of St Martin-Le-Grand in nearby Coney Street. Pre-Norman Conquest in origin and partly destroyed in the same 1942 air raid that did for the railway station, it sits on an alleyway with the rather scruffy City Screen cinema tucked in at the end. St Martin's, extensively rebuilt complete with distinctive clock, is well worth a look. Particularly as, in 1939, some bright spark had the foresight to remove its glorious 'Great West Window', sticking it to Hitler. The thirteen scenes of St Martin of Tours on it are now 'rehoused in the quasi-transept of the South aisle'. The church's peaceful little courtyard - the access to which is 'non-direct and intended to reflect life's long and winding pilgrimage' - was created in the 1960s from the ruins of the bombed nave.

This might be a good time, too, to venture onto those castellated city walls that, even on a grey day, offer a more leisurely, reflective and literally uplifting take on the city. The stretch from Micklegate Bar to Barker Tower has a wonderful view of the Minster towers, as fine a morning stroll as any. Give or take the odd break, the walls encircle the old city over three miles and, though medieval in origin, stand on the same earthen ramparts that once held the Roman and Danelaw versions, strengthened by the Normans. The only danger of assault nowadays is from the weather; the stone being well beaten, as today are a host of golden daffodils.

Daffs are trying gamely to reach Clifford's Tower, too, in the grounds of Castle Museum. And while the Yorkshire Museum is a must-visit, it's here you must come for a broader sweep of York history. A gaggle of plump geese waddle from a bedraggled, grassy traffic island past the museum's imposing front entrance where, once inside, a 400-year or so journey awaits - Elizabethan soldiers to Victorian debtors, Georgian dolls' houses to Swinging 'Sixties, Civil War to the Space Age.

We are here for Roundheads and Cavaliers, but how can you not get sidetracked by fascination at every turn? First up, in the North Building, are replica period rooms from the 1600s to the 1950s, atop a Victorian street peopled by actors in costume 'going about their daily business'. The parlours and moorland cottages are enlightening, while the sound and smell effects ('hmm... eau de horse?) of gas-lit cobbled Kirkgate are another pleasing twist to what Rick Steves' *Great Britain* guidebook calls: '...the closest thing to a time-tunnel experience'.

Amid the ironmongers, pawnbrokers, taxidermists, milliners, tobacconists and cocoa rooms, who would not be tempted by theatrical posters advertising such delights as *Turpin's Ride to York* and *The Death of Bonnie Black Bess* alongside a padded cell: 'Dick Turpin played by Mr T Fossett

{The Best Representative of this Character}. Tom King, who he shot, played by Mr J Fossett' ...it's a family concern out of *Nicholas Nickleby*. Appearing in the market place at Shaw for one October day only, at each performance of this traveling circus: '...six great clowns headed by "Funny Harry" will appear, two perfs daily at 2 and 7 o'clock.' All that is missing is an infant phenomenon.

Upstairs on this side of the museum is an exhibition *Toy Stories*, its entrance watched over by a lovely figurine that wouldn't quite fit under my coat of Victorian comic star Ally Sloper. Toys and games from the past 150 years over which he stands guard include such Proustian rushes as chemistry sets; Meccano planes and Bayko building sets of the 1930s; Matchbox cars; a 1970s Action Man; rubber ducks; Sonic the Hedgehog; water pistols; a Sindy doll; kick-boxing Bratz; Singer sewing machines; toy soldiers and, of course, a castle.

There are also two very nice signs on the walls. One describes Gilligan's Galloping Carousel: '...made in Yorkshire around 1905. Lawrence Gilligan and his horse-drawn roundabout were well known on the streets of Yorkshire for forty years. Children paid for a turn with glass jars and rags if they had no money. The roundabout was hand cranked by Mr Gilligan and his wife Hilda. He turned the crank and his wife collected the glass jars and rags. They were known locally as "Ma and Pa Jingle Bells."'

The other sign says: 'Please do not leave your child unsupervised.'

From there, the route downstairs goes from *Cradle to Grave*, an exhibition dedicated to rites of passage and how people marked the big events in their lives, i.e. funerals, love, marriage, hearth and home. The wedding section is funniest and intentionally so; it's rare to discover a museum with such a keen sense of humour. One book on display, *How to Master*

Slouching towards Blubberhouses

A Wife, published by William Walker & Sons of London and Otley, gives the flavour. Another nice touch are the wedding presents and stories donated by local people.

With the North Building conquered it's time to visit the adjoining half of the Castle Museum, via an obligatory foyer gift shop. Here can be purchased such classy delights as Thomas Crapper emergency plumbing kits, 'Keep Calm and Carry On' biscuit tins, and kettles bearing the mantra 'Yorkshire born wi' nowt teken out'. The South Building covers three floors with a prison exercise yard, complete with stocks, the first port of call. It's from here, from 1717 onward, that iron-clad convicts were transported to the colonies, initially America and then after the War of Independence in the 1770s, Australia, before such barbarism ended in 1867.

A whistle-stop tour of an entertaining if weirdly juxtaposed exhibition *The Sixties* follows, complete with Beatlemania, mods, hippy fashion, counter culture, summer of love, women's lib, Pop Art et al. It's here where the middle-aged may get another jolt of personal antiquity, many of the artefacts familiar from yesterday. There's a painting in the dining room of an exotic woman making a basket; Polo mints 'now in four flavours'; the theme tunes of *Robinson Crusoe* and *Crackerjack*; the cover of a *Sound of Music* album on RCA Victor, upon which Julie Andrews in pink dances over a hill tracked by a gang of children in canary yellow and watched by a disapproving Christopher Plummer, hands on hips. Whatever happened to black and white? Weird too to see electric fires with plastic coals, Sunbeam blenders and that hated Sunday afternoon pressure cooker - sprouts and turnip, ugh! - as museum pieces.

But then, with a hop, skip and a jump past the King William IV pub, we are in the cells of York Castle Prison itself.

They have been locking folk up here - and worse - for almost 1,000 years, since William the Conqueror built the first castle in 1068 in fact, complete with en suite gaol. Today, what was once the 18th century courthouse is York Crown Court, complete with holding cells and regular trials of alleged serious offenders. There has been a museum of social history here since 1938, originally based in a female prison added in 1780. In 1952, that expanded to the so-called debtors' prison, where we stand now.

A re-build in stone in the 1300s coincided with the arrival of Yorkshire's Assize courts, staged every spring and summer, and some extremely intimidating dungeons. These were in use until 1700, when the then existing buildings, with the exception of Clifford's Tower, made way for an imposing new County Prison serving the whole of Yorkshire. One of Britain's first multi-purpose prisons, it opened five years later and with a couple of exceptions looks much the same today.

The exceptions are a radiator throwing out welcome heat and ghostly holograms projected onto the walls with monologues read by actors playing rogues, robbers, killers, debtors and revolutionaries, all of whom were inmates here. Once again, the star attraction is Dick Turpin, legendary highwayman and one-time inhabitant of a city that seems to value its bad boys - and girls - more than any other.

The first such virtual character we encounter, suitably enough, is Mr Turnkey: 'Debtors upstairs, thieves and vagabonds down here,' he says. Back then, men and women were kept separately. For 21st century purposes they are neighbours, held in adjoining cells. People like Mary Burgan, a woman jailed in 1706 for killing her first baby, a crime for which normally she would have hanged. Mary was spared the gallows, however, after again falling pregnant as she awaited her trial, most likely by that aforementioned turnkey, Thomas Ward. The result was a son, Tom, who upon his mother's pardon four years later stayed behind bars until 1718 because the money wasn't there to buy him out. 'Who'd have thought a pardon could break your heart?' she asks in a cell the size of an outside toilet. Us Yorkshirefolk, of course we had it tough.

Along with Tom, Dick - actually born in Essex and fleeing to York under the name John Palmer, before being charged here with horse theft - and Mary, other residents include Ward himself, 'a bully and extortionist, forcing prisoners to buy food and drink from him at inflated prices'; William Hartley, a machine-smashing radical Luddite; Simon Hargreaves, 'a 19th century lager lout'; and to confirm that not all the crooks were in the cells, Richard Woodhouse, the keeper intent on making a profit from the suffering of others.

Between 1705-1835 around 15,000 Yorkshiremen and women faced cold, hunger, filth and degradation here, charged or about to be charged with heinous crimes. And there were just four ways out. Found not guilty - around half that number eventually were - you went free. First-time offenders like Mary might also be released, in time, upon payment of a fine, whipping or branded hand. Around 4,000 convicts were transported to America or Australia. Elsewhere in these catacombs, mounted on a wall, is a flagstone from their exercise yard of departure, with graffiti of a man shooting a pheasant while out hunting with a dog. Dated 1831, the artist was 23; his work resembles the doodling of a child. The remaining 500 or so prisoners went out 'feet first', condemned to execution.

Today, you just amble through more exhibitions. One, a costume gallery, has clothes, accessories and household textiles worn or used over the previous two hundred and fifty years. The other, *York in the Second World War*, has more detail on that 1942 air raid, ration books, National Service and Britain's subsequent baby boom. There is also the story of conscientious objectors sent not to York, but the jails of Armley in Leeds, Manchester and Wakefield.

***

IT took an awful long time for Yorkshire to get over William's Harrowing of the North - devastation compounded by the subsequent Black Death that killed anywhere between 75 million and 200 million people across Europe in the mid-14th century, depending upon whose account you believe. By the 16th century, however, the recovery was all but complete.

A burgeoning wool industry encouraged by Edward IV from 1461 found its centre in the west of the county. Towns like Leeds began to flourish, as did the likes of Halifax and Wakefield through cloth, their populations rising accordingly. In the south, Sheffield's cutlery industry too gathered pace, with better days for rural communities also, on account of agricultural recovery.

Better days for those at the top end, anyway. The majority of non-land owners in town and country remained poor, with growing numbers working as labourers for little pay. That, coupled with on-going rows between the King and parliament over who could and could not raise taxes, and the religious divide instigated by Henry VIII in which the people were by now mostly Protestant but with King Charles I seen as backing the Catholic faith meant that things were once again about to get very nasty indeed.

Soon Yorkshire would be divided, Royalists on one side, Parliamentarians the other. And if you thought the various Wars of the Roses were complicated...

The English Civil War broke out in 1642, when Charles I - second in the Stuart dynasty after succeeding to the throne in 1625 upon the death of his father, James I, son of Mary, Queen of Scots who had, as James VI of Scotland, become the first monarch of a United Kingdom upon the death of Elizabeth I in 1603 (phew), tried to enter Hull and the city gates were shut against him. Before long, they were scrapping in lumps, the Royalists capturing Leeds and Wakefield, while using York as their base. Bradford and Halifax, though besieged, stayed untaken.

Then, early in 1643, it was the Parliamentarians' turn to attack. They regained Leeds and Wakey before, in June of that year, the Royalists again landed a mighty blow by winning the Battle of Adwalton, thereby capturing all of Yorkshire with the exception of those stubborn beggars who remained holed up in Hull.

And the Parliamentarians there it was who, in October, finally lifted the siege on their city by driving back the King's troops. In the spring of 1644, they retook Bradford and Leeds before routing the Royalists once and for all in the north of England by winning the Battle of Marston Moor on the outskirts of York, though the Civil War itself rumbled on in one form or another until 1651, when it ended with Parliamentary victory at the Battle of Worcester almost two years after the public beheading of Charles I, in January 1649.

This, of course, is the bare bones of a military death toll the like of which has never been seen before or since on British soil. Yorkshire was by no means the only region to suffer, but it certainly has one of the best museum exhibitions dedicated to the subject. And from the Siege of Hull via the Storming of Selby to the Siege of York and beyond, much of it is seen through the eyes of one very ordinary yet, given the times, extraordinary man.

William Marshall was a university-educated Catholic, married with two sons, and a partner in the Black Dogge Inn, Petergate. As a display in the South Building of the Castle Museum explains: 'In November 1642, he joined Sir Harry Slingsby's regiment of foot. William guarded the city walls and food transports. He found this work so dull that, looking for adventure, he joined Sir Marmaduke Langdale's cavalry regiment in February 1643.' He also kept a diary, whose extracts, describing the writer's feelings and activities during and after 'these bloody days', pepper the rest of the room. Normally this spiteful point in British history is told from the viewpoint of its Crown and Parliamentary leaders, known popularly as Cavaliers and Roundheads. It is a refreshing change to experience it from the ground up.

Not that there is any absence of military detail, along with a cast list of the usual suspects like Charles's nephew Prince Rupert, whose army of 15,000 men famously forced Yorkshire Parliamentarian leader Sir Thomas Fairfax and his troops to break off their siege of York in 1644 and beat a temporary retreat.

Or William Cavendish of Handsworth, Earl of Newcastle and 'Master of Yorkshire', made a marquis before going into exile after Marston Moor, returning with the English Restoration and living to the ripe old age of 84.

Then, of course, there is 'Old Ironsides' himself, Oliver Cromwell, commander of the New Model Army and future Lord Protector of the Commonwealth of England, Scotland and Ireland, hero to some, genocidal megalomaniac to others, whose body was dug up, hung in chains and beheaded upon the return from exile of Charles II in 1660, ending an eleven-year republic, or Interregnum.

We gasp at the sheer carnage of that bloodbath at Marston, 'the greatest battle of the Civil Wars', wherein 28,000 Scots and Parliamentarians met less than 18,000 Royalists and fought until dusk, destroying the loyalist forces in the process. We see musket shot and cannonballs from the Siege of Helmsley in 1644 (sieges being as ubiquitous during the English Civil War as Go Compare adverts are today) and hear how Cromwell and Co arrived at York in June of that year intent on ousting a Royalist garrison that was 8,000 strong.

Among their number, of course, was one William Marshall, musket and diary at the ready and doomed to... well, I'll let you make that discovery for yourself.

***

IN early March 2014, a judicial review to decide the final resting place of King Richard III's remains was deferred after the Plantagenet Alliance challenged a Ministry of Justice licence to re-inter the bones in Leicester Cathedral.

The city's university said it gained the exhumation licence in line with archaeological practice. Its representative Anya Proops told the court: 'The current, very undignified, squabble - a squabble, we should say, not of our making - should now come to an end.'

But Gerard Clarke, counsel for the so-called 'relatives' of Richard, retorted: 'It would be fanciful and absurd that if the Queen died on a visit to a primary school in Lowestoft she should be buried there.'

Mayor of Leicester, Peter Soulsby admitted: 'It is not surprising the courts want to rule on this as it's not every day a king is found tucked away in a car park.'

The University further pointed out there were an estimated one million relatives of Richard III alive today and that one of the most significant, Michael Ibsen, whose DNA identified the skeleton, supported Leicester's claim.

It is estimated that ticket sales to Richard III's tomb - having already been designed by Leicester Cathedral with a deeply carved cross, resting on a floor inlaid with a large Yorkist white rose - could be worth up to £4million a year.

5. Dales of the Unexpected

◇

A Yorkshire Landscape

YORKSHIRE, then, is long fermented. From the first recorded mention of its name in the Anglo-Saxon *Chronicle* of 1065, the uprisings, rebellions and bolshiness evident in England's largest ancient county have commanded column inches and attention in equal measure. But what there doesn't seem to have been, until relatively recently anyway, is an enveloping and almost nationalistic sense of unified pride under one flag.

Why? How? And when did this happen?

Dig deep into the nitty-gritty of Yorkshireness and there is a strong whiff of heavenly myth. Differences arise from city to city, town to town, village to village. You could not mistake Bradford for Leeds. Barnsley does not remotely resemble Ripon. Ilkley could be a million miles away from Keighley. And Hull... well, Hull isn't much like anywhere.

Politically too, Yorkshire is a county divided, not only in terms of who votes where and for whom, but with regard to administrative boundaries after local government acts in

Slouching towards Blubberhouses

the 1970s saw 'old Yorkshire' divided into metropolitan, non-metropolitan and ceremonial counties. These were in turn derived from its original ridings, or thrydings as the early Norse-speaking inhabitants would have said. In this context, the word 'riding' means 'third part' and is unrelated to the popular misconception that these places could be covered on horseback in a single day, M62 roadworks notwithstanding.

To begin with subdivided into wapentakes - Danelaw administrative 'hundreds', often found at crossroads or fords in rivers - the West, East and North Ridings of Yorkshire were always distinctive in character. In some ways, they operated as separate counties, particularly after the Restoration in 1660. When a matter could not be resolved in the wapentake, it was brought first to the riding and then, if an outcome still could not be determined, to the court of the shire. From 1888, each riding also had its own elected county council, before these were abolished in the aforementioned local government shake-ups of 1972 and 1974, with responsibilities scattered across the newly created districts of West Yorkshire, North Yorkshire, South Yorkshire and Humberside.

There never was a South Riding, unless you count Winifred Holtby's novel of that name, posthumously published in 1936, that spawned many a film, radio and TV drama, the most notable perhaps being Wakefield writer Stan Barstow's adaptation for Yorkshire Television, in which Dorothy Tutin and Nigel Davenport appeared in 1974. And even that was actually based on the East Riding.

The shadows of those original wapentakes can still be traced. Skyrack in the West Riding, for instance, was centred on modern Leeds, but had upper and lower divisions encompassing the likes of Kippax, Thorner, Bingley and Otley. Today, it gives its name to the pub that stands opposite the spot of the 'shire oak' from which 'Skyrack' is derived and which only fell in 1941. It was under this tree - the 'Original Oak' that also gives its name to a pub in the location - that the wapentake's administrative meetings were held.

This idea of pub as historical clue pops up rather a lot in Yorkshire.

***

WHILE urban Yorkshire is marked by contrast, the geological and topographical nature of the county, from which so much human activity is derived, is every bit as distinct, if not even more emphatically. And as with the ridings, we are once again under the rule of three.

With its western Pennines of Carboniferous origin (large coal deposits laid down in that prehistoric era giving rise to the Industrial Revolution), a central vale that is Permo-Triassic, north east Jurassic and south east laid on Cretaceous chalk, each area's geography is distinct. And all of it drained or served by an array of rivers whose names are as evocative as any bluff fast bowler or pint of best bitter.

The majority of those rivers serve the Ouse. The Swale is furthest north followed by the Ure, Nidd, Wharfe, Aire and Calder. Also flowing into the Ouse, which empties into the North Sea via the Humber Estuary, are the north-flowing Don in the south and Derwent in the north east. Higher still, the Esk makes its own way to the sea at Whitby, as does the Tees downstream of Middlesbrough. The River Hull flows straight into the Humber Estuary, while the Ribble helps drain the west of the county into the Irish Sea in the vicinity of Lytham St Anne's.

At its most basic level, what we are walking through, gazing at in wonder and increasingly trying to capture on canvas are moors, wolds and dales: Yorkshire moorland most commonly in the west, south and north of the county, dales to the north and wolds in the south east uplands.

And of that trio, it is the first where you are most likely to stumble upon one particular Holmfirth-based artist.

***

FEISTY as hell beneath a blizzard of white hair, the painter Ashley Jackson is a pent-up ball of artistic expression. On a promise with a land he knows intimately, a force of nature, you might say.

And as with all elemental energies, he brims with unpredictability, on occasion menace. It is there in over half-a-century's worth of landscapes, as moody and defiant as the moors he will never quite pin down. And it is there in his engaging pugnacity during the art of conversation.

Jackson is an old-fashioned Yorkshire icon too. It says so in *Yorkshire Ridings*, a magazine he hands over proudly as we make our way up to a second floor 'garret' atop his Holmfirth gallery, situated on the main route through town. It is an ascent shared with paintings and photographs of the artist-in-residence alongside a host of well-known figures, several local, some not.

Here he is with legendary cricketer Fred Trueman. And here with Prince Charles, Bill Clinton and US civil rights activist Jesse Jackson - no relation.

With his inclusion, the *Yorkshire Ridings'* hall of fame has a membership of seven: York-born Dame Judi Dench, supermarket tycoon Ken Morrison, Fiery Fred, William Wilberforce, the late charity campaigner Jane Tomlinson and Sir Michael Parkinson being the others. And each has been voted in by a notoriously hard-to-please Yorkshire public.

Thus begins a chat that somehow manages to be

simultaneously rambling and to the point. How about this for an opening gambit, apropos of nothing?

'I am a member of the working class and have been all my life. I define working class as being where you have to go out and earn a living. If that's the case, you're working class. If you lie in bed and money comes to you, you're not working class. That's the difference. None of this snobbish stuff, upper middle class, lower middle class, all that bunkum and bullshit, we're all in the same boat. All we are doing is paddling up the same stream with a different canoe.'

Not just a force of nature, then, but a force of Yorkshireness too.

Ashley Jackson is as dry and funny as he is intense. For him, creativity, poetry, pride and bluster are urges that will not be denied, bestowed by the county of his upbringing. Spirituality and common sense are but two sides of the same coin and no one gets anywhere in life without coin, do they?

Sometimes, your head is in the clouds simply because you are up there painting them on Cartworth Moor.

Ashley - born in Penang - spent his earliest years dodging Japanese warplanes rather than the rainy gales of West Yorkshire. His father, managing director of Tiger beer, had been posted to Malaysia with British Intelligence.

'We were colonials,' he says, revealing how he is named after Leslie Howard's character Ashley Wilkes from *Gone With the Wind*. 'My father was captured at the fall of Singapore but, before they got him, he made sure that all the family, mum, grandma, his mum, everybody, was on a French ship that sailed for India. At the age of 18 months, I was sleeping on deck with my mum while missiles rained down. We arrived in India just before partition in 1947. We had servants and all that. We were the Raj.'

He speaks with pride of the man who, despite his

predicament, managed to escape his captors' clutches four times before being machine-gunned into a grave he dug for himself in Labuan, Borneo.

'My dad is mentioned in many war books of the Far East, as he belonged to a platoon called Engage and Destroy,' his son says, recalling heroic adventures that left their mark in a variety of ways, some emotional, some practical.

Along with Dame Vera Lynn and the late Harry Secombe, Jackson junior would much later be made a patron of the Burma railway - as seen in the film *Bridge Over the River Kwai*. More immediately, after a spell in Scotland as an evacuee - 'my maternal grandfather was a Scot' - young Ashley was destined for Huddersfield after his mother's remarriage to Hedley Haigh, a Yorkshireman.

'I was nine years old. Fate is fate, you know. They wanted me to be educated in England. We'd had a lot of money, but because of the war everything was taken away. I've no chips on my shoulder about it.'

Either way, the displaced boy was soon getting to grips with the gritty realities of Yorkshire life. 'I'd been to England before, when I was six. But when we went back for good I went to a junior school in Huddersfield. My stepfather said: "We're not calling you Ashley. We'll call you your dad's name, Norman." He didn't want me to get brayed, you see.'

From there, it was on to a secondary modern in Barnsley - '...never took an eleven-plus, never had one put in front of me, because I was too young in Huddersfield and too bloody old in Barnsley...' - where he began a stint as a Roman Catholic altar boy that lasted until the age of twenty-two.

'The greatest gift I ever had given was when I used to bring the dead in with the priest when I was thirteen or fourteen, for *Die Profundis*, the requiem mass. It hit me then that I'd better get on my bike and work if what I really wanted was to be an artist. I am bloody glad I did. The realities of existence hit me when I was fourteen; many people don't wake up until they are forty. And then, when they do, they say: "What I have done with my life? Well, I'll get rid of her, and I'll get a new house, let's start anew..." And then they don't realise that they are chasing rainbows.'

In fact, Jackson and his own wife, Ann, have been wed for fifty years - '...And we were courting for seven years before that. We lived in a one-up one-down terrace at first and then, just when we were about to move into a semi-detached bungalow costing £2,400, I was invited to put on a one-man exhibition in Mayfair. Bloody hell, I thought. But they wanted £3,000 for the week, even though they were taking money off my paintings.

'So I went back to the Yorkshire Penny Bank, who had tailor-made a mortgage for me, and they loaned us more money; the building societies wouldn't have anything to do with us. If the exhibition hadn't done anything we would have been wiped out. We would have had no house to live in and we had a kid by then. In all, we did that seven times in the bungalow and eight times in our house in Holmfirth.

'Nobody ever believes that. Eight times. To get my works recognised, for six or seven years I was going down to London and sleeping in a second-hand hump-backed Morris post office van, or in Hyde Park. Then, after getting washed and changed and having a brush up at Paddington Station, I would go knocking on the doors of galleries. Tell me, who's got the balls to do that today? Nowadays, if you sneeze you'll get a grant. I've never had a grant in my life, never wanted one. And yet we've risked it all. Now, I can afford to be cocky.'

So far, so Yorkshireman. But then bluster gives way to glassy-eyed nostalgia at thoughts of childhood bus trips to paint the surrounding moors.

Slouching towards Blubberhouses

'I was going up to Langsett and on the tops of the Holme Valley - Wessenden, Saddleworth, Greenfield Moor, places like that,' he says of the time when his love of painting was kindled. Aged sixteen, Jackson enrolled at the Barnsley School of Art where he wanted to 'do with brushes what the Brontës did with the pen.' And even now, when it comes to describing his own painterly motivations, his language is no less picturesque.

'I paint in the cathedral of the open air. I was very, very fortunate that the moors spoke to me. My mistress, I call her. I can read her love letters, which I turn into paintings.'

Not that everyone appreciates the correspondence. Although Jackson's creations are enjoyed by a large audience, the contemporary British art world, perhaps distrustful of landscape and his favoured medium watercolours, have hardly clasped him to their bosom, his 1967 election as a Fellow of the Royal Society of Arts notwithstanding.

It is an attitude that this 'People's Artist', as he is often called, professes not to let bother him one jot. 'I have never really got on with the establishment. Art is not for the pseudo-intellectual, it is for ordinary folk with tattoos on their fingers... us..." says a man whose popularity was cemented by *A Brush with Ashley*, a television show that ran for eleven series from the late 1980s, along with regular slots on the BBC lunchtime strand *Pebble Mill at One*.

'You see, I am not a herd animal. I know that if I sleep with the right person I'll get something, you know? But I couldn't stand the pain. I'm not a social beast. I don't go to champagne parties and hold my glass as though there's a vine growing up the side of the stem, I can't stand that. I can't stand snobs and I can't stand big heads. The worse thing of all, though, is a working class snob. An aristocrat only knows one way because that's how they were brought up, but the working class should know better. Our crowd shit on their own when they get a position. That's why unions don't work now, because they are all shitting on one another. Playing as a team, they could force the boss's hand. That is so sad today. Very, very sad.'

Another Yorkshire figure to whom stubbornness clung like Cuban cigar smoke, was Trade Union leader Arthur Scargill, in whose cause Jackson was only too pleased to rally back in the industrially-troubled 1970s and '80s.

'I helped the miners' families and children in galas for nearly thirty years and I have marched with all the big union men in the front line,' he says. 'What I really wanted to do was take art to the kids and I still do that. The art world is so snobby. A pile of dung is a pile of dung, whichever way you want to put it. Now, if you want to do an abstract of a Yorkshire landscape, or you want to do an abstract of a woman, and you put her backside on her head and part of her head down in the bottom of her backside and you've got a model who you have been using to do this design, well then, fine. Fantastic. It does make good carpeting patterns. It does make good curtains. But don't tell me that it's *Aphrodite at the Well*. The beautiful thing about the abstracts is that there is skill in it. They used to call them happenings. Now we've got "conceptual art" - putting a pile of bricks together that they haven't even made. We have come from making sandcastles to mud pies.'

Nor are Ashley Jackson paintings certain to attract the admiration of more traditional art buyers, for whom pictures of the countryside are supposed to mean blue skies, fields of golden barley, virginal clouds and pretty baa lambs.

What Jackson has most often delivered since opening a gallery of his own in 1963, is brooding, apocalyptical scenes of bleak and barren Pennine wildernesses, rolled out under dark forbidding skies. Not so much *Last of the Summer Wine*, as the end of the world is nigh. And that he chooses - sepia and indigo studies and pencil sketches apart - to realise his vision in watercolours, so often deemed conventional and twee, is one more contradiction among many.

'People who like pictures don't like my works,' is how he sees it, defining 'picture' as an image that is mechanically constructed rather than the product of a true artist's craft. 'They say they are morbid, dour, windswept - there are no sunny scenes. Well, I say that if you go to a champagne party, great. You go to a champagne party every bloody week, though, and you'll be bored stiff. You would be bored of the people they attract too. It's the same with sunny days. I am an earthy lad. When I go up on the moors, my hairs stand on end when I begin to paint or draw. I am beckoned to that piece of landscape. I don't go looking for it.'

What about the medium? 'I had some good teachers at art school for skill, but we never did watercolours as they thought that was just for aristocracy women working behind screens in front of a fireplace. Well, I contend that watercolour is the English school of painting. There's no white paint in my paintings. The white is the white of the paper. That is English. Once you put white into watercolour it becomes gouache, it becomes body colour and that is French.'

He gestures at a rendition of a snow-covered moor, populated by a handful of grazing sheep. 'So this is English and if you make a mistake you pray to God, because you may as well tear the bloody thing up. And it takes me ages. I put about thirty washes on. The books tell you to put no more than six washes on, because it will go opaque. Well, I've never been one for following rules. If a sign says: "Private. Moorland. Keep Out," I'll climb over the bloody fence and paint inside anyway. The sketchbook is your passport. The

104

gamekeeper will come up, see that I'm painting and say: "Come on, lad, I'll show you a better place." That's what the sketchbook does for you.

'I paint the largest watercolours you will see, without any gimmicks. Eighty per cent today use a camera, a process that leaves people looking at their work and saying: "Ooh, wow, look at that, it looks just like a photograph." Well, that's because it bloody well is a photograph, but with watercolour or oil on top to give it a glaze. And they are getting away with it. There's no skill in that. It's a copy. They are good tracers. What I want to put on my business card is "done freehand". I don't use masking fluid, I don't scratch out. It's instinct.

'You see, when you are making love, by the time you reach a vibrator it's too bloody late, isn't it? I'm being crude, but you know what I'm getting at. I prefer it natural.'

And nowhere, to Ashley Jackson, is more 'natural' than Yorkshire.

'People ask me why I don't paint in Cornwall. Well, to me, that countryside has all been coutured. The Pennines of Yorkshire and Holmfirth aren't coutured. What you see is what you get. If you don't like this drizzle rain which is dank and you think, "Oh, I'm not getting wet," but then, at the end of the day, you're sodden. Or you don't like what's called lazy wind, when it prefers to go through you than around you, then maybe it's just not for you. Me, I love going up on these moors because there are so many people who aren't up there.

'She's only there for those who love her. I have been all over the world, to China, Malaysia, India, America, Vancouver in British Colombia, all of them fantastic, and I have painted all those places, but my heart is not in them. It's like, many people tonight will have sex, but only a few will make love. I make love to my Pennines of Yorkshire. It's not a con. I have been very fortunate and I can see why the

Brontës were so attracted to it. It's forbidding. It's like the seas. You can wander out on a lovely morning and die on them that afternoon. Four seasons in a day.'

Which must, I assume, apart from their ease of reach, produce its own particular set of artistic difficulties? 'Most of the paintings in my gallery were done less than six miles away,' Jackson says. 'Why would I have to go any further? I'm telling you, it's very easy to paint Scotland because Scotland has got mountains. As the peaks go back into the distance - call them pyramids if you want - they go back smaller in perspective. So it's easier to paint that sort of thing; the Rockies are just the same. The Yorkshire moors, the Pennines, are very difficult because you are sat on a table top and there's nowt in front of you. There's no verticals taking you in. All you've got is horizontals. And then what you have to rely on is the heavenly light. And it's the light that takes you into the painting. The painting has the soul of the artist and of the atmosphere. And if it moves you, I am glad it has.'

From time to time, there are health-related issues too. 'If there is thunder and lightning and I'm the only thing up there, I am going to get off the moors as quick as I can because I am the tallest thing there is. A lot of people go up without a map or a compass. You can do without your map, but you need your compass. Have your compass like your watch. If anything happens - it becomes dark or anything like that - you've got your bearings and you know how to get off.

'Easiest way, they say, is to follow a stream. But if you are on flat moorland, you can't see streams. If one of your feet is stronger than the other, you end up walking around in a circle. That's what happens on Kinder Scout in the Peak District and it's the same on Greenfield Moor. You've got to know your moors. You've got to feel the bracken. It's like cowpat. It's crispy and if you go through that, you will go in up to your thighs. When I go on the moors, I always tell my wife where I'll be. Mobile phones - although they don't work everywhere - are useful, because you can always ring in your whereabouts off your compass, if you've broken your leg or something.'

By way of a parting shot, I mumble something about Yorkshire breeding a strange combination of practicality and romance in its sons and daughters.

'Correct. You might think I am a maniac, but when I get up on the moors I can talk openly to them. Generally, I like to go where there are no Wallace Arnold tours. I am not being awful. When I am making love to mother nature, to my Yorkshire, I don't want an audience. I only want an audience when I am doing my telly. And when I am doing my telly I don't do paintings, I do pictures. You can't write a love letter and talk to somebody while you are writing it, can you?'

***

THE Craiglands Hotel, Ilkley. One gothic edifice among many, perched like a raven on a steep drag up to the famous moor under whose stoney ridge the town is sheltered.

It is a Sunday afternoon in autumn. The sun is out, casting genteel dappled shadows over the gravel of a car park crunchy with rubber and feet. Lovely day for it.

Inside, the place is packed. This is the Ilkley Literature Festival, an annual treat, and we are here to listen to Hannah Hauxwell, the latest speaker in a couple of hundred. Louis de Bernières, sans mandolin, sits reading in an adjacent bar.

Hannah, of course, was a household name in the early 1970s when, as the 46-year-old subject of *Too Long A Winter*, a Yorkshire TV documentary produced by Barry Cockroft, she brought the High Pennines into the living rooms of a nation.

Slouching towards Blubberhouses

The programme detailed her spinster's life alone on Low Birk Hatt Farm, back then North Riding of Yorkshire, nowadays County Durham. It was an existence marked by extreme weather, frugality, toil, struggle, isolation, poverty and, more often than not, bitter, bitter cold. With a lot more snow on top. Seldom has farming looked less glamorous.

Now over 80, she will talk about all of that and more in the company of Bill Mitchell, former editor of *The Dalesman* magazine and author of several books about Yorkshire and the Dales, who has known her for over thirty of those years.

She will tell of how, after the deaths of her parents and uncle, she ran the family farm from age 35, with no running water or electricity on what would now equate to around £3,000 a year, or less, clad in rags; of how, with the broadcast of *Too Long A Winter*, her life was subsequently transformed.

Touched by her gentle humility and uncomplaining nature, financial donations and good wishes flooded in, not only from across the UK, but from viewers who had watched the documentary around the world. The old farm soon had electricity. Hill walkers - just passing by - knocked on her door.

Twenty years later, in 1992, the same programme makers were back for an update. *A Winter Too Many* revealed how Hannah's lot was at least superficially improved. The extra brass had been prudently invested in more cattle. She was about to attend a 'Women of the Year' gala in London, where this 'simple' - one hopes in the very best sense - northern woman would be guest of honour. The spotlight, should she wish it, was still hers to enjoy.

Away from all that, though, the winters remained hard, as did the work. And Hannah, who had a perfect grasp of literacy and numeracy thanks to a good old fashioned elementary education at chapel and Sunday school - was not getting any younger. By the end of the second film she reluctantly decided to sell up and move to a warm and comfy village cottage instead. There followed a TV series, *Hannah Hauxwell: Innocent Abroad,* in which a maiden grand tour of Austria, France, Germany, Italy and Switzerland was embarked upon, before a televised visit to New York in 1993, all of it faithfully recorded by Cockcroft.

Doubtless, here at the Craiglands, she will reminisce about all of that. And maybe of how, latterly, she has spent the epitome of well-earned retirement in Cotherstone, a village five miles away from Low Birk Hatt Farm, whose fields, 'Hannah's Meadows', now belong to the Durham Wildlife Trust and are a designated Site of Special Scientific Interest; that's a nature reserve to you and I.

The omens, though, are ominous.

To begin with, I am seated behind a post. No matter. Showing Hauxwell-like levels of adaptability, I spot a rare empty chair nearer the front and stake my claim there, only to have my view immediately blocked again by the arrival of the sponsors, a half-deaf retired colonel and his wife.

'Have you heard of him?' asks the former of the latter a little too loudly, when Mitchell, shifting uncomfortably in a solitary top table seat, is introduced. And therein lies the big problem: the headline act has cried off.

'Poorly,' says her would-be interviewer, Bill. 'She's over eighty now. Mind, so am I.'

It's disappointing, but as his opening line hints this long-time Dalesman is a more than capable deputy. His dry wit calls to mind Alan Bennett. 'Goodness,' he says, in mock recoil at the size of the audience. 'If there were this many in Giggleswick, where I come from, they'd read the Riot Act.'

A handful of photos are passed around. Hannah, in the old ones wearing her trademark greatcoat and bonnet, more latterly clad in bright blue anorak and red tartan headscarf, hair all white and wispy. She's still got the wellies on, mind, her one-time 'favourite friends'.

Though she's getting on a bit now, Hannah still has her austere little routine, we are told. She goes to the chapel on a Sunday evening, pops to the village shops, has a little walk... and then we are off with how it all began.

'Years ago, there was an organisation set up in the North Pennines to help Dales farmers,' Bill recalls. 'I was editor of *The Dalesman* at the time and remember getting their first report. It pointed out the various problems and hardships of life, how things were very difficult - as they are, indeed, today - and mentioned a nameless lady, living alone on an income of £170 a year.'

This, it turned out, was Hannah Hauxwell. The one-time *Yorkshire Post* journalist who found her 'living in a solitary state with just half a dozen cows' was Darlington-based Alex Donaldson. And the dale on which she resided was Baldersdale, an offshoot of Teesdale, where Hannah had been born on Yorkshire Day, 1926. According to Donaldson, and as all would very soon witness for themselves, it was a little world of 'spent grasses, snow and shrieking wind.'

Almost immediately, Hannah was projected as a character. She looked, wrote Donaldson, 'feminine in masculine clothes'. The coat on her back was from the First World War: 'It belonged to one of my uncles. I found it hanging behind his bedroom door.' The bonnet once sat atop a great aunt. And she displayed '...a woman's concern for the ritual of tea making and serving, despite her tweed jacket, breeches and gum boots.' Then came Barry Cockcroft and his images of trailing through mud and snow to draw water into an empty bucket, damp paraffin-heated rooms and tugs of war with frisky cattle.

Bill Mitchell's own first encounter with Hannah came

at the suggestion of his late wife, Freda: 'It was Bank Holiday Monday and everyone was going to Morecambe or the Lakes, so we had the northern Dales to ourselves. Off we went, north of Settle. Dale after dale, high road after high road, hardly any traffic. I remember we popped in at the Tan Hill Inn, the highest licensed premises in the land.'

Eventually, they wound up at Low Birk Hatt Farm, far from empty-handed. Freda brought a sponge cake, and so off they went, lapwings circling overhead, across the pasture, down to a reservoir and then up the hard path that led to her gate. 'Have you ever tried carrying a sponge across such terrain,' asks Bill, and no one had. 'It was a rather unusual wooden gate, really. Broken in at least a dozen places. But instead of being replaced or patched up, Hannah had very carefully tied all the little bits together with binding twine, the farmer's best friend. Each piece of twine had a little bow.'

And the initial meeting? 'Usually, you knock on the front door, so we wandered around to the front of the house and there was the finest crop of nettles I've ever seen, almost waist high. We went up to the front door, no answer. It hadn't been used for ages. We went around to the back door and knocked on that. The dog started yapping and we heard a voice commanding it to be quiet. She put it in another room and there was our first view of Hannah in the flesh. She had a beautiful cherry complexion. You don't get that from a chemist's shop. You have to douse yourself in cold water every day and get the capillaries working. That's what she did. She was in a healthy state, although the rest of her was a little on the shoddy side.'

Once inside, the couple were invited into the living room, the centrepiece of which being one of those big old open fireplaces, '...absolutely vital in Dales farms, because you need that draft through to keep the place dried and aired.' Here, though, the chimney was stuffed with material and jackdaws nested on high. At the end of the 1970s, all Hannah had to heat her dwelling was a tiny one-bar electric fire '...which wasn't doing much for the dampness. It was a spring day and you could see it glistening on the wall.'

Given that Freda was also a farmer's daughter, soon the trio were chatting merrily about their respective mothers making butter in the kitchen. Mum, dad uncles and any other relatives were long gone now, of course, although two Victorian photographs in big heavy frames, complete with aged types in their Sunday best, hung prominently.

'Is that your grandfather,' Bill says he asked.

'No, not really,' Hannah replied. 'But my mum said it looked like him, so we left it up.'

Piles of unopened fan mail also lay around, bound up by farmer's twine.

The departure was long. Hannah saw the couple out and stood at the gate as they wandered back down that circuitous pathway. 'We had to turn every two or three paces and wave.' Separation, however, was short. Mitchell returned regularly, whether in a professional capacity as a writer, with curious fellow visitors in tow, but always as a friend.

'I planned to write an article on how she planned to celebrate Christmas. It didn't take long to discuss that; she wasn't going to. The previous Christmas Day, no one had turned up.' Not far from the farm is a stretch of the Pennine Way walking trail that goes from Derbyshire up to Scotland. 'Occasionally, she would have a chat with walkers. Otherwise, she spent every winter very much alone in the cold. She didn't like winters at all - it was a cruel routine.'

So cruel, in fact, that on one particular day, with the electricity having gone off and her paraffin lamp burned out, the temperature was such that as bed-time approached

Hannah felt chilled to the bone. 'So she went out to the byre and there was Rosa, her favourite cow. She milked a pint of warm milk, drank it and then, as an afterthought, laid down beside Rosa and fell asleep.'

***

SO vividly painted are Bill Mitchell's word pictures that Hannah Hauxwell might well have been in the Craiglands Hotel as planned.

'Whenever I took people to see her, they wanted to get away as quickly as possible,' he says. 'Not because they didn't enjoy the visit, they just wanted to begin talking about it.' And peeping through his vignettes are bittersweet indications of a secondary inner life unexpressed, perhaps inevitably in such a solitary figure.

One wet and cold day in 1988, Mitchell knocked on the farm's back door with the rain falling and no one, apparently, in. Then came a scraping sound. A bedroom window nudged open and Hannah's head appeared. 'One of my off days,' she said, before adding: 'It's a poor do about Russell Harty, isn't it?' Her only spoken companion was radio. The broadcaster had passed away that morning.

Still, says Mitchell, he didn't think Hannah was necessarily lonely: 'In the back of her mind, she was still living with her family.'

With her defining pragmatism and taciturnity - summed up by her friend as 'the ability to say nowt for a long time' - Hannah had at least two supposed characteristics of Yorkshireness wrapped up. There was friendliness too, and a twinkle in the eye.

Every literary festival worth its salt has a question and answer session at the end and Ilkley is no different.

First up, a woman at the back.

'Has she still got her own teeth?'

It's as well Hannah couldn't make it, after all.

'I'm not sure actually,' Bill replies. 'I'll ask next time I go see her. We'll put a notice in the *Ilkley Gazette*.'

'Would she have made a dry-stone waller?'

'No.'

'Did she have any suitors?'

'I once asked her that, cheekily, and she said: "No, I've never formed anything in that line..."'

'Does she miss the old life?'

'She'll talk about it, but it reached a stage when she had to make a break. That was an emotional time, but she never harps on nostalgically about those winter privations now. She does have a romantic touch about her, though. She talks about how she misses the moonlight sparkling on the reservoir.'

***

WOLD. It's an odd little word, isn't it? And a bit of a struggle onomatopoeically.

Moor, being room backwards, sounds like what it is. Open, yet confined somehow. Ruddy. A tad threatening. As other-worldly and, well, Moor*ish* as Heathcliff.

Dale, too, brings to mind broad sweeps of space, at altitude perhaps, but less rough and contained, lulling the senses with a lush pallet of greens.

To hear either word in anything but high summer is simultaneously to hear wind whistling through bracken or whipping over the tops and country lanes. Both invoke awe beyond their size. They are mighty in their way, profound.

Wold, though. What picture does that paint?

The lolling swell of ocean waves? Possibly. The North Sea isn't so very far away. But then the North Sea doesn't so much loll as glower, grey and leaden, when its storm surges aren't flooding the Wash and Fens of lower eastern England, that is, or its shipping lanes aren't bustling with the marine traffic that puts them among the busiest in the world.

Maybe Wold carries connotations of sturdiness and good health? The coastline adjoining this third aspect of the Yorkshire landscape - its Anne to the Moors' Emily and Dales' Charlotte you might say - is long associated with curative and restorative holidays. People have come here since the early 19th century with the explicit purpose of letting the sea air improve their circulation, strengthen immune and respiratory systems and generally activate the body's natural defences.

Well, if it worked for Count Dracula...

But no. As it turns out, Wold is derived from ye Olde English 'Wald', meaning forest. As indeed is the area known as The Weald, that traverses the south-eastern counties of Sussex, Hampshire, Surrey and Kent. With the retreat of the trees, the meaning changed over the centuries to 'open high ground', presumably because the original forests in question were up in the hills. The word survives in the Cotswolds too.

As it happens, the Yorkshire Wolds are relatively low-lying. Their highest point is Garrowby Hill, 807 feet (or 246 metres in new money) above sea level. You'll find it on the Wolds' western side, which rises to the escarpment on which it is situated before falling away suddenly into the Vale of York. To the north, across the Vale of Pickering, are the North York Moors; to the east the hills flatten into the Holderness plain; to the south the Humber estuary.

And below that, the Lincolnshire Wolds, part of the same chalk formation, but we are here to talk Yorkshireness, aren't we?

Slouching towards Blubberhouses

Less obviously dramatic than the Dales and lost in comparison with the literary moorland motif, the inland Wolds have long attracted creative types, usually locals in tune with their hidden secrets and their confounding of expectations. Mass popularity though has largely escaped them; for many the Wolds are simply a picturesque - on a good day - route to the Yorkshire coast.

Viewed from above, we are told, the Wolds' deep and steep-sided flat-bottomed valleys, the product of glacial ice ages past, are difficult to pick out, giving the impression that the gently rolling plateaued landscape is flatter than it really is. Chalk is good for drainage, too, leading to a scarcity of surface water that belies the temperate and changeable maritime climate and 128 days of rainfall, on average, a year.

All of which means that the farming here, too, is quirky. The area's sheep, cattle and other livestock will most often be found grazing down in the valleys, while crops are grown on the hills above.

Meanwhile, what painters, writers and tourists there are around here roam just as they please.

***

THE man most likely to popularise the Wolds is David Hockney, godfather of British art, sometime resident of Los Angeles, Kensington and Bridlington, formerly in the Borough of North Wolds, sheltered by Flamborough Head.

He will though have a job on his hands, if one *Daily Telegraph* story about the Bradford-born icon is anything to go by. Design and culture critic Stephen Bayley - Liverpool-raised, Manchester-educated - took the death of the artist's young assistant Dominic Elliott, early in 2013, as his cue for a charming bout of cosmopolitan condescension.

'Who is not struck by the haunting oddness of David Hockney's Bridlington house,' Bayley's piece began, under a photo of the home in question, a red brick 'seaside villa of little charm and no architectural distinction whatsoever,' snapped on a wet and dreary day, obviously. 'You can almost smell the damp and the must, sense the ghosts of unhappy holidays past. The property used to be a hotel, but not - if appearances are anything to go by, which they are - of the better sort. Apparently, faded room numbers remain on the doors. It is impossible to calculate, but easy to guess, how much the existential horror of such a building might have contributed to Hockney's gloriously cheerful accounts of the local countryside.'

There followed a helpful comparison in transatlantic property prices, with the average for an 'East Riding resort, famed for not much other than a half-hearted reputation for shellfish' coming in at £145,000 and similar detached homes in Mulholland Drive, 'the painter's last locale', nearer $7.3 million. 'You might as well compare Harry Ramsden's fish and chips to Wolfgang Puck's spicy tuna tartare in sesame miso cones,' opines Bayley. Well, quite. So why bother?

And this by way of reflecting upon the tragic demise of a 23-year-old man. Is it really any wonder that folk up here can get a bit chippy?

***

TO be fair, the rest of Bailey's article was a thoughtful and well written debunking of the myth of artist as solitary struggling genius, '...in a cockroached and frozen garret with only a crust of bread and syphilis for company.'

From Michelangelo to Rembrandt to Warhol to Gormley, he points out, most artists could not have achieved what they have without teamwork. Hockney is no exception. Yet no matter what the collaborative regime: '...art is also ultimately the product of a single, unique imagination.'

A provocative - and once again loaded - question was floated too: 'What is it about Yorkshiremen that makes them want to return home? Liverpool ... can claim as many talented offspring but, while excessively and eternally sentimental about their hometown, Liverpudlians leave emphatically and never, ever return.' Bayley has no answer to his own conundrum, doubtless because there isn't one, chuntering vaguely instead about the 'mysterious allure of suburbia'.

In the specific case of David Hockney, notwithstanding his emotional and/or private motivations, one response is clear. Given the artist's lifetime fascination with colour and light, then why on earth wouldn't he want to live in and interpret a place where those features change so radically with the passing of each season? Almost eerily empty, one critic called it - with a resonance all of its own.

Provincial is as provincial does.

To take a summer Sunday afternoon drive to this part of Yorkshire or set foot on its 79-mile walk from Hessle on the Humber to Filey via the Wolds Way National Trail, is to be faced with a corner of the region that is all too often neglected. As the Tour de France winds its way through the best views that North, West and South Yorkshire have to offer over two days and 390 kilometres, the county's eastern secret will remain a distant rumour.

6. Up and Humber

Laughing Stocks - Part One: Hull

WHEN Kingston upon Hull announced it had bid to become the UK's Capital of Culture in 2017, much of the rest of the UK - those who took any notice anyway - laughed.

So business as usual then.

Along with Bradford, around sixty miles away, back inland along the M62, the East Yorkshire city is one of the nation's two longest-standing jokes. In the case of the former, that is largely about racism, either out in the open or buried deep within even those of a supposedly liberal disposition.

Hull's reputation is mired squarely in ignorance.

Let's start by debunking just a few of its myths.

Hull is no more riddled with crime and pregnant teenagers than any other British city. Its citizens are not necessarily fat benefit scroungers. Sadly, since the demise of a thriving industry, the place no longer reeks of fish, even at The Deep, '...one of the most spectacular aquariums in the world [and] home to a whopping 3,500 fish, including

Europe's only pair of green sawfish, sharks and rays.' The world's only submarium, indeed. Far from everyone is thick.

Friends who reside in Hull report that it is actually a great place to live, with a relatively low cost of living, lots of bars, restaurant, sport, parkland and other cultural pursuits. And these latter are driving a Capital of Culture bid that hopes to place even more emphasis on the city's rich theatrical, political and literary heritage, while promoting all that's good and creative in the here and now.

Thus is it possible to take a morning walk in the steps of William Wilberforce, Andrew Marvell, Philip Larkin and Andrew Motion in the so-called Museum Quarter, before an afternoon stroll around the burgeoning Fruit Market.

The development of this latter part of Hull, down on the waterfront in the old town, and sited over eight acres from the city's beautiful Humber marina to the east bank of the River Hull, is a relatively recent phenomenon. Plans to revamp it first took flight around 2008, when a number of its empty old warehouses and other buildings were re-invented as café bars, art galleries, theatre spaces, music venues and the like. But with the crash of the financial markets, the entire £100m regeneration project stalled.

As such, and notwithstanding how in September 2013 a fourth annual Freedom Festival to celebrate the talent of local artists was about to be staged here, the area has a half-finished look. Dripping with potential, the City of Culture bid was viewed as a key driver in seeing it all to fruition, pun very much intended.

Especially on the back of news that those original plans would be revived, the search for a development partner put out to tender. Up to seventy homes, shops, offices and an arts centre were back on the agenda.

'Our vision is to create a vibrant cultural and

residential quarter that will bring more people to our stunning waterfront and become a world-class visitor destination,' announced councillor Steven Baynes.

***

THE place has already attracted at least one visitor: me, on Good Friday, 29 March 2013.

Clichés and stereotypes rarely gain traction without a cog of justification, and Hull's caricature as a left-field oddity stuck out in the middle of nowhere does have at least some basis in geographical fact.

To end up in Hull, you really do have to be going there. The only thing it is en route to is a scrotum-shrivelling North Sea dip, and even then only if you possess a scrotum. Then there are the creamy white phone boxes, visitors from some alternate universe in which the author got a tiny detail wrong. They are here, as it happens, because a renegade city council has operated its own telephone network, Kingston Communications, now partly privatised, since 1902. And they didn't want red.

Leafing through Dave Hadfield's 2004 rugby league travelogue *Up and Over* recently, I rediscovered the following quote from Bradford's finest J.B. Priestley who, in his *English Journey* of 1933, wrote: 'These people are pleasant but queer. They are queer because they are not quite Yorkshire but not quite anything else.'

As for Hadfield himself: 'The architecture often has more in common with Holland, Scandinavia and the Baltic than with Leeds and Bradford. For most of its history, you would be more likely to bump into a Russian or a Swede in the city centre - and certainly around the docks - than you would a Lancastrian.' He goes on to add, after a trip to the

Maritime Museum, that these days only five trawlers operate out of Hull as opposed to 365 in its heyday.

'In what seems like a calculated insult, most of the fish sold in Hull chippies is flown in from Iceland - clearly the victor in the Cod Wars - to Humberside Airport.'

And then there's the twang. Along with this being a city of very unusual fern boxes, Hull is a place where perch degs come on terst, the Perp is the head of the Catholic Church and where, in winter, it's colder than the Nerth Pearl.

The accent of my friendly guide for the day, Hull playwright Dave Windass, isn't quite so broad, but he does have a love for the city of his birth that flavours just about everything he is - or has ever been - involved with.

We meet in the Lion and Key, an independent pub with beer mats on the ceiling and an impressive choice of local ales and ciders. Situated just up the road from slave trade abolitionist Wilberforce's house, now a museum, it turns out to be a perfect spot from which to commence the Fruit Market circuit.

'The accent is something of a disadvantage,' Dave admits, opting for lager rather than a pint of Pricky Back Otchan (something to do with hedgehogs) from the Great Newsome Brewery, based in nearby Frodingham. 'We've all heard Scouse, Manc, Geordie and Cockney, but it comes as a shock to some people because its unique vowel sounds haven't been in the public domain as much. It has flattened out quite a lot lately, though. We've got the 1980 Challenge Cup final DVD in our house and it's got all this hilarious pre-match stuff. The accent is completely "owld ull", where it all comes from the back of the throat. If we'd just carried on doing that no one would have argued with us.'

The final referred to is a still talked about occasion when the city's two rugby league clubs and fierce rivals at that, Hull Kingston Rovers to the east of the river and Hull FC to the west, met at Wembley stadium. Rervers it was who triumphed 10-5 in London that day, before a capacity crowd of 95,000. Hull, they say, was a ghost town.

It's further confirmation, too, of the individuality of a place where a sport - no, make that an obsession - that is most often on the undercard elsewhere, is a regular on the front page of the daily paper as well as the back. In this way at least, Hull is like Sydney, but with less sunshine and where a surfer is the piece of furniture you recline in to watch telly.

And yet, for all that, a reputation as 'the land that tarme forgot' clings stubbornly, certainly in comparison to other big thriving northern cities like Manchester, Sheffield, Liverpool, Newcastle and Leeds. True enough, concedes Dave, but the tide is already turning.

'They had been talking about doing something with Ferensway, where the Hull Truck theatre is nowadays, since the War,' he says. 'It was a barren wasteland with a grotty old ABC cinema on it.' A new shopping centre and a schools rebuilding project also squeezed through just as other regeneration projects were scrapped. The opening of the new Hull Truck at a cost of £14.5m, coupled with Hull City's first promotion to football's Premier League in 2008, seems to have kick started a fair bit of heady optimism, culminating five years later with a first-ever trip to the FA Cup final.

Says Dave: 'You just felt: "...we can do stuff here, we're all right." But yes, Hull is the poor relation. When you go to Leeds or Manchester, the cities seem sprawling. Our city centre is in a very tight geographical area. We don't have much land to play with, never mind anything else. It could have gone one of two ways. They could have just left us to die or...'

It was Hull Truck, in fact, that gave Dave Windass his own start in drama, in a roundabout way anyhow. A theatre founded in 1971 by out-of-work actor Mike Bradwell was, by the time young Dave came on the scene, about to become a 'national institution' with the arrival of artistic director John Godber in 1984.

Godber it was who, having packed in a well-paid teaching job to take charge of his own theatrical destiny, cannily wrote and staged the play *Up n' Under*, turning around Hull Truck's long-standing financial struggles and lowly audience figures at a stroke. It was about rugby league, you see. Couldn't fail.

After which came many another popular production, including the still widely performed by professional and amateur dramatists alike, *Bouncers*, the last play performed at Truck's old Spring Street home.

'I have always written,' says Dave. 'I nicked my sister's typewriter when I was about eight. An Imperial one - made in Hull - gone but not forgotten. I didn't really know what plays were until I was about 14 and we did Shakespeare in English. It bored me to death. I thought, that's not for me, I'm not going anywhere near that. But then a girlfriend of mine worked at a café that the Hull Truck mob used to go in, back in the early 1980s so, with her, I saw two or three years of plays there, before Godber arrived. A series of unfortunate incidents then left me working as a theatre critic for *The Stage*. Without really knowing what I was doing, I had seen a lot of theatre and just started churning out plays myself.'

After a couple of 'short things,' Windass got involved with Truck properly in the early 2000s, with the arrival of new artistic director Gareth Tudor Price. 'I was bombarding them with unsolicited scripts, which they quite rightly didn't respond to,' he says. 'They must have thought I was some kind of nutcase, there was a new one every other week. Then I did a slightly longer thing, then a thing that was slightly longer than the slightly longer thing, before the first full piece I wrote called *Kicked into Touch*, which was about the 1980 Challenge Cup final.'

Rugby league was also the centrepiece of *Sully*, the play that brought Windass to wider attention in 2006. A biographical take on the life and times of Hull and Great Britain's World Cup-winning captain Clive Sullivan - after whom, incidentally, the Hessle to Hull section of the A63, originally the South Docks Road, is named - it played for three-and-a-half weeks with every performance sold out.

'We got all the supporters from both clubs,' Dave says. 'They were for the rugby, obviously, but Sully was more thought provoking than that. And because a lot of rugby folk are big, they couldn't get out of their seats to run away.'

Next was *On A Shout* in 2008, about the lifeboat crew at Spurn Point, the only full-time one in the country, which serves the Humber.

These days, John Godber - the third most performed UK playwright after Shakespeare and Scarborough fixture and fitting Alan Ayckbourn - is no longer around. Since 2011, he has filled a similar role at Wakefield's Theatre Royal. Dave Windass, though, isn't going anywhere. Months before, your author was in one of the new Ferensway theatre's 440 seats as his latest hit, *Ballroom Blitz*, packed in the punters:

Bernie (*to audience*): The local MC for regional events was none other than Frankie 'Fishtail' Mowforth - he had a legendary quickstep, a glass eye and a style all his own...

Bernie raises the mic and becomes Fishtail.

Bernie (*sings; as Fishtail*): Oh, I do like to be beside the turbines, oh I do like to be beside the wind ... so, ladies and gen'lemen, here we are; the Rumba ... on ... the Humber; and how lovely you all look; how lovely ... it's nice to be back in Hull, it really is. Although, last time I was here, I got into a bit of bother; a bloke asked me, "do you smirk?" I said, "yes, if the occasion dictates." He said, "give us one then." So I did. (*Bernie smirks*) And I started to walk away. He said, "Where are you going? Where's me smirk?" I said, "You want another?" (*he smirks again*) He said, "Are you taking the piss? I want a smirk I can smirk." A smirk you can smirk? I said, "Okay then; watch me." (*very exaggerated smirk*). "How's that?" Well, he got so annoyed; I had to give him a cigarette just to calm him down.

'Hull is an honest and truthful place,' says Windass. 'It doesn't take prisoners. It's unpretentious, which is good. And for me the medium of theatre is just that, a really honest way of telling a story. There are no frills to it here. It's just a bunch of people on stage with a bit of lighting and maybe some music if you are lucky. And you've got to tell a story in a simple, stripped-down, effective way. So maybe that's it really. I know theatre can be a different thing elsewhere.

'We had John Godber here for a number of years and he is indelibly linked with Hull. The type of theatre he did, which is kind of very minimalistic, breaks down the barriers between the audience and people on stage. You've got to write stuff that resonates with the locals as well, whether that's rugby league or whatever. Alan Plater, who was born in the North East but based himself here and considered himself an adopted son, wrote a play about Hull City. He was quite involved before Hull Truck even existed, when it was Humberside Theatre. Barrie Rutter, who went off and founded Northern Broadsides in Halifax, was born here. There's a dramatic tradition.

'Richard Bean, who has just kicked up a storm at the National Theatre with *One Man, Two Guvnors*, is an East Hull lad. West End run ... Broadway ... his bank account is filling up. Last time I was in London I had a pint with him. He was saying how demotivated he is now he's got money. He's always been a miserable bugger, but that's what the people of East Hull are like.

'And that's another interesting aspect, this east-west thing. We are a city divided by a river. I know elsewhere cities are built on rivers, but it's a dynamic that does affect the Hull psyche. I'm not sure an outsider would notice; I'm not sure the differences are even there. It might be another thing we like to create an illusion about, but people do identify themselves by it. Whenever I meet someone elsewhere and they ask where I'm from, I have to stop myself saying "West Hull". Richard's website has a bio saying he's a writer from East Hull. What does *that* mean to anyone in the world? Meaningless. I don't think there's much difference really, other than West Hull's better.'

A tendency to self-mythology, coupled with a roll-up-your-sleeves mentality; it's becoming a Yorkshire theme.

'Hull is a good place just to sit down and get on with stuff,' Dave continues. 'And there's a feeling here that we kind of want to keep things a little bit secret. The people in Hull know it's good. Those of us who are engaged with all the cultural activity know it's comparable to anywhere in the country. But we don't like talking about it because we don't want loads of people to come and fuck it up for us [chuckles]. Which would happen, wouldn't it?'

So would it be fair to describe Hull's cultural scene as thriving?

'That might be over-egging the pudding; we are kind of getting there. Loads more could happen. We are in what you might call a transitional phase, where everybody is really supportive of each other. But that can only go on for so long. We're all being nice at the moment, going to each other's things because the community needs to grow. But once we've got critical mass, we'll get a bit more competitive and try to be better than everyone else. Thriving is an exaggeration, but we are definitely in a better place than we were five years ago and it's beyond recognition from what it was a decade ago.

'We have a lot of venues who are interested in entertainers or artists or musicians or theatre-makers coming in and doing stuff. It's easy in Hull to set up those kinds of links. In other places, there's not as much activity because there's not the legacy and history of people doing it. Here, you can ask a landlord if you can put stuff on and the landlord will invariably say yes.'

And that must be a good thing in a city as mired in recession as anywhere.

'It's one of those situations where tough conditions inspire artistic endeavour. You just think: "Fuck it. I've got no money. No one is going to fund me, if anyone's going to make it happen it has to be me. So there's loads of people like that now cropping up here, there and everywhere. The old Fruit Market ... when you see it you'll know what I'm on about. It could become a real hub of activity. It's kind of getting there, but nowhere near where it could be.

'Before the plug got pulled, the council and regional development agency 'Yorkshire Forward', as it was then, had bought up all the properties, compulsory purchase, ready for the developers to come in. So then they were left with loads of empty buildings on their hands. There was like this big public meeting of artists and basically everyone came out of the woodwork. The intention was to find expressions of interest. They had all these empty spaces, plagued with problems, but said they might be able to provide funding to get the buildings up to scratch if we could find a use for them; a big ideas session. Out of that was born the venue Fruit, that I'm involved in, and the galleries that have cropped up since.'

***

IT's time for the tour. We leave the Lion and Key and head off into what if this were New York would surely be called the Warehouse District.

Once a densely populated residential area until all but obliterated by the Luftwaffe, on this Good Friday morning our starting point has a ghostly, derelict vibe. Maybe it's just my age or the time of day, but it feels like it's on the verge of awakening from a coma, and somewhere you wouldn't want to stroll alone after dark.

Emerging from under the A63 flyover, though, traffic grumbling on high, and we soon head along Humber Street, focal point of the Fruit Market, in the direction of the more obviously mainstream and photogenic Marina. The route, a grittier and more demanding panorama, begs to be snapped in black and white. Sights include the Hull Art Club, now defunct after being burnt down, where according to Dave: 'There was this collective of artists who didn't want funding and one of them used to live in it. He liked the impermanence of art and would destroy everything.'

Here is a 'dinosaur museum', there a microbrewery or deli, and everywhere empty warehouses, some put to use - or at least that's how it looks from the signs, even if few of them are actually open for business. 'It's happening,' says Dave, 'but organically, on a shoestring.'

Almost immediately, we happen across a gallery - kag - that does betray a flicker of internal activity, though only if the word 'activity' can be held to mean a bloke stood on his own waiting for someone to come in. He is Geoff Keen, long-time member of Kingston Art Group, a charitable co-operative. 'This is my exhibition,' he says. 'We provide studio space for local artists and this is a sort of shop window.'

The kag gallery has been open for eighteen months now, while Geoff has been in the group itself for fifteen years, '...this is a new departure for us.' On the walls hang his own paintings, eye-catching adventures in abstract expressionism intended, reveals the former London student, to investigate where knowing ends and the unconscious starts. 'It's something I've been involved in for nearly 30 years. The impulse came from an idea about deconstruction. Opposite my studio at that time was a building that was being demolished, and it was just interesting going in every day and seeing each structural layer revealing itself. That was the initial idea, layering, putting things on top of each other and having the first mark to the very last mark still evident.

'Every stage of the painting should show itself at some point. It's a process in which you look for exciting elements or colours or just a set of brush strokes that begin to resonate or mean something. For me, it's about getting as many of those things happening as possible, because then it stimulates you to look at it and make your own associations. So I suppose it's about mood or a feeling. Primarily I use the paintings as memory, a kind of diary if you like.'

And with every scribble, every rhythmic gesture that emerges from what might commonly be seen as a mundane industrial landscape, one can only wonder what Ashley Jackson would make of it all.

'The movement of colour is influenced by the city,' Keen goes on, warming to his theme, which is just as well as the temperature indoors is several degrees colder than outside. 'It's not a direct portrait in a visual way, you won't recognise images of Hull in these. It's more about inspiration and the feeling of the place. I think it's about the way things change, the possibilities of change and, hopefully, can in some way kind of inspire that change.'

Is there a lot of interest I ask, a clumsy attempt to confront the room's fourth inhabitant, a rather large elephant.

'Well, even in the depths of winter we've had two hundred visitors here,' says Geoff. 'So that's an improvement on last year when we barely reached one hundred. The gallery is becoming more popular. In the summer, if there's an event in the street or at the marina, a thousand people can walk through in a day.' Kag operate a rolling programme that is full right up until December, '...and then we'll close through January and February to re-seal and re-line the walls. The only things we haven't done yet are heating and lighting, but tracking is going in next week so we'll have spotlights to make it a proper gallery space.'

A little further up Humber Street, opposite a Welcome to Yorkshire banner pinned randomly on some tatty old blue double-doors and on the other side of the road, hangs Fruit.

With an entrance painted a cooler shade of grey and whitened pillars supporting red brick walls, this live music venue and airy performance space, with recording studio Fruit Trade Music alongside, is exactly what Hull's cultural hub as a whole aspires to be. It is here that Dave Windass curates and comperes a night called scratch@fruit, wherein new writers are given a chance to show their work on stage, allowing them to develop it based on audience response and feedback. Since early 2011, more than eighty such creative types from Hull and East Yorkshire have put on plays.

A little further along is the Studio Eleven Gallery, run

Slouching towards Blubberhouses

by painter and printmaker Rob Moore and designer Adele Howitt, its resident artists, set up to offer specialist studio space for printmakers and ceramicists. And next to that, across the way from what was once The Humber Fruit Brokers and is now an antique shop and further music venue, sits The Museum of Club Culture.

As we pass, timely shutters rattle up and owner Mark Wigan, veteran of the city's nightlife of several years' standing, welcomes us in. Everything from '...prohibition speakeasies and jazz age flappers, to zoot suits and French Zazous, from beatnik hipsters to teddy boys, rockabilly rebels, discotheques, mods and scooterists, rockers, ton up boys, hippies, skinheads, soulies, punks, new romantics, Rastafarians, rappers, breakers, fetishists, goths, cybergoths, metalheads, casuals, ravers, UK Asian underground, riot girls, skaters, rappers, grunge, drum 'n' bass, scenes such as trance, queer, emo, garage, burlesque, grime, music super clubs and virtual internet clubs...' is here.

Or if not immediately apparent, then walls literally papered in clubland memorabilia will get to them at some point. Quite some mission statement.

'We have exhibitions every month or two,' says Mark, 'all related to club culture or sub-cultures. We have had exhibitions of Japanese club culture, things from New York, London ... this exhibition is based on clubs in Hull from the 1960s onwards and is on until the end of April. Clubs like the Skyline, Gondola, Kontiki, right through to an institution like the "Welly", whose centenary it is this year.'

As with so much popular culture, it's a story all too often overlooked by those for whom history means only the hatches, matches and dispatches of power-crazed kings and queens, the fortunes of empire, generals, field-marshals and the attendant political and battleground intrigue. And yet the real secret of how any society ticks is most likely to be lined with toil and sweat.

The Welly, for example, began life as the Wellington Assembly Rooms just before the First World War, initially as a ballroom. Later it became a cabaret bar and private members' club, before its more modern evolution as home to acid house, punk and just about every other musical trend available. It's easy to see why Mark, who has spent around twenty years running such places '...and quite a lot of time promoting them...' should find the idea of a museum devoted to championing 'the cultural significance of nightclubs and streetstyle' so appealing. Thanks to its key themes of memory and collective identity, I could rootle about in here all day.

'I worked at *i-D* magazine [dedicated to fashion, art, music and youth culture] as a journalist and photographer and accumulated an archive of flyers and photographs of clubs over several years,' he says. 'So we set this up in 2010 to house the archive but also to put on exhibitions. In the time since, more things have gradually happened in the street. The biggest things for us are the festivals; that's when we get the most visitors. But we are open on weekends, so we get people traveling here from the likes of Leeds and Manchester, they even come up from London, so it's not just Hull.'

Still a keen clubber himself, he will be DJ-ing at the Welly this coming Sunday '...until three in the morning with my Northern Soul records.'

The name, I suppose, should have been a giveaway. Was there a big northern scene in Hull?

'Oh yes,' Mark says, gesturing towards a photographic display. 'There were regular coach trips in the 1970s to the Wigan Casino all-nighter. We used to travel there and also up to Cleethorpes for their all-dayers. Bridlington used to have a lot of events too, there's always been a strong following. The Hull Soul Club still attracts about five hundred people.'

But though Northern Soul records fill the bulk of Mark's collection his musical tastes, like those of a city that is home to three hundred bands and in which Paul Heaton and Norman Cook formed the Housemartins, are eclectic.

'House, punk, ska... there's been a vibrant club scene in Hull for ages. Clubs like the Skyline had a 2,000 capacity in the mid-'sixties. Around a thousand people would sit and eat in the cabaret section, with two hundred standing, while bands like The Who played. Another seven hundred danced in the adjoining Café de Paris. In the 1970s, as Romeo's and Juliet's, it was still Hull's biggest venue.

'You've got people like Jacko [Paul Jackson - said once to have had a deaf dog] at the Adelphi, characters who just set up clubs and run them; he gets acts from the States regularly.' Bands like Oasis, Radiohead and Franz Ferdinand plus plenty of up and coming talents too have all graced a club that, in 2014, is 30 years old: '...so he's built up something of a reputation. Jarvis Cocker used to play quite a bit at the Adelphi when he was in Pulp.'

Onward, ever onward, and at the corner of Humber Street, on cobbled roads lined with redundant tramlines just across from a jewellery workshop, where the 'Marche des Fruits', 'Mercado de Frutas,' and 'Mercado della Frutta' are helpfully signposted for overseas visitors, and glinting waters lap gently against a swankier Marina frontage, we bump into Paul Dennis, founder of 'brand design consultancy' Consul.

Paul, it seems, senses in the Fruit Market a business opportunity, as exemplified by his creation 'The 1 Gallery - Discovering and Celebrating Art from Yorkshire,' sited in some vacant Humber Quays offices, one originally having been built for the World Trade Center organisation.

It is here too where the outdoor stages and bars of the Freedom Festival (named in honour of Wilberforce) will once again stand: 'John Cooper Clarke played in that car park.'

The best place to discuss Paul's plans, of course, is in a pub and so it's off to the Minerva Hotel we go, passing a renovated smoke house, complete with colourful chimneys, and a kids' fish trail - 'blistering barnacles!' - underfoot.

I later read that this 'historic maritime' gastropub is situated 'on Yorkshire's only pier'. It also boast's Yorkshire's smallest theatre, so there goes Yorkshire, even boasting about inadequacy. It's certainly next to one of the finest public toilet blocks anywhere ... brass pipes, hanging flowers and ornate ceramic cisterns and urinals (made in Burnley, Lancashire), hand-written poems on the walls ... erected in 1854, they offer a better class of graffiti.

The land on which the Minerva stands once wasn't here at all. It was reclaimed from the Humber in 1801 for use as a ferry boat dock, Humber Street having prior to that been Hull's southernmost extent with only the town defences and the riverbanks beyond it. A blue plaque tells us that although the Humber Ferry operated between here and New Holland from 1825 until the completion of the Humber Bridge in 1981, 'a ferry between Hull and Lincolnshire was recorded in 1315.'

But back to Paul, now leaning on a bar that must have supported one or two swaying passengers of its own given the range of real ales on offer. 'The gallery began as a project to help artists promote themselves online,' he says, 'so it was nice to secure two thousand square feet on the Quays. The whole idea is about discovering and celebrating art from Yorkshire. There's so much going on that could be promoted, not just in the UK but globally. The 1 Gallery can give Yorkshire artists a sense of place as a group, and help them be part of something unique.'

Slouching towards Blubberhouses

Across all genres? 'Absolutely. It's for any artist who has a body of work - there are a lot of people with studios stacked full of stuff that never gets seen. So it's about finding them, getting them to show themselves, and telling them there's something here they might want to participate in.'

Again, though, the key word is potential. One dot on a bigger picture of dots that haven't quite been joined up yet.

'Footfall to my galleries is very poor,' Paul admits, 'because it's not got all that other stuff around it. What I'm keen to do is use it as a space where seventy to eighty people can gather in the day; where every month artists, poets, writers and so on network. There's nowhere else where you can actually sit down and listen to a talk or see the work.'

Though confident it will come to pass one day, Dave Windass, listening intently, reckons the cultural hub desired is '...probably a decade off. What's been good about having been involved from the start is that I've seen how once there was nothing and now there's stuff going on. The City of Culture bid will kick-start more activity and that can only be a brilliant thing, whether we win or not. The idea is that you have to put a programme together for the year, but then there has to be an increase in activity. Everyone is working together on that. There's meetings about getting involved. If everyone follows them up with actual work, whatever happens with the actual bids, we're all doing the right thing.'

And as the *Guardian* reminds us, just four weeks later, in a piece headlined 'Hull braces itself for the jokes with a bid to be UK City of Culture 2017', Tracey Thorn, another of the city's musical big guns, attended the same Hull University where former poet laureate Andrew Motion taught English. The group she made her name with, Everything But the Girl, borrowed that moniker from a junk shop in Beverley Road. These days, it's the chamber of commerce.

***

WHETHER or not Hull is voted *the* City of Culture will have to wait until the end of this chapter. That Hull is certainly *a* city of culture, though, should go unchallenged. Though many have admittedly seen better days, its boulevards bustle still. And the artistry isn't just confined to the Fruit Market.

Philip Larkin lived in a house on the park off Princes Ave, which now has 'a sort of boho feel about it,' according to Dave Windass, 'with all the artists and entertainers and pseudo-intellectuals. It's full of pubs providing entertainment on a night, café bars and there's a nice urban residential area just off it. Newland Avenue has more of a coffee shop culture and a couple of live music venues. We get some good people coming here.'

Like Glasgow, though, Hull does have a reputation as a challenging place to play, and not only for bands. Famously, the comedian Les Dawson was given such a hard time here early on that he almost packed comedy in entirely.

'Yeah, there is that,' Dave chuckles, 'and I think we still are quite a tough audience to please. We sit there with our arms folded saying "go on, funnyman, entertain me..." There is definitely that vibe. The people here are not afraid of saying what's on their mind. There's a lot of not having the filter through which to edit what you are thinking or saying.

'The people of Hull don't give a fuck really about what the rest of the country thinks about them. We've struggled on and got through some very tough times - the Blitz, the decimation of the fishing and before that whaling industries - and just carried on regardless. We don't care. And that manifests itself in the treatment some entertainers get when they come to the city [laughs]. We're not bothered whether you play here, mate. You died, so don't bother us again.'

Even so, as we speak, a major lump of Hull's future prospects do appear to hinge on the opinion of one bunch of outsiders in particular; the judges who to widespread relief shortlisted a bid that includes 1,500 events, twenty-five festivals, twelve artist residences and other projects in a package costing £11m alongside those of fellow contenders Dundee, Swansea Bay and Leicester on June 17. Bloody Leicester again! Haven't they caused enough trouble?

'The bid celebrates our resourcefulness, creativity and pride of our people,' read the promotional manifesto, *2017 Hull - Tell The World*. 'We aim to change perceptions of the city by telling our untold stories and demonstrating our place in the UK as a gateway to Europe.'

Culture minister Ed Vaizey, whose government does not provide direct funding, added: 'The events in [current incumbent] Derry-Londonderry highlight just how much of an impact being City of Culture can have. It brings together communities, encourages economic growth and inspires social change.' The seven other bidders to miss out were Aberdeen, Chester, East Kent, Hastings and Bexhill on Sea, Plymouth, Portsmouth/Southampton and Southend on Sea, with the winner due to be announced in November 2013.

In the meantime, if Hull is really so different to the rest of the UK, I ask Dave, how does it fit in relation to Yorkshireness? Over on England's west coast, the city of Liverpool betrays a split personality when it comes to being in Lancashire, can a similar scenario be detected here?

'When everywhere else bought into the telephone exchange we fiercely didn't and there are other examples of that mindset,' he says. 'We invented the Liquid Crystal Display in Hull, when everyone else liked LEDs. The Venn diagram was invented here too, of course, and that's very useful isn't it? We were the starting point for the English Civil War and if there's a spirit that runs through the city it's that of being autonomous. I do have mates who are fiercely proud of being from Yorkshire, but my personal view is we're not part of that; I don't know how representative that is. I don't feel like we are in Yorkshire, which is weird because we are, kind of. And I think that affects how we behave.

'There's that feeling of ... yes people do come here, port city, trade passes through, so we are kind of outward looking as well. We are looking out over to Rotterdam and all those places. I go to Leeds and feel like a stranger in a strange town. They don't behave like we do.'

And as for the drama: 'As much as you think, I don't want to write plays that are specifically about the city, or Hessle Road ... I don't want to be that, there's nothing worse than a professional northerner, is there ... I'm kind of kicking against that all the time ... you can't escape what you are. You can't step outside of that and be someone else without stuff becoming completely and utterly meaningless.'

***

EIGHT months later, on Wednesday 20 November, comes the news. Hull has indeed beaten Leicester, Dundee and Swansea Bay and will be the UK's next City of Culture in 2017.

Hull council leader Stephen Brady tells the media that being chosen to follow on from Londonderry is 'a real game-changer. It will give Hull a platform to tell the world what this great city has to offer and transform perceptions.'

TV producer Phil Redmond, chair of the judging panel says Hull was a unanimous choice after putting forward: '...the most compelling case based on its theme as a city coming out of the shadows. This is at the heart of their project and reminds both its people and the wider world of both Hull's cultural past and future potential.'

As 2013's City of Culture, Derry was able to attract high-profile events like the Turner Prize and BBC Radio 1's *Big Weekend*. It is revealed, however, that sponsorship income and ticket sales had been lower than expected. Not that any of that put a dent in Hull City Council's celebrations.

The cultural programme, they said, would be built on the poems of Philip Larkin. 'Inspired by Larkin's poem *Days*,' a statement read, 'the ambition is for each day of Hull 2017 to make a difference to a life in the city, the UK and the world.' A £60m boost to the local economy in 2017 alone was on the cards, along with a longer-term legacy for the city.

Plans include an opening ceremony complete with theatrical elephants, dancing white phone boxes and four rivers of light flowing into the city. The annual Freedom Festival will boast an aerial show based on the last line of Larkin's *An Arundel Tomb*: 'What will survive of us is love.'

And hope, the poet might have added.

7. Spinning a Yarn

Talking Yorkshire's Language

THEY are by no means exclusive to Yorkshire, of course, but if any phenomenon confirms language - written or spoken, dialect or otherwise - as key to the county's personality, it is the current explosion of literary festivals.

In Leeds alone there are several, perhaps the fastest growing to be found in Morley, market town birthplace of former Prime Minister Herbert Asquith but otherwise as far removed from Bloomsbury as cocktails are from best bitter.

Since 2006, its thirty or so events and rising not only give up-and-coming local writers a chance to meet and attract readers, run workshops and escape the computer keyboard for a while, they attract many of the publishing industry's bigger fish too, especially those with a book to promote.

More pertinently, for our purposes, they are a chance to celebrate and climb into the psyche of those Yorkshire-born talents whose influence has always stretched much further afield - a centuries old river of words that is still in full spate.

Slouching towards Blubberhouses

Think Alan Bennett, Tony Harrison, Willis Hall, Keith Waterhouse, Kay Mellor and Barbara Taylor Bradford - who, like the others, is actually from Leeds - along with wider flung authors, playwrights and poets such as the ubiquitous Brontës, J.B. Priestley, John Braine (who *were* from Bradford), Barry Hines, Phyllis Bentley, Stan Barstow, Susan Hill, W.H. Auden, Ted Hughes, John Godber and more recently Blake Morrison, Simon Armitage, Ian McMillan, David Peace, Joanne Harris, Gervase Phinn *et al*. Then there's Laurence Stern, Philip Larkin, Alan Plater, David Nobbs and company who, though born elsewhere, pitched up and stuck around.

They and many many more can, when not in Morley, be found either sharing their genius in person or having it discussed in old theatres, church halls, schoolrooms or rugby clubs the length and breadth of the UK. In Leeds, that might mean the 'Big Bookend' or Headingley; in the rest of Yorkshire, it could be Harrogate's Crime Writing Festival - the biggest of its type in the world - or similar jamborees in Beverley, York, Scarborough and Grassington.

***

THERE is, however, no doubting the daddy of all Yorkshire Literary Festivals, the county's very own Cheltenham or Hay-on-Wye. It would have to be Ilkley, of course, with or without Hannah Hauxwell.

Launched in 1973 and held every October to the bosom of the Cow and Calf rocks, this particular literature festival is now as warming a presence on the calendar as the russet moors that stand guard over the town on the drive in.

Ilkley, like Harrogate up the road, is a spa town, albeit much smaller in size if not ambition. It sees itself as posh, with a defining avenue called The Grove, a Betty's Tea Room as in Harrogate, a Winter Gardens... the place has gentility, sometimes shabby, often not. It's ripe for bracing walks and healthy strolls, short weekend breaks, fine ale and an hour or so browsing through a very pleasant bookshop.

The ideal spot, then, for a middle England gathering of comfortable cardies, pashmina shawls and knitted wraps that these festivals always seem to attract, being none the worse for that. In any case, it's best not to press the old urban credentials too hard when, upon glancing down, you notice that you're wearing a tatty pair of charcoal grey corduroys.

And, as it turns out, in conception the Ilkley Literature Festival had a devoutly anti-elitist and utilitarian intent. According to its first director, Michael Dawson, quoted in *An Outpost of Progress - 25 Years of the Ilkley Literature Festival* (ILF Books, 1998), the idea had its roots in the 1971 postal strike.

Lacking mail, Dawson describes how while reading various British arts festival brochures in his possession, he twigged that only Cheltenham dealt predominantly with literature. Books, in other words, were the arts' poor relation. 'Why not a first class literature festival in Ilkley,' he reasoned. 'One which would whisk the dust off the written word and provide entertainment for the man in the main street.'

And so, with a £750 grant from the Ilkley Urban District Council and a promise to 'stimulate public interest in writing; encourage authors, particularly those in the region, and attract more visitors to Ilkley,' it all began. Looking back some forty-odd years, it is safe to say that those targets have been hit on all counts. Among the festival's first 'big gun' guests - indeed the original presence of Howitzer size - was W.H. Auden who, the book says, agreed to come only on the understanding that his partner and collaborator on *The Rake's Progress*, Chester Kallman, '...be offered a lunchtime poetry slot.' It turned out to be Auden's last public reading.

Slouching towards Blubberhouses

J.B. Priestley, too, was scheduled to attend but in the end could not, nevertheless writing at length in support of the venture, particularly as '...the Festival club is licensed.'

'A literature festival is very difficult to organise,' Priestley began. 'A music festival and a drama festival have attractive performances to offer their patrons. Authors have little to show and are no treat as a spectacle. So anybody trying to organise a literature festival really has to work at it.' He concluded: 'Like Malvern - and very, very unlike Edinburgh - Ilkley is the right size for a Festival town.'

In the years ahead, the enterprise grew, albeit not without the odd hiccup - often financial - and biennially. In 1975, the second event, Ted Hughes gave the first public performance of a poem specially commissioned by the festival, *Cave Birds and Lumb's Remains*, in the King's Hall.

According to the *Yorkshire Post*, it made quite an impact: 'A blood-curdling scream pierced the heart of Ted Hughes' new poem sequence at its world premiere ... it came from a member of the audience. Shortly afterwards a woman vomited and was led out. There is no doubt that *Cave Birds* is a very powerful piece of writing.'

Or maybe she had just been told the price of a special printed edition of the poem, complete with facsimiles of rough drafts and illustrations: £125. It wouldn't be the last time the festival met accusations of elitism and profiteering.

Yet such critics are most often those with little or no knowledge of the realities of an actual balance sheet. And there is absolutely no doubt that right up until the festival's 40th celebrations in 2013, as costs have risen, for audience and organisers, so have the levels of diversity.

Also in 1975, a public symposium featured John Braine, journalist James Cameron, Auberon Waugh and playwright and screenwriter Henry Livings. Melvyn Bragg made the first of many visits in 1977. After appearing to be on its last legs, things perked up a little in 1984 thanks to appearances by Alan Bennett (who set his film of that year, *A Private Function*, here), Tony Harrison, Michael Palin, Terry Jones, Christopher Fry, Graham Swift and Roy Hattersley. The first appointment of a full-time director, Steve Dearden, fended off that mood of crisis in 1988, whereupon the event went annual and 'something for everyone' became its rallying cry.

The continued adoption of that philosophy - whether in terms of age, sex, ethnicity or cultural taste - together with a steady supply of, particularly in later years, 'box office' celebrities, has been a winning recipe. Clive James, Kate Adie, Maya Angelou, Carol Ann Duffy, Andrew Motion, Benjamin Zephaniah, Louis Theroux, Nick Hornby, Fay Weldon, local boy gardener Alan Titchmarsh ... all have trodden and continue to tread its boards and pavements. Most recently, around two hundred and thirty events were watched by thousands of people, many local but with sizeable numbers travelling in for the occasion.

Yet it's easy to see success looking backwards, isn't it?

Certainly, novelist Angela Carter didn't have the benefit of hindsight in 1977. Where papers like the *Financial Times* condescended - '...It was all over. Not many hours later it was Band Night at the Craiglands. People in sensible clothes danced sedate fox trots. Ilkley, if not exactly asleep, was back to normal...' - Carter's reflections in *New Society* were more doubtful, perceptive and, well, literary.

'The Transylvanian backdrop of West Yorkshire hangs oddly behind the small clean pleasant town of Ilkley with its boutiques, its discretely reticent proximity to the darkly handsome, polyglot, multi-racial cities of Leeds and Bradford,' she wrote. 'The notion of a literary festival is in itself an odd one. Books are inner-directed things. There is a direct, one-to-one silent, private relationship between writer and reader. Reading aloud is something else.' But, she concluded: 'You could write [like] Balzac if you lived in a town like that.'

***

PRIOR to 2008, I was adrift in a sea of ignorance, unaware that the Ilkley Literature Festival even existed. Nowadays, I'm a regular. You can't keep me away, as audience member or, on occasion, participant.

There's something about the timing that chimes with the appeal of the written word. Winter is coming, harbinger of inward retreat. Soon, it will be firesides and cosy nights in. Leaves chase after passing cars like gangs of giddy children - nature's pages raging orange against the dying of the light.

And as with so much about Yorkshire, the event's split personality is engaging, marrying the cosmopolitan and local with little hint of contradiction. Highlights? So many; but here are three from the year I lost my festival virginity.

Exhibit one: Graeme Garden and Barry Cryer, here to flog a Hamish and Dougal book. Having quelled the nagging doubt that you have paid over a tenner to be advertised to (or is that doubt just an issue in Yorkshire?), an hour or so of amiable Sunday night wisecracking would win anyone over.

Cryer on the perils of writer's block: 'I couldn't think of another word for two weeks. And then I got it! A fortnight.' At which, Garden takes an imaginary pencil and pad from his pocket and 'makes a note'. As the evening progresses, he will do this again and again before eventually proclaiming: 'I'm not writing them down. I'm ticking them off.'

Humphrey 'Humph' Lyttelton, long-time host of the pair's radio home *I'm Sorry I Haven't A Clue*, has only recently

died. 'Humph' never swore, except once, upon receipt of a
breakfast dish not to his liking after a recording in Harrogate:
'How can you fuck up a prune?' Asked who might now host
Clue, since they have decided to keep it going, the Leeds-born
Cryer says a woman could do it. 'Do you have a woman in
mind,' asks interviewer Paul Blezard. 'Always,' quips Garden.

Exhibit two: *Priestley's Wars: Soldier, Broadcaster,
Pacifist*, with local author Neil Hanson and Tom Priestley, son
of Manningham's very own pipe-puffing, free-thinking John
Boynton (J.B.) Priestley, whose white rose roots were mined
so memorably in *The Good Companions* (1929) among myriad
other now classic novels and plays, and who, notoriously,
spent a good lump of the Second World War getting right up
the nose of Winston Churchill with his hugely popular
Postcript broadcasts on the BBC.

The typical 'Yorkshireman' then; straight-talking;
opinionated; distrustful of authority; outward and yet
simultaneously inward gazing; a trouble-maker in the eyes
of the powerful, yet the reason 16 million people gathered
around the wireless every Sunday night, an audience on a
par with Churchill's own. And, as taped transcripts read in
Ilkley by Huddersfield actor Patrick Stewart reveal, capable
of endowing what might appear to be the most mundane of
objects or events with morale-lifting lyrical beauty.

Nor was Priestley averse to turning the trick in reverse,
bringing as awe-filled and awful an event as Dunkirk down
to the level of the everyday, the better to be grasped by all. In
Hanson's words: '...the ordinary men and women of Britain
feel that their contribution to the war effort was both valued
and understood.' As so often in Yorkshire, surface simplicity
belies emotional depth.

Also within the book is a collection of previously
unpublished matter-of-fact letters from the Front, written as

a younger Priestley soldiered in World War One - '...we were in the fire trenches, twelve consecutive days ... up to the knees in water...' - plus his anti-bomb *New Statesman* writings of the late-1950s that led directly to the founding of the Campaign for Nuclear Disarmament, CND.

But it's his ten-minute *Postscripts* that resonate sharpest in a modern ear. Not only have they since been credited with humanising Britain's plight in an America that had initially seen WWII as a chance to get rid of the British Empire forever, thereby rallying public opinion and diverting history in our favour, they expose the machinations of an Establishment that is every bit as fearful of threats to its status from 'enemies' at home as it is from opponents abroad.

As the first regional voice to present on the BBC, Priestley was always likely to ruffle feathers. But certain to put him on a crash course with the Conservative party right wing were beliefs he took from life experience, namely that, as Hanson puts it: '...if people were to give their all in the War they needed to be reassured that, this time, there really would be a country "fit for heroes" when they came home...'

It was an attitude guaranteed to put him on the wrong side of Churchill, whose view was that you won a war first and worried about its aftermath later. Priestley, on the other hand, insisted that anyone fighting for democracy had to be democratic during the war also: '...let the voices be heard.'

It was all there, most often between the lines, in those colourful pictures with words.

In any case, the upshot was that after five months as a monumental public favourite, J.B. Priestley was taken off air, listening figures plummeting as a result. Did Churchill himself get Bradford's finest fired? It's tempting to think that he might but, citing a lack of hard evidence, *Priestley's Wars* supposes not. Safe to say, though, that 'Jack' to his friends wasn't the first Yorkshireman to have a, shall we say, uneasy relationship with 'that lot in charge'. And he certainly was not going to be the last.

Exhibit three: well, a couple really. Howard Jacobson and, two hours later, Will Self. Intellectual pyrotechnics galore.

Jacobson is plugging his novel, *The Act of Love*, about an antiquarian bookseller who gets off on knowing his wife is being unfaithful. As usual he is very funny, promising 'all the sex you can think about for £4'. But the philosophical sparks also fly - ruminations on human nature, shame, the meaning of love and the like - demanding speed of thought and absolute concentration from the listener or all becomes noise. One 'shall I do Yorkshire puddings' and you're gone.

There is something similar about the closing event of 2013, Sir Jonathan Miller's majestic riff on the 'point' of opera. On this occasion, though, the level of intellectual engagement required from a packed Kings Hall reaches such a pitch that it is the audience who, on the quarter-hour mark, suddenly start becoming the distractions themselves.

There are widespread shuffles in seats, stifled yawns, glazed upward gazes - 'ooh, white alabaster roses around the arch, but how many..?' - a growing mood of desperation. One row in front, a father and son, book-ending trapped wives, exchange telepathic glances. 'What is THIS,' they want to say, 'and how can we escape?' Eyes betray inner screams, their owners fighting to keep a lid on their own boredom and dismay. 'An HOUR? I can't sit here listenening to THIS for an HOUR!' And yet, only one elderly lady on walking sticks is 'courageous' enough actually to get up and leave.

So you see, Yorkshirefolk *can* be painfully polite.

Six years before, after killing time between shows in a pub that had best stay unnamed lest it incurs the wrath of the tobacco police (it is possible, I suppose, that B&Q do sell nicotine-coloured ceiling paint), I joined another Kings Hall full house in listening to Will Self.

Already, there had been profoundity in the boozer, from a drunkard balanced horizontally on a bar stool singing along to the jukebox with grim fortitude: 'Elvis ain't dead; Elvis played for Leeds...'. While this was going on, a group of Welsh lads, a pint or five behind him, tried to chat up the young woman serving on. 'She's pregnant,' our well-oiled crooner interjects. 'She's not just a fat Yorkshire lass.'

I take refuge behind my bitter and pork scratchings before later, up the road, the lady sat next to me in the King's Hall, wearing twin set and pearls, tries to grind her way out through the floor. It's the comedy of embarrassment.

Self, like Jacobson and the singing drunk, is not only willing to risk offence, he seems to view it as an occupational hazard. And so it is. In previous books, Howard Jacobson has sought humour in the Holocaust. With this latest, he braves sex, jealousy and a reader's inherent voyeurism, comparing writing to masochism. His sparkling wit and ease of literary reference, however, make for a delightful afternoon.

'Bring us a glass of red,' he jokes as a member of the Ilkley Playhouse audience attempts to sneak off to the loo. Of course, she does. Happy even to oblige a Lancastrian.

A sour southerner to Jacobson's naughty northerner, Self, though, is quite another beast. Literature festival events tend to include readings and the two he performs here seem designed to unsettle. In the first, a story about a London drinking club's day trip to the theatre, he says 'cunt' three times, with a couple of 'fucks' for good measure. There is an audible mass intake of breath. Then he tells a nice little tale of liver cancer, a trip to Switzerland and assisted suicide.

When the question and answer session comes around, a voice from the back calls this Ichabod Crane-like figure in cardigan and jeans 'gloomy', before asking whether, in his view, there is any hope at all for humanity.

'I'm not gloomy at all,' Self responds. 'It's the rest of the world that is ridiculously optimistic, tying the truth up in little pink bows.'

Perhaps in a dig at his supposed social conscience, someone pipes up that she once saw Self eating oysters in a posh London restaurant. 'I know,' he replies. 'What you probably don't realise is that I remember seeing you there.' He then trashes, uproariously, 'the party she was with.'

'Do you know,' I say, as he signs my copy of the *Book of Dave* in next door's Winter Gardens later, 'that might be the first time anyone has used the word "cunt" in Ilkley.'

'Really?' he says. 'Well, I'd never swear gratuitously.'

And do you know what, he wouldn't, would he? Though unfailingly comic by design, there is always a point to any Self narrative. Life is absurd being chief among them, a philosophy with which at least one bloke laid horizontal on a pub stool not far from here would very definitely concur.

***

WITHIN the pages of *An Outpost of Progress - 25 Years of the Ilkley Literature Festival* is an old black and white photograph dated 1988. It features four gaudily clad loons in loud shirts and braces: The Circus of Poets.

On the far right of the shot, a little more substantial than the rest, in need of a few early morning strolls one might say, mouth wide open and making an open-handed gesture to the camera, is a chap who looks just like Ian McMillan.

True, there's no shock of white hair yet, but the exuberence is unmistakeable. A little rootling about on the the internet reveals that the Circus of Poets were a poetry performance group in which McMillan appeared alongside John Turner, David Harmer and the late Martyn Wiley. According to one source, they: '...achieved success, renown and popularity performing for over ten years together in front of audiences in their thousands.'

And that in turn, as web surfing tends to do, leads on to further 'research' regarding the fabled Barnsley Chop, a delicacy I've always meant to have a go at but never quite got around to. They are huge, by all accounts; too much for most folk in one sitting. Yorkshire's very own version of those monster burger challenges in Waco, Texas: '...weighing in at ten pounds, topped with cold pork and red onions, if you can finish this burger in sixty minutes or less without puking we pay for your meal and give you a FREE T-shirt...' that sort of carry on.

Happily, The Beatson House restaurant, situated in the 'picturesque village of Cawthorne, near Cannon Hall, Barnsley,' offers a more culinary and historical perspective on this true South Yorkshire delicacy, according to its website. 'While many restaurants have often claimed they serve the genuine lamb chop,' they write, 'few keep to the actual cut of the meat which was introduced over eight decades ago. The art of cooking the meat is a slow and loving process which few have the patience for... This fantastic meal is part of our heritage in Barnsley and it is only right that we keep it in its original form, and give people a real Barnsley treat.'

The site goes on to explain that the chop's creation is accredited to master butcher, Albert Hirst. 'He wanted to create a special dish to be served to HRH Edward, Prince of Wales, when he came to officially open Barnsley Town Hall on the 14th December, 1933.' It weighed 1lb 6oz and, no, HRH, the big soft southern Jessie, couldn't finish it either.

Someone else who is yet to tackle a Barnsley Chop,

remarkably, is Ian McMillan, still pulling in big audiences if nowadays mainly as a solo performer and presenter of BBC Radio 3's *The Verb*, billed as a '...cabaret of the word, featuring the best poetry, new writing and performances.'

'I never have,' he admits in January 2014, a couple of months after we meet on the panel of an Arts Council-backed forum intended to encourage adult reading. 'I've been put off by just the size of them. I didn't want to be defeated by it and known for evermore as the bloke who can't finish one.'

That 'Try Reading' event, staged at HM Hatfield open prison and Young Offenders Institution near Doncaster, where Ian also shared a table with England's first Muslim rugby international in either code, Ikram Butt, journalist Neil Barraclough and author and publisher Phil Caplan, had been linked with the Rugby League World Cup; one of many such autumnal nights more usually staged in public libraries throughout the north of England. As such, it attracted one or two audience members perhaps best described as 'testing'.

The Bard of Barnsley, as he is long known, was on the front foot from the off, leaning into his sentences like a man braving a gale, winning over the room's tougher individuals with wit and vitality. And the fact he was there at all - football being rather more his thing than egg-chasing - said lots about a career-long devotion to taking poetry and a love of language to the masses, wherever that may be.

Today, his diary no doubt packed already with a fearsome amount of future appearances and train rides, we discuss the important role that words have in the creation of Yorkshire identity. And he likes the Texas analogy.

'My mate [the cartoonist] Tony Husband, who's a Lancashire man, says that as soon as you start talking to Yorkshire people they will relate anything you say to them to Yorkshire, in the same way that Texans do. You'll say "that looks good" and they'll say "yeah, but it's not as good as that one in Yorkshire." Another thing he says, which I've noticed myself, is that we always put it at the top of our conversation... "Speaking as a Yorkshireman..." which people from lesser counties don't.'

All of which, of course, begs the question why?

'There's many things. Partly it's because we've always had an oppositional thing to us, Yorkshire people. We've always felt far away from centres of power. And we've always been a crucible of industrial and technical and artistic thinking, yet it's never been acknowledged. When the pits, the mills, the steelworks were providing a lot of wealth for the rest of the country, the power was still down south. I think we've developed this hard carapace of brusqueness that says: "Look, we're as good as them if not better." That's what it is. We feel that we are far from the actual economic, cultural and social power, so we make a lot of noise about it.'

As someone not averse to wandering far and wide, by foot or rail as his thousands of early-rising Twitter followers would testify, McMillan is also ideally placed to distinguish between different types of Yorkshireness within the county itself. Often, that will show itself in Yorkshire's supposedly dry comedy. Always, he points out, it is laid bare by words or, in some cases, their absence.

'Our humour is self-deprecating by and large,' he says, 'but that is itself regionalised across the county. I wrote a play many years ago about some pigeon flyers. It was set in Barnsley and I tried to write it in Barnsley language. We took it all over the place. At miners' welfare clubs here they laughed their heads off. In Sheffield, nobody laughed. That's the other thing: Yorkshire contains multitudes. Sheffield is different to Barnsley is different to Heckmondwike is different to Hull. It contains all these different things; it's not just one thing.' Especially when it comes to talking, yapping, chelp and chunter...

'The South Yorkshire thing is much less loquacious - they don't talk much. As a Barnsley lad who makes my living through talking, I'm quite unusual. Barnsley folk don't speak. They do that sideways movement of the head: "Is t'awreet?" "Ahh..." But once you get towards West Yorkshire, the vowels start to widen a bit and people talk more - "Now then, morning, all reet, 'ow are yer?" - a lot of brighter and open, a bit more of that. Once you get to North Yorkshire, because it was mainly farming country, you get that thing of people who want to stand there and tell t' tale. There's a difference in language. It's kind of the minimalism of South Yorkshire, the openness of West Yorkshire and the storytelling nature of North Yorkshire, owing to the fact that they spent a long time not seeing anybody. It's a lot to do with the industries people worked in. When you worked down t' pit, you didn't want to waste your breath. If you worked in t' mill, it was that loud you had to compete. Differences in where you worked defined how you talked.'

Nor is it just about the old ridings. 'In terms of towns, Harrogate - quite posh - isn't like Rotherham, which was a steel town. And the thing is, wherever people live, they think that their bit is the "true" Yorkshire. They'll say: "Look, I come from Driffield. That's *proper* Yorkshire." Pateley Bridge ... Hull ... wherever ... there's that kind of micro-racism within Yorkshire. When I go watch Barnsley, if we play a team from another county, they'll all shout "Yorkshire, Yorkshire..." If we're playing Huddersfield, we shout "South Yorkshire" and they shout "West Yorkshire..."'

It's a point supported, appropriately, by poetry itself, or at least the Yorkshirefolk who have made a living in it.

'It is, it is. The first Yorkshire poet I read, really, was

Slouching towards Blubberhouses

Ted Hughes. He was born in West Yorkshire and moved to South Yorkshire. What struck me about Ted Hughes was that he used short words and rounded vowels, the rhythm spelt Yorkshireness. Tony Harrison is a fantastic example of someone who writes in a Leeds accent and always about that idea of how he was educated out of his class. Then someone like Simon Armitage has that wonderful West Yorkshire voice that sort of can handle longer lines. For a while, Huddersfield was seen as the poetry capital of Britain.'

There are, though, McMillan insists, poets and writers all over Yorkshire. 'People like Barry Hines, Stan Barstow, people like that, who have written down the language of the way we speak in prose. But what I want to find, and haven't yet, is somebody who can write Yorkshire down serious, handle big political ideas in it. A lot of Yorkshire dialect, like Lancashire dialect, is comedy. As Tony Harrison says, we are the ones Shakespeare gave the comedy bits to. It's not that you have to write in dialect - I'm not talking about the old t-apostrophe - but there should be a way of writing in the Yorkshire language that is serious and intellectual and full of ideas, I reckon.'

What of the sound itself? Take the Brontë sisters, who somehow manage to capture the landscape and geography of Haworth in the actual words on the page or tongue. How the heck does that work?

'I did a dictionary years ago for a publisher of Yorkshire dialect. There were words I'd never heard before, that are very local. For example, there's a word in Doncaster, grod, which means an old pushbike. Get on thee grod. And we can say words that aren't dialect words and make them seem that they are. If we say: "That's a beautiful sunrise..." - because we say it in a Yorkshire accent, we colonise standard English. Words are very important to Yorkshire people. Less so in South Yorkshire because "we dunt talk as much", as I say. One of my vivid memories of the miners' strike is coming back upstairs on a bus from Wakefield to Barnsley and a bloke standing up and saying: "I've written this poem about t' strike." Go on then, read it to us. That wouldn't happen in Bexleyheath ... it wouldn't happen in Cirencester. And yet this fellow gets out this folded poem and reads it out. It wasn't a great poem, but for just a few minutes the upstairs of that bus was turned into a sort of literary salon.'

And there it is again, poetry for the people, from the one-time or current poet-in-residences as diverse as Barnsley Football Club, Humberside Police, Northern Rail and the English National Opera. In a bottom note accent the *Radio Times* has called 'fruity', he lays clear his manifesto.

'Everybody has poetry in them, whether they can read it or write it,' he says. 'A lot of people can certainly talk it. That's what I like, just the celebration of the way we speak - they can write it down if they want. They can turn it into a song or they can tell you a tale.

'I'm just really interested in the way people will stand there and tell you something, tell you a story. Once they know that you are interested in them, they open up. Writing and language belongs to us all and a poem about a walk down the street is just as important as one by Shakespeare. The problem you have is that a lot of people collar you and there just isn't time to read the stuff. Someone turned up at the house the other month with a carrier bag saying: "I've been translating Greek." I've had it ages and I know he'll be disappointed, but when am I going to get around to it? You get caught in the slipstream. If you encourage people, which you want to do, then they will keep showing you their stuff.'

Another drawback of coming from Barnsley and being in the public eye - perhaps the main drawback - are the accusations of being a professional Yorkshireman that invariably follow. The poet's fellow Barnsley product, former television interviewer Michael Parkinson, certainly cops a fair amount of stick in this regard and Ian McMillan is no stranger to such finger-wagging either.

For what it's worth, my view is that, especially when it comes from outside, such criticism is condescending, a way of keeping us northern - or in this case Yorkshire - oiks in our place. It is diminishing personally and denies the right to investigate - or even celebrate - a background and culture.

While such accusations clearly sting, Ian's response is more light-hearted than polemical, with a twist. 'I find that phrase so interesting, professional Yorkshireman,' says a man who still resides in the county and shows no sign of being shaken off. 'My throwaway response is that I'd rather be a professional Yorkshireman than an amateur Lancashireman. You never hear people saying, "...aye, he's a professional Northamptonshireman" or "...a professional Devonian", do you? I think, because we live here we are allowed to do it. I do get cross with old Parky, talking about Yorkshire and living outside it. I can take the mickey out of Barnsley because I live here. That's all right. I get rung up by the BBC when they want a Yorkshire voice and I'm sure they've got me on a list that says 'professional Yorkshiremen'. There is that. It happens to people like Ian Clayton, Dickie Bird ... you can get defined by the way you talk and their perception of who you are.

'I wish there was another phrase or word for it. You do get tarred with that brush. What I don't like is when people think it's put on - that *is* a professional Yorkshireman - and that in the house you talk like Prince Charles. To which I always reply, no. In the house, Prince Charles talks like me. My mate's mother-in-law says: "That Ian McMillan, he puts that voice on."'

And of course a northern English tendency towards self-deprecation does tend to help those critics out.

'Well, it does. We are good at taking the mickey out of ourselves. But in some ways we are just getting in first, because for so long we've been told that talking like this means we are not as clever as everyone else. We are not as loving, we are not as deep...'

All of which takes me back to a couple of other Ilkley talks, one with Ian himself and one with Simon Armitage, another festival regular. It was after listening to the latter that I decided to pose the question direct: why do northern poets so often resort to humour?

'What, you mean like Tony Harrison,' he replied. Armitage – one. Questioner – nil. 'Or Ted Hughes?' Two-nil.

'In my case, I think it's to do with upbringing and background,' Armitage, to my relief, continued. 'I didn't come from a bookish family, but they were - still are - very interested and active in amateur dramatics, getting on stage and entertaining, singing for your supper and giving value for money. I also think that there is a strong tradition in the north of the dissenting voice. Part of my poetry comes out of that. Dissent to the extent that it doesn't even reach the right-hand margins. It doesn't even reach the bottom of the page. It stubbornly goes out there and occupies a piece of paper, but it won't conform to the normality of prose.

'At readings for example, I quite often explain poems more than some other poets, because I think if you know the story then you can just enjoy the language and not spend ages wondering about what's going on. Sometimes, humour is just a way of offering a bit of relief and the humour I use is often quite dark. It might just be a way of grabbing the attention, so that I can smuggle the meaning of a poem in through the back door.'

Slouching towards Blubberhouses

Then there was Ian McMillan's own talk when, beforehand, we were told by a compere that there would no longer be a half-time break as promised. At which point, the star turn poked his head around a heavy velvet curtain and said: 'That's because they all bugger off home.'

***

DEAN Clough. A name that ought to belong to a no-nonsense Northern Premier League centre-half, but which is in fact the jumble of old buildings you might well drive straight past on the flyover that leads into Halifax town centre.

Once at the heart of industry in the metropolitan borough now known as Calderdale, it is a mill complex that once liked to boast of housing the world's largest carpet factory, but which has in recent times been put to far more creative use. In common that is with other such venues like, say, Salts Mill over on the outskirts of Bradford, with which it shares some direct common ancestry.

Viewed from above, it has the look of one of those jungle traps that threatened to dispatch Captain Scarlet, a vast hole in the ground in a town that itself feels like a hole in the ground, with chimneys spiking upward, ready to impale the unwary on art, culture and something they hadn't known.

Descend to the ground level car park and, watched over by Bradford-based artist Frank Delaney's sculpture of a ram made from aluminium strips, it's all stone pavements, iron railings and stairways, metal plates, rivets, ginnels, gaps and passages, stained but unbroken by time. There are workshops, row after row after row of windows tinted with something other than soot, doorways disused, new entrances commandeered, photogenic alleys and cellars holding dark promises of secret hideaways and hidden depths.

It was in one such corner that actor, director and all-round impresario Barrie Rutter stumbled across what is now the Viaduct theatre, home to Northern Broadsides, the award-winning touring company that has carved such a strong national reputation with authentically northern interpretations of Shakespeare and classical texts, a number scripted and adapted by the Skipton writer Blake Morrison.

Though born in Hull, Rutter - a familiar face of TV sitcom and drama throughout the 1960s and '70s - has been based in the west of the county since the early 1990s, but more of that anon. We meet in the reception area of 'D Mill', all cream plaster, wooden beams held aloft by iron pillars, walls and comfy sofas loaded with promotional paraphernalia of exhibitions and performances gone and on their way. As second impressions go, it says busy regeneration, a visitor's first impression being the giant 'E Mill' building behind it, DEAN CLOUGH written in capital splendour, Hollywood hills style, on the roof.

My notes say Rutter not long since suffered a prostate cancer scare and, it transpires, he has a stent in his heart too. But when he lopes down a staircase he looks healthy enough, vital even. And as we head back up into the street and over to the mill that holds his office, I'm reminded of a *Guardian* interview from 2012 that had him as '...bull-necked, forthright, equipped with a voice that could drill holes in millstone grit...'

He's at an age, 67, when most folk would either be thinking about or taking retirement. Not him. 'I've just come off nineteen weeks as Rutherford', he says of his part in the touring production of Githa Sowerby's *Rutherford and Son*, directed by Jonathan Miller. And at the end of our chat I am rebuked for asking, half as a means of making small talk, whether, as an actor, he is contemplating slowing down a bit and maybe just concentrating on the organisational aspect.

'Well,' he huffs, 'I might be a bit of a dinosaur, but I'm still going...'

But to get the ball rolling, I wonder out loud why the city of his birth, Hull, has such a strong theatrical tradition?

'Has it?'

'I think so, yes. There's Hull Truck, John Godber, Alan Plater, Tom Courtenay, Maureen Lipman...'

'I don't see it as a tradition - out of half a million people, you'd expect a couple to...'

Hull does seem to be lumped with theatre though?

' Yes, it does, because it's a freak city in that there's no hinterland. Alan Hardaker - who was from Hull and used to be chairman of the Football League, Hardaker's of Hull was a removals firm - said Hull is on the right wing of England waiting for a pass. They thought that pass was going to be the Humber Bridge but, interestingly enough, it might be the City of Culture. Which would be great.'

Nowadays, the idea of re-energising a town or city by recourse to the arts is so widespread as to risk becoming a cliché. From Gateshead's Angel of the North to Liverpool's Albert Dock to Portsmouth's Historical Dockyards, it is the phenomenon that just keeps on giving. And it's a movement of which a vibrant Dean Clough is quite obviously a part.

'Yes,' Rutter says, 'and it's been going on ever since the big industries stopped - coal mining, fishing, all of that. The problem is at the very, very top level where governments have always been terrified of us. They can't corral us, you see. They can corral soliders, but they can't corral the arts, therefore they diminish them by not giving them a place at the cabinet table, except with sport and media.'

And if there's one thing Yorkshire folk like to pride themselves on, it's not being corralled.

'Yeah, except with other Yorkshire people. I do think,

living and working in the West Riding, that there is a distinct difference between east and west. The north tends to be much more rural, as does vast swathes of the east. All that basin is very fertile farmland. And then you have 'Ull, which sits within that area like its own internal monolith. That's why the sounds are flat, because the area's flat. When you come further west, into the hills of the West Riding, the language changes. The limestone and the granite and the millstone grit affect it.'

Is it strange that it should do that? Or natural? Does it happen elsewhere?

'It's a perfectly natural thing. How much does Ireland infiltrate into what Scouse is? A real bedrock Dubliner and a bedrock Scouser are very, very similar.'

And that then feeds into the theatricality of the place.

'Indeed. Although a lot of the theatricality is in the recorded writings. So when you get famous West Riding people like J.B. Priestley, a great writer, Ted Hughes, who was a great poet ... the greatest for me, of course, is Tony Harrison ... they write in the metre of their stones, as it were, the heartbeat of the area. Blake Morrison is a much gentler poet and a much gentler man, but he still has that quality. And Simon Armitage: he has that wonderful, ironic sense - oh, astoundingly good. He never misses his targets, doesn't Armitage. He's terrific.'

But let's beat a retreat for a moment. Hailing from a classic two-up, two-down in Hessle Road, Barrie Rutter was perhaps not the most obvious candidate for the National Youth Theatre, where he went aged 17 in 1964, before a decade or so later joining the Royal Shakespeare Company. When did he think 'theatre is for me'?

'Well, I was enjoying it at school, doing the plays, and then when I went back for 'A' Level it was the staff who really decided that would be a path for me. To my delight, Mr John Siddal, my former English teacher who is still alive, lives in Filey and comes to see all our plays, him and the head got together and said we should help this guy. Which in 1962-63 was quite rare.' There then follows the first in a succession of little playlets that sprinkle the Rutter discourse.

'Them: "We've had a circular from the National Youth Theatre." Me: "What's that?" "You go down to London and have to act..." Me: "Well, I'll get in..." "No, no, you have to pass an audition..." Me: "Well, I'll pass. What's an audition?" My naïveté was incredible. But the experience ... once I got there and then got to drama school ... there was always that thing of "Ooh, bloody hell, if I find myself out of my depth, I"ll get out..." but I'm still swimming.'

Rutter's entry into the actual profession came with *The Apprentices* in 1968, in a part specially created for him by the playwright Peter Terson.

'Literally the next morning, after the performance, I had seven telegrams and six letters from agents. It would have been a whole different life if I'd cashed in and gone straight into television or film, because that was available to me. But I went away into theatre to learn my trade. I love what I've done on screen and radio particularly, but I've always been a stage animal.'

He also stubbornly retained his Yorkshire accent.

'I couldn't do anything else. I wasn't good enough to change it. I could do other accents ... a passable attempt at Geordie ... but I couldn't do received pronunciation. I was picked out at college, went to Glasgow, and got told my "RP" was shocking - the only English kid in a group of Scots! I couldn't do it. It is a simple fact - I could never do it,' he says, betraying another Yorkshire impulse, repetition of words and phrases for emphasis. 'There are people out there who can, so you ain't gonna cast me if you want a Noel Coward. I'm not bothered by it. There's other stuff for me to do.'

The entrepreneurial urge, Rutter says, kicked in at the National, which he joined in 1980, initially commuting in from Stratford. '*Animal Farm* was a very big success, the only play to perform in all three auditoria at the National Theatre in 1984, 1985 and 1986. Although still playing Napoleon, I became assistant director on tour and there was a little bit of a feeling of organisational stuff going off.'

The real road to Damascus moment, though, or rather road to Saltaire, came during the 1990 tour of Tony Harrison's *The Trackers of Oxyrhynchus*, a headline-grabbing adaptation of Sophocles's satyr play *Ichneutae*, at Salts Mill. 'A part was written for me and the other lead was Jack Shepherd, from Leeds. The classical language, written for a Yorkshire voice but in classical form by Harrison, met its natural audience. We played in London, we played in Delphi, we played in Denmark, we played in Austria... but we'd not played in Yorkshire, where the sound of the text was. And that gave me the idea.'

Northern Broadsides was on its way. 'I thought: "I want to do more classics, in my own voice in places which aren't theatres," revolutionary. If someone suggested it now, they'd get told to piss off. But in 1991 nobody else was doing what I proposed and, to begin with, I just saw it as one good idea: do *Richard III* with an all-northern cast in what I call non-velvet spaces. That meant a marina boat shed in Hull; the old transport museum in Bradford, where all the armies came off the 43 bus from Wibsey; a transport warehouse in Barrow; and Middleham Castle, Richard's favourite home.'

Over twenty years on, Rutter says, he is 'as surprised and delighted as anyone' that the company formed 'to get that one good idea out' is not only still around but thriving.

Slouching towards Blubberhouses

The road to Dean Clough, meanwhile, came via a connection with Sir Ernest Hall, the mill's owner and friend of visionary Jonathan Silver, whose dream it was to reinvent Salts Mill before his tragically early death, aged 47, in 1997.

'When we put *Trackers* on, I asked Jonathan if he would let me work out of Salts [named after Sir Titus Salt, the Victorian industrial philanthropist]. In his utter candour, he said: "No, but my friend Ernest Hall will," because they started this place together. So I came to see Ernest and he said: "I like your idea, I like your thoughts, and by the way I'm chairman designate of Yorkshire Arts. Come to my mill and have an office." An office was a desk in someone else's office, but gradually it grew and then I sort of discovered the place downstairs.' It was a place that became the Viaduct Theatre.

'I say discovered, it was already there. But I phoenix-ed it from the numbing banality of being an underground car park.' Does he remember the first time he walked in? 'Yeah, I'd plagued Ernest to find me a performance space: "There's seventeen acres here, there's got to be one." Him: "There's nowhere." Then, apropos of absolutely nothing, six months later, he said: "Did you see the fire engine yesterday?" I said: "What fire engine?" He said: "Oh, we had a fire downstairs in the space we call the viaduct." "What viaduct?" "Well, it's got a ramp to the ground level and we stored an old car and a kid got in and set fire to it. There's nowt to burn, it's just stone and iron." I said: "Show me." He said: "Why? It's cold." I said: "Show me." We walked down into it and I said: "Oh, Ernest, we can play this." He said: "How?" I said: "I'll show you."'

The Viaduct opened officially in 1995, with *Antony and Cleopatra*. 'Ishia Bennison was Cleopatra, I was Antony, Dave Hill from Skipton was in it... Conrad [Broadsides producer and director Nelson] was in it. He did all the

166

drumming, because we did the warfare percussion on oil drums.'

And the subsequent blossoming of Northern Broadsides is perhaps all the more surprising because it was launched at a time of major economic recession.

'What idiot would start his own theatre company during that? Me, and I got away with it. I didn't get away with it in a cynical fashion, naïveté was courage, I didn't know. I said to my agent: "Nobody will let me go into their theatre and take it over with this idea, Northern Broadsides," and she said: "No bloody wonder. Why don't you do it?" I said: "What do you mean?" She said: "Start your company. Ring your accountant." I said: "What's that got to do with it?" She said: "You pay him some money, he'll register you at Companies House in Cardiff, give you a number, you pay him £600 and you're a company." I said: "Oh."

'Actors and actresses like Polly James, who played Queen Margaret in the first production, said: "He's fucking mad. But what he's proposing ... I'm going with it." Ishia rang up Polly and said: "Has Rutter been on to you?" She said: "Yeah, he's raving, but it sounds wonderful." And Brian Glover said: "This is a crazy idea, Rutter, it just might work. All right, I'll play Buckingham for you," because I asked him to. When we came off after the first night he said: "You've done summat here, Rutter. You've really done summat here."'

So how much of that longevity would he put down to Yorkshireness? By the question I mean obstinacy but, again, he brings it all back to language.

'Totally, that's what I insist on. Kings will speak as commoners, but kings are marked out by their syntax. That's why, when we came to do *A Midsummer Night's Dream* three years later, I chose to play Oberon and Theseus. I wanted Oberon to say "luv" and "much" and "blud" honestly for the stage, clearly so the audience could understand it, as well as Bottom and the mechanicals. But it is a different syntax. The number of people who still think we adapt the text to suit Yorkshireness - or northernness - we don't touch a word. We sometimes muddy it, but then Richard III says: "I tell you what," in the first scene. He says to his brother: "I tell you what..." And yet still you hear [adopts actorly Olivier-like rhythm] "I tell you ... what?" - fucking hell. It drives me mad.'

And there it is again, that conflictory Yorkshire urge to look both inwards and outwards at one and the same time.

'We like to think Yorkshire reaches the world, there's nothing wrong in that,' Rutter counters. 'The importance of this region during the industrial revolution for cotton and cloth, there were more millionaires in this band of England, and over into Lancashire as well, than there were in the rest of Europe. It is a county that continually impacts the world.'

And how about audiences? How do they differ, if at all, both within Yorkshire and without?

'I'm often asked that. The pleasure is the same nationwide, but there is a certain familiarity of family about what we do because we never not play in Halifax. We never not play in Scarborough. We always take two weeks at Easter at Leeds. So there is a warmth that, in some other places, is just a tenth of an inch less. Simply because we live here, we work here, they get the local news about us and there's that recognition, that umbilical cord. It doesn't make them any better as audiences necessarily. It's marginal and not something that dissuades me from going to Winchester or Southampton or anywhere else.'

And no, he says, he does not intend to leave the stage anytime soon. 'On a journey of twenty-odd years, how many secretaries of state for culture have we seen? How many drama officers? How many cub reporters on the East

Grinstead fucking Mercury or what-not, who call it *Coronation Street* Shakespeare? Well, you could wring their necks.

'There's a book on there [points to some well-stocked shelving] about Tony Harrison, which he says he hasn't read. It has everybody writing pieces about him and he calls it his tombstone. In it I say: "There's many people written about Tony, but I got to speak the bloody stuff." When you get with him it's like a burning bush, the sheer wonderful classical muscularity of the language. That's what was so wonderful, just the sheer pleasure of wrapping your gob around language based on short vowels and granite on a classical range.

'Very interesting that, when all that furore happened about *V* [the 1985 poem written after the gravestones of Harrison's parents were desecrated with obscene graffiti at Holbeck cemetery] and those idiots in parliament and the *Daily Mail* were saying "Who's this unknown poet", and fucking, shit, piss and cunt were in the film of it Richard Eyre shot for the telly, when he got back from abroad to his house in Newcastle, Tony just closed the front shutters because the papers were all camped outside his house. He walked out the "ten foot" at the back, went shopping and came back in, nobody knew. He wrote a letter to *The Times*: "I'm sorry I was away during the furore of my filmed poem *V*, but a classical education helped me to write those four-letter words." And do you know how he signed it? President of the Classical Society of Great Britain. That was his shaft. That was his arrow to the idiots condemning him.

'Because actually, just like Tony, who it helped in his poem to write fuck, cunt, shit and piss, and use them properly, equally I'm not a mug. I'm a classicist by practice not education, but I know what a rhyming couplet is. I know what iambics are. And all those wonderful rock 'n' roll creations the poets have given us, alive and dead, you know, I really encourage. I'm not one for chopping up verse as if it's some fucking sausage and indulging in psychological claptrap. I'm still here, still plotting and scheming because we start the next one in January. Just this week I'm getting a change for one scene in the final draft and then I'll start casting, helping the designer and everything.'

***

DIALECT - Yorkshire writhes with the stuff and, just as Ian McMillan says, each region boasts its own. Some of it, though, does appear to be universal... 'laik' for play, 'brass' for money, 'spice' for sweets and the like. Book after book has been written about dialect and indeed *in* it, some by Ian himself.

Similarly, with the invention of this here new-fangled internet jobby, access to such vernacular is now unlimited which means we don't need to go through all of those words here. Even the *Huffington Post* has got in on the act, devoting a whole page to 'Yorkshire's most amusing turns of phrase', though one doubts that 'chucking your guts up', 'arse over tit' and 'not enough room to swing a cat' actually qualify. Similarly translating 'very dirty' as 'black as t' face o' spades' is an eyebrow raiser in all respects, but kudos for giving the definition of 'eeh by gum' as OMG.

The problem with writing too heavily in dialect, of course, is that one person's recognisable idiom is another's absolute jibberish - which is why this is a 'right grand Tour de Yorkshireness' rather than a 'reight', 'reet' or 'reyt' one. In the interests of universality, I'd rather give it all a swerve.

It was, though, fascinating to learn that 'spanish', our word for licqourice growing up, comes from Spanish monks having brought such a tree to Rievaulx Abbey. Chew on that.

8. Heart of the Laik District

This Yorkshire Sporting Life

IN March 2013, Sheffield's own Michael Palin is on the BBC4 TV programme *Mark Lawson Talks To...*

'I never think of you as a Yorkshireman...,' says the eponymous London-born but Yorkshire-raised interviewer, '...in the way of Alan Bennett, Geoffrey Boycott, Michael Parkinson... Do you think of yourself as Yorkshire?'

'I do, really,' Palin replies. 'And I know it seems a bit odd because I don't [puts on broad accent] talk Yorkshire... until I go back to Sheffield and then it's all around you and you end up talking like people used to. But I was born and brought up in Sheffield and I'm very fond of Sheffield.

'There are certain things about that particular city that I still value. The fact it had a really strong character... entirely of the city itself. It didn't think of itself as being cosmopolitan in any way. It wasn't as successful as Manchester or Leeds, but there was a kind of dogged feeling that 'we produce what the country really needs, iron and steel, knives and forks...'

and all that. Sheffield people still have that ... optimistic stroppiness. I'm fond of Yorkshire cricket, the Sheffield United football team ... because you have to be ... but, no, I'm not the sort of Yorkshireman of the ilk of Boycott and Parky...'

Although Parky does appear to have enjoyed the Eric Olthwaite episode of *Ripping Yarns*, Palin's 1970s comedy series co-written with ex-*Monty Python* colleague Terry Jones. The one in which shovel fan Eric lines up one shovel next to another, just for the thrill of it.

'Someone contacted me and said: "Michael's leaving the BBC. We want to give him a shovel. Would you write something on it and give [it to him] at his leaving party because he loved the sketch so much?" So I gave him the shovel and wrote on the shaft: "To the second most boring man in Yorkshire, love Eric Olthwaite."'

As Palin says, we like sport in Yorkshire: '...because you have to...' But why do we have to? The opportunity it presents for proving white rose superiority? Perhaps.

Yorkshire's medal haul in the Olympics ... the fuss around the Tour de France ... indeed, as I write, the regional media is again wallowing in how Sheffield's Matt Fitzpatrick is the first English golfer to win a US Amateur Championship title since 1911 (the last time Bradford City won the FA Cup).

'With his 14-year old brother Alex as caddie, 18-year-old Fitzpatrick led for the majority of a 36-hole play-off at The Country Club in Brookline, Massachusetts. Guaranteed entry in the US Open for reaching the final, victory also earned him a place in the Open at Royal Liverpool and an invite to the Masters in Augusta, thereby guaranteeing a busy 2014.'

Maybe Yorkshire's sporting obsession is a by-product of its tendency toward taciturnity. Men in general we are told would far rather dissect football results than discuss anything so messy and uncomfortable as emotions, certainly in each other's company. Maybe sport is Yorkshire's way of getting it all out there. But then again, Yorkshire women love it too.

Or could it just be a manifestation of the human urge to gang together. With Yorkshire being the largest specimen, might a dollop more pride than usual be in the mix?

Sport is an arena where uplifting, heroic and quasi-miraculous deeds take place. But it is also a receptacle for less edifying displays of human behaviour - homophobia, drink, gambling, racism, nationalism, violence and drug abuse among them. Might it be a place where anti-social aspects of ourselves are removed safely from our collective system? Better football, surely, than terrorism and war?

At its most fundamental level, sport is about me against you, or when it comes to team sports, us versus them. Maybe that's also behind Yorkshire's obsession with sport; such identity issues are heightened there.

Then there is the extent to which a competitive Yorkshire personality became tied in with the codification of recognisably modern sport in Victorian England.

What better way of cocking a snoop at the London-based Establishment than by a) sticking it to the MCC and Co with what, until 1992, was proudly hailed as an exclusively home-grown cricket team; b) driving the burgeoning growth of a once Corinthian football league courtesy of its very first professional club in Sheffield; or c) telling a hypocritical Rugby Football Union in Twickenham to ruck off while setting up a completely new rugby football code of our own at the George Hotel, Huddersfield, instead?

***

IF there is one sport that epitomises Yorkshireness in tooth, claw and fondness for butterfly buns at teatime, it is cricket.

Slouching towards Blubberhouses

Elsewhere, expectant fathers pace maternity wards fearful only for the safe delivery of new baby and the welfare of a pregnant partner. In Yorkshire, for so long the delivery of cricket balls might also be thrown into the equation.

Indeed, for much of the 20th century, such a scene as that above might be staged with the couple in question racing to a hospital safely within the county limits, thereby ensuring that Yorkshire CC might not be denied their next Len Hutton, Raymond Illingworth, Freddie Trueman or Geoffrey Boycott. Line and length were as important as pounds and ounces.

The great midwife change did drag Yorkshire kicking and screaming into the modern era eventually - in 1992 with the signing of India's Sachin Tendulkar to be precise - twenty-four years' worth of Championship failure for a one-time glamour club that won thirty of the first hundred titles saw to that. In fact, so much of what might constitute traditional Yorkshireness is either mirrored or exists as metaphor in a sport that the one time Archbishop of Canterbury William Temple described as 'organised loafing'.

New-fangled forms notwithstanding, the players are clad in white. It is a game in which you can cross boundaries without actually leaving the field. It encourages individual effort, skill and concentration, but constrained within a wider group ethic. To indulge in ostentation is to court mistrust. At the crease, you must never let an opponent know you are hurt. Quiet courage is admired, with actual cash rewards for outstanding achievement. In cricket, fast bowlers roll up their sleeves and get on with it, polishing the ball with hard-earned sweat, the projectile in question, like life, hard. Take your eye off the ball and a split-second opportunity may be wasted.

And, more latterly, a growing South Asian influence is being felt that threatens not only to usurp old certainties - if they haven't crumbled already - but to bring noise, colour and exciting cultural diversity to an activity in which, once upon a time, and particularly in the Test arena, a certain dour stubbornness brought not only respect but acclaim.

The Godfather of that, of course, was one Geoffrey Boycott OBE - known variously in his home county as 'Sir' Geoffrey, Boycs or by the acronym GLY (Greatest Living Yorkshireman) - Yorkshire and England opener extraordinaire. With 8,114 runs in 108 Tests at an average of 47.72 in a career stretching from 1962 to 1986, he knew what his right hand is for and, as such, you might imagine would be universally revered. If so, you would be imagining wrongly.

Sportspeople always divide opinion, it's in the nature of the business, but few have divided and continue to divide it like Boycott, on or off the field. By and large, it's a spilt that might be rendered thus: Yorkshire (aye); elsewhere (nay).

In his pomp, if you can apply such a description to so supposedly dour a batsman, his fellow professionals often berated their team-mate for a level of crease hogging they judged selfish, even as Boycott himself saw it as devotion to duty. This Yorkshireman's wickets weren't going cheap.

'Given the choice between Raquel Welch and a hundred at Lord's,' he is said to have remarked, 'I'd take the hundred every time.' Ms Welch's thoughts on the matter have gone unrecorded.

As such, the perception grew of a career built on practice and dedication rather than talent, but then talent can come in many guises can it not, and no one ever scored so many runs without shots. Many a good judge, including perhaps the finest England captain of them all and certainly the most thoughtful, Mike Brearley, saw something to be admired. In 1979, Brearley wrote that: 'As I stood at the non-striker's end, I felt a wave of admiration for my partner; wiry, slight, dedicated, a lonely man doing a lonely job all these years.'

Slouching towards Blubberhouses

When the boots were hung up and the whites folded away, a perhaps even more controversial career then began on talkSport, Channel 4 and, since 2005, the BBC's long-running *Test Match Special*, upon which his 'straight-talking' style continues to raise hackles where the bowling of Fiery Fred (who, until his death in 1999, was also not averse to a caustic, downbeat opinion) once raised divots.

'If Geoffrey had played cricket the way he talked,' Trueman said in 1993, 'he would have had people queuing up to get into the ground instead of queuing up to leave.' And it is certainly true that his less than sympathetic approach to critiquing those in the middle combined with a stout refusal to socialise with players and colleagues has resulted in many a barb being chucked his way too.

One recent Test bowler, Durham's Steve Harmison, in responding to Boycott's brusque view that England should 'forget him' in 2008, told the *Mail on Sunday*: '...within the England dressing room [Boycott's] views are regarded as a joke. People who only have a passing interest in the game hear the famous Geoff Boycott accent and may think it gives some status to his opinions. But inside the dressing room he has no status, he is just ... a caricature of a professional Yorkshireman. Quite a few of us cringe whenever he comes near.' Ouch.

His *TMS* colleagues, meanwhile, despite no end of provocation, particularly for poor old Jonathan 'Aggers' Agnew who seems to bear the brunt, have proved in public at least a little more tolerant of Boycott's foibles, eccentrities, arrogance, old fashioned Yorkshire bluntness, call it what you will. In fact, on Yorkshire Day 2011, Boycott even apologised on air to Aggers for having been 'too forceful' the day before, calling him 'my best friend' after an Ian Bell run-out controversy against India. There may even have been affection.

It should come as no surprise then that, as with

anyone from anywhere - a stereotype is a shallow net - there are contradictions. The man rebuked for 'rudely interrupting' a French barrister during a distasteful court case alleging assault of a former lover in 1998, subsequently married and had a daughter. His reluctance to give ground proved helpful enough during an extended bout of throat cancer in 2002-2003, since overcome.

And his reputation with some listeners for an 'in my day' mentality belies a modernising streak that has seen him argue in favour of innovations like Twenty20 and push the claims of overseas players from Pakistan, India and the West Indies in particular. This from a man who in 1982 helped organise a rebel tour of apartheid South Africa.

He even has his own website. And, no, it's not Friends Reunited.

***

BUT now there is another Test Match hero in waiting. This time, however, rather than emerging from the one-time West Yorkshire pit village that is Fitzwilliam, near Wakefield, England's next great white rose hails from cricket's South Yorkshire nursery, in Sheffield.

During the 150th anniversary of Yorkshire CC, a year incidentally during which the club president is one Geoffrey Boycott OBE, I am at Headingley on the third day of the second in a two-match Test series with New Zealand.

Having already won the First Test at Lord's, England are in the box seat but the bigger barramundi, out-of-form Australia, loom. Back-to-back Ashes series follow, the first on these shores and the second to be held down under over the winter, on account of the next World Cup buggering up the schedule.

Slouching towards Blubberhouses

In Leeds, though, aside from a one-day clash with the old enemy in September, this is the only international clash Yorkshire fans will get to see on their own doorstep - the Ashes Tests are scheduled for Lord's, Trent Bridge, Old Trafford, Durham and the Oval - and eighth-rated New Zealand aren't Australia. At least partly as a result, the ground is far from full and those who are here seem chiefly to have come to cheer on a couple of local lads; middle order batsman Jonny Bairstow, son of ex-England and Yorkshire wicketkeeper David, plus man of the hour and soon to be England opener, Joe Root.

I say man. Root is 22 years old but, even allowing for the aren't-policemen-getting-younger phenomenon, he has the fresh-faced look of a precocious cub scout. But for a boyish grin where a lop-sided mouth used to be, he and a youthful Boycott are not dissimilar in stature, even if physically, and maybe also temperamentally, Root more closely resembles a young David Gower.

He knows how to belt a cricket ball too. Coming into this match, he has already amassed going on 1,000 first class runs in 2013 and it's still only May. Root is just the sort of player President Boycott is on about when he bemoans how county sides seldom see their finest young talents these days.

'When I was a kid, everyone used to talk about Yorkshire cricket and its special players,' he told the *Yorkshire Post* in January. 'It's all you ever heard. For those of us fortunate to play for the club, it felt extra special because we were the only one with homegrown players. It's all changed now, and it had to for the club to be able to compete with other counties. The problem now is that when our best young players get into the first XI, England take them away and we never see them again. Consequently, the modern player cannot possibly have that same level of connection with the club that my generation enjoyed.' Maybe not in terms of on-field domestic influence, but if crowd reaction is anything to go by, a connection there very much remains.

There's an old cricketing adage: 'When Yorkshire are strong, England are strong,' doubtless dreamt up by a Tyke and no longer much believed anywhere. Yet, historically, the white rose county has indeed provided the national side with more Test match players than any other and this England squad, in which Root and Bairstow are at five and six, and bowler Tim Bresnan hovers unselected on the sidelines, is hyped as among the most formidable in recent times.

With day one wiped out by rain, the host nation reaches 337-7 come close of play on day two, Root and Bairstow at the heart of the attack. The latter hits an admirable 64 - including a third 50 in his eight Tests so far - before being caught McCullum, bowled Boult when England are 279 for 6. But it is Root - in only his sixth Test and with whom Bairstow clocks up a 101-run partnership - that really catches the eye.

At the start of a day watched by this writer on Sky Sports ahead of the Headingley trip (impeccable timing as ever), England's innings does not begin brightly. Opener Nick Compton, under pressure after recent poor performances, is caught in the slips for one run and his team are already 11-1. His departure, though, has a muted response, presumably because it will hasten the arrival of the dynamic duo with only Jonathan Trott and Ian Bell to come. Anyway, the Sky commentary team is preoccupied with the low turnout.

It's Saturday and only 12,000 tickets have been sold at a 16,000-capacity stadium. Does it, wonders David 'Bumble' Lloyd, have anything to do with Yorkshire folk being tight? He might have a point. My own Sunday ticket cost £40. 'Forty quid?' grumbles Accrington's finest with exaggerated Yorkie incredulity as the camera scans by some unfortunates in the West Stand. 'You'd get a fortnight in Scarborough, wi' full use of t' cruet for that.'

In *The Guardian*, Andy Wilson treats the matter with more gravitas, hinting at the potential opening up of a north-south divide. 'One of the unique factors in English cricket is that the national teams gets taken around the country,' he quotes Yorkshire's new chief exec, Mark Arthur, as saying. 'It's very important to understand that not everybody has the spending capacity of those people in the south east of the country. That has to be factored in by the [ECB's] Major Matches Group when allocating matches.'

Back in the middle, meanwhile, the home fans who have emptied their pockets don't have long to wait for Root to come to the crease. When Trott and skipper Alastair Cook fall just before lunch, England are 67-3 on his arrival. And when Bell is then out at 146-4 at around 3.30pm, the cheer from the western terrace tells you Bairstow is on his way too.

There follows six and a half overs before tea in which Bairstow gets off the mark with a four and Root completes his third England half-century with five fours and no sixes. 'He looks about 12,' says Sky's Nasser Hussein.

Cue chants of 'Yorkshire, Yorkshire' from men in sombreros, carrying trays of Tetley's Bitter.

On TV, Sir Ian Botham is full of praise for a lad following in illustrious Yorkshire footsteps by doing so well on his England Headingley debut. At this stage, only Michael Vaughan's 76 in defeat against the West Indies in 2000, Herbert Sutcliffe's 83 against South Africa in 1924 and Len Hutton's 100, also against the South Africans in 1947, stand above him.

'There is a very, very rosy future for Joe Root,' says Botham who, in 1981, famously lit up this very turf against

Australia himself. 'Everybody enjoys watching him play. He's very pleasing on the eye and uncomplicated.'

According to David Gower, Jonny Bairstow '...needs to capitalise on a nice day and a flat pitch that he made runs on not so long ago in the Championship. He'll be itching to cement his place.'

Fellow pundit Mike Atherton, meanwhile, points to a discrepancy in style of two players who have come up together through the Yorkshire ranks. 'Batsmen are typically products of their environment,' Atherton says. 'That's why we say Root plays late and soft, because he's brought up on the slower pitches of the north. But Bairstow is also a Yorkshire lad. Root is a touch player and plays the ball late, yet Bairstow goes hard at it. If you saw Bairstow as a young kid for the first time, you'd say: "Where's he learnt his cricket, on hard pitches down south?" They are different types of players, yet brought up in the same area.'

Which might lead some to doubt the value of pigeon holing theories in general and the tendency of everyone in sport to expound so much intellectual energy on what is essentially a trivial pursuit, nowhere more so than in cricket. But then life *is* essentially a trivial pursuit, isn't it? Humankind must have its distractions. Oops. Seem to have come over all philosophical. Cricket can do that to a person.

'The young 'uns are enjoying themselves,' Bumble says, as 200 comes up for England, shortly before Root ends a 19-run over by sweeping the four that makes it 206-4, with Bairstow on 24 and Root a personal best 78, having returned with a 73 from India over the winter and scoring 71 at Lord's.

There are a couple of dodgy moments as Root passes 1,000 runs for the season. First, Bairstow's straight drive hits the bowler's hand and dislodges the bails en route to the boundary for four. Happily, video evidence confirms that

Slouching towards Blubberhouses

Root is back in his crease. When the ball then clips his pad before landing in the keeper's gloves down the leg side, another nervous wait is endured until survival is confirmed by infra-red imaging system Hot Spot. And then, after Bairstow completes his own classy 50 with a seventh four in 73 balls, a boundary of his own writes Root into the record books as the first Yorkshireman ever to score his maiden Test 100 at Headingley. 'In twenty years time, there'll be a million people who were here to see it,' says Botham.

Given the county's love of mythology, he's not wrong.

As the white rose flags fly and the crowd sings his name to the tune of 'Hey Jude', Root holds his bat in one hand and punches the air with the other, before lifting off the helmet that reveals the cheeky smile beneath. Unflustered, if in this heat a little red of face. But after that, he doesn't last long. Four more runs, in fact, before Trent Boult takes the new ball and, with his first delivery, tempts an edge to Brendon McCullum behind the wicket.

'What a great day if you're a Yorkshireman,' says Atherton, as Root walks off with England on 270-5. A poster on the BBC's online blog chips in: 'Joe Root and Jessica Ennis went to the same school in Sheffield. What are they putting in the school dinners?'

***

AFTER which, day three was always going to be something of a let down, though for the author it does at least offer a chance to study the natives up close.

On the field, England's remaining three wickets are mopped up for 17 runs, before New Zealand openers Hamish Rutherford and Peter Fulton put 50 on the scoreboard in only 74 balls. Might we have a game on our hands? No. With 6ft

7" Middlesex paceman Steven Finn and Nottinghamshire spinner Graeme Swann to the fore, the Black Caps are skittled for 174 in 43 overs and only a belligerent last wicket stand of 52 from Boult and Neil Wagner adds a touch of respectability.

To the surprise of many, however, and perhaps eyeing a bit of batting practice with the upcoming Aussies in mind, captain Cook elects not to enforce the follow-on. 'Any bowler worth his salt would have been queueing up to have a bowl at them,' says Sir Geoffrey on *Test Match Special*.

As it is, Cook himself then bags his 30th Test 50 off 63 balls on his way to an unbeaten 88 in a total of 116-1 by the close. The one wicket in question again being Somerset's Nick Compton, whose scant seven runs leads some to wonder if Yorkshire opener Root might not be a better option.

In the sun-kissed Headingley stands, meanwhile, they are mainly contemplating another pint.

At £4 a pop, received wisdom dictates that, in these parts, this is not a decision to be taken lightly. Yet having been fired up by a blast of 'Jerusalem' as yesterday's highlights get another airing on the big screen, the pre-match nets are removed and the umpires, New Zealand and English batsmen stride out onto the lush outfield, here is a crowd determined to enjoy itself whatever the cost.

Are you familiar with the concept of the beer snake? They grow in reverse proportion to the level of amusement attained. As the day progresses, the general raucousness and reach of the 'snake' - i.e. line of empty plastic beer 'glasses' stacked end upon winding end - expands with every drop downed. When things get out of hand, the stewards do occasionally step in. But given that most of these look like students who would far rather be reading Wittgenstein or playing on the Xbox 360 than earning a few bob from trying to control ruffians who have to a man - and it *is* usually young men, rather plump ones at that - long forgotten any parental advice to 'act right in their head' upon leaving the house, such interventions prove ineffective.

As bedlam proceeds, like Yorkshireness itself, some are borne ale, some achieve ale and some have ale thrust upon them. Some are thrown out; some are carried out. And whenever activity around the main 'snake' lulls, outriders are cheered as they come jogging along the front of the stand holding aloft smaller plastic towers of their own, eager to conjoin with the beast at its irrepressible heart. Which, obviously, after six hours solid, can start to get on your tits.

All in all, though, and particularly in the morning session, it's good-natured and even a welcome distraction when the on-field action dips. A chap along the way has brought his ukulele and the bloke manning the Sky Sports speed gun at midwicket - there to compute the mph of each delivery (that's bowling, not beer) - is ribbed aplenty.

'Up a bit, left a bit, down a bit ... fire!' shouts one wag, though how at his age he remembers *The Golden Shot* is beyond me. Hopefully, it's the Bob Monkhouse rather than Charlie Williams series. Or, to the tune of 'Chirpy, Chirpy, Cheep, Cheep': 'Get a proper job ... get a proper job ... far, far, away.'

At lunch, along with standing in line at one of various catering stands, there are the usual fancy dress attempts to gawp at, among them video game Marios, a collection of Mrs Browns and several cross-dressers with exaggerated camel toes. There is also a geeky group done out like droogs from *A Clockwork Orange*. Shouldn't they have been stewarding?

At this juncture, a conscientious author would gather the odd vox pop: 'What is most important to you, Yorkshire or England?' That sort of thing. But frankly, it is obvious.

Back on the battleground, a quieter day for Root and Bairstow is nonetheless enlivened by a roar of 'Yorkshire,

Yorkshire' whenever they field the ball. And these folk have a long memory. One umpiring error - far from a rarity during the coming Ashes also - leads to the cry: 'Bring back Dickie Bird!' With uncanny accuracy as it turns out, Bird soon being chosen to follow Boycott as Yorkshire club president in 2014.

A young lad waits, oh so patiently, by the boundary fence for the autograph of 'Jonny! Jonny! Jonny!' which, at an appropriate moment, he receives to wide admiration. One of us, is Jonny. And with the day's play all but done, Headingley becomes one of the few sporting venues in the world to boast a fully-clothed streaker, who manages a single lap before one side-wobble too many sees him bundled up the tunnel.

By contrast, day four on a TV screen is a quieter affair, even with the Sky Sports commentary team for company. England press on with Cook scoring his 25th Test match century before Root wanders in again at 214-3, collar up.

Rain is expected tomorrow, so the hosts are chasing enough runs to enable them to declare with enough time to finish the job. And Root is still there at lunch with the score at 249-3 and England leading by 429, having played some nice shots including an eye-catching reverse sweep. The tactics, though, seem strange, what with the weather forecast and the fact that 418 runs is the highest total ever caught in a fourth innings in Leeds. But when Trott is out to the second ball of the afternoon, Bairstow is back.

A partnership of 124 in the first innings is unlikely to be replicated today and the new man is almost run out on a duck egg, but somehow survives. Root, though, is caught for 28 at extra cover trying to pile runs on and the declaration follows on 287-5, with Bairstow 26 not out from 22 deliveries and with a lead of 467. The only danger now is from the clouds. By tea, New Zealand are 68-3, with Root having nabbed a very popular catch off Hamish Rutherford at short leg. As the light worsens, with the umpires insisting on the abandonment of pace, he gets in a little gentle off-spin too.

From the commentary box, meanwhile, comes a reminder that cricket is a great sport for folk who like to chunter. You can chunter away all day, in fact, most often about nothing at all. 'This is the weekend Yorkshire folk plant their annuals,' says green-fingered David Lloyd, in assessing another low Bank Holiday Monday turn-out and educating his audience on the county's nine-mile 'rhubarb triangle'. 'They've got a statue of a stick of rhubarb in Wakefield.'

Come half past six and off the teams go, with New Zealand having reached 158-6. Will England be punished for not going for the throat? No, as it happens. A painful stop-start day five, in which the teams twice leave the field for rain, is finally wrapped up just before tea, as the few dozen people left see their national side win by 247 runs. And in Joe Root, England has a new hero.

In advance of all that, however, BBC Radio Leeds led its morning sports bulletin with a couple of different stories entirely: Yorkshire's six-wicket defeat at Middlesex in the Yorkshire Bank 40 and today's County Championship match in Taunton. And two weeks later, in a YB40 match against Leicestershire at Scarborough, 15-year-old Matthew Fisher becomes the youngest post-war cricketer to play in a county competition. The right-arm seamer from York scores ten runs and takes one wicket as Yorkshire post 258-9.

That white rose production line rolls on.

***

NOTE to Bumble: rhubarb isn't the only thing grown in this part of West Yorkshire. It's an area that might also be seen as the heartland - or maybe hinterland - of rugby league.

For an overview of Britain's class system, its so-called North-South divide and traditional gender roles, the history of rugby football offers a rich study, particularly with regard to the North of England. It's a picture often painted in broad-brush strokes. Posh Twickers refuses to allow payment of players, so clubs whose players can't afford to take Saturday off, go their own way. Goodbye rucks, mauls and pockets in your shorts, hello play-the-ball and Eddie Waring.

Of course, it's a lot more complicated than that, as a Pennine range-worth of literature (some by this author) will make clear. There is a sense in which the twenty-one clubs who split to form the Northern Union in Huddersfield on 29 August 1895 were manoeuvred into doing so, chiefly by a southern-based RFU keen to assert its control of 'their' game in the face of rugby's growing popularity with the oiks.

The recompense sought by those predominantly working class northerners might well have been primarily for lost earnings - i.e. 'broken time' - at an individual level, but the club owners, generally local businessmen, did indeed have a commercial agenda. Whatever the public protestations and an initial agreement that the standard broken time sum would be six shillings, they had star players in their eyes.

That said, the vast majority of those participating in what would become known as rugby league (there were few, if any, distinguishing on-field features separating the two 'Unions' to begin with, fifteen-a-side, line-outs, the lot) turned out for the fun of it. That and the fact that money and payment in kind (a job, say) were covertly commonplace in the 'Corinthian' south also, meant that one set-up was really no more amateur than the other in truth.

What's the difference between league and union, as the old joke has it. In league, the players pay their taxes.

Before the split, the most successful clubs were in the

north; the best - often international - players were in the north; the biggest crowds were in the north. Easy to see where all this was leading. Yet unlike association football - 'soccer' to rugby football's 'rugger' - who embraced modernity and thereby emerged as the true national football code, those Twickers sticks-in-the-mud could not countenance any such move towards rugby becoming a spectator sport.

The rallying cries of empire and *Tom Brown's Schooldays*, having originated on the same Rugby School square upon which Salford-born William Webb Ellis is said to have first picked up a ball and ran (another myth) - 'Play up! Play up! And play the game!' - were not so easily surrendered. Thus did a schism already broad widen.

Idealism versus pragmatism then, though far messier and subtle than that, and just who belonged to the 'right' and 'wrong' side remains a matter of debate. After all, it is as easy to pontificate on the evils of money when you've got plenty or at the very least aren't worrying about putting food on the table. Just as it is all too easy to portray an amateur idealist as a hypocrite, especially when he preaches moral purity from a pulpit mired in duplicity and sanctimoniousness.

It is also a fascinating pub topic to wonder at what might have transpired had the 'northern twenty-one' not voted to break away at all and, instead, gone on chipping away from the inside, letting progress take a more natural course. Would the chief football code of England now be the one played with an oval ball, as in Australia, New Zealand, South Africa and the USA?

They know what they think in Wakefield, represented at the George Hotel by one J.H. Fallas. And with him in the white rose corner, delegates from Batley, Bradford, Brighouse, Dewsbury (who later - temporarily - changed their minds), Halifax, Huddersfield, Hull, Hunslet, Leeds, Liversedge and

Manningham. The lion's share then, with nine clubs - Broughton Rangers, Leigh, Oldham, Rochdale, St Helens, Tyldesley, Warrington, Widnes and Wigan - having caught the train to Huddersfield station in Lancashire.

'The clubs who struck a blow for freedom,' wrote the *Hull Daily Mail*, 'are to be commended for throwing off the cloak of hypocrisy, conceit and subterfuge, and standing out for those essentially English characteristics - honesty and straightforwardness.'

Almost twenty years on from when rugby union itself turned openly - note: openly - professional in 1995 (nice tidy date), Wakefield's Belle Vue still bristles with indignation. There have been great days here. Most notably in the 1960s, when Trinity as they were once known without the modern appendage 'Wildcats', vanquished all before them. A fifth Challenge Cup win in 1963 was followed by the club's first Championship title in 1966-67, this being the days of winter seasons.

In the side back then were such greats as Gary Cooper (without cowboy hat), Ray Owen, the Fox brothers Neil and Don, and skipper Harold Poynton. A year later, they did it again. In fact, they almost did the double, denied only by 'poor lad' Don Fox's now infamous missed conversion in the 'Watersplash' Wembley Challenge Cup final of 1968.

In the summer era, things have been tougher and not just for Wakefield, but near neighbours and closest rivals Castleford and Featherstone. It wasn't supposed to be this way. Back in 1996, with the birth of Super League and all the promised expansion, razzamatazz and money that might in hindsight be seen as the inevitable outcome of events one hundred years before, these three clubs were supposed to merge as 'Calder' in a brave new world.

It didn't happen. That and the proposed mergers of

other long-standing northern clubs to make room for new top-flight concerns in London, Paris and Barcelona, in return for millions of pounds from Rupert Murdoch's Sky TV chest, never made it to the starting line. The natives, restless as ever, weren't having it. As one memorable banner of the time put it: 'Fev is Fev. Cas is Cas. Stick your merger up your..!'

In short, a compromise was reached with less money in the pot and the same old names - London and Paris aside - at the starting gate. In this neck of the woods that meant Castleford, who finished in the bottom four during the first two summer seasons and reached their first play-offs in 1999, the same year as Wakefield belatedly joined the party.

After five seasons in the bottom four, Wakefield's debut play-off spot came in 2004, the same year as Cas finished bottom and were relegated before returning in 2006 and then going down once more before rebounding up again in 2008. Both clubs have battled on in the top flight since, albeit with financial worries seldom far from the surface.

Chiefly, these have been exacerbated by a Super League licensing system that, since its introduction in 2008, put more emphasis on facilities and salary caps than tries and goals. Partly intended to save clubs from themselves by marshalling their boom and bust tendencies, licensing has indeed had the effect of levelling the competition and has forced some clubs - mainly in Lancashire it has to be said - to either improve or build new stadiums fit for the 21st century.

Mainly, though, the ambition of that project - with its abandonment of promotion and relegation that soon after our visit would be overturned - has not been matched by the capabilities of those supposedly policing it. In essence, and in an unhelpful economic environment, the ruling body has sought to develop rugby league according to the world as they would like it to be, rather than the one that actually exists.

The result: where homely little clubs like Wakefield and Castleford might once have spent cash they couldn't afford on players intended to keep them in the top-flight, they have instead left a credibility-sapping trail of broken promises en route to as yet undelivered new stadia.

Only this week, amid rumours of an advance in Sky TV monies to ward off the latest in a line of tussles with the Inland Revenue, Wakefield chief executive Andrew Glover has made way for a new man at the helm. And this in a competition that has for the past two seasons lacked a paid title sponsor, with lurking administration either a fact or creeping fear for a number of clubs, together with the demise of one, the Wrexham-based Celtic Crusaders.

Despite their best efforts, meanwhile, Featherstone Rovers have spent the entire Super League period doing rather nicely thank you in the level below, nowadays known as the Kingstone Press Championship. Perhaps they are better off there. Not that they'd admit it themselves.

Along with less ambitious stadium developments that have indeed come to pass, Rovers have somehow also landed themselves a sugar daddy in majority shareholder Feisal Nahaboo, whose ambitions know no bounds.

Amid rumours that London Broncos may be the latest club to go under, he announced in August 2013 that: 'The sport is starved of funds and we've made it clear we have the funds available to build Featherstone Rovers into a rugby league powerhouse and we should be encouraged, not discouraged. We own our ground, we have a strong board with at least two key shareholders generating seven-figure profits from businesses they run successfully and own. It all bodes well for Featherstone Rovers to show that entrepreneurs can enter the sport of rugby league and commercialise the game and attract investment. Roman Abramovich started this in football and now the money in football has gone crazy. Rugby league is ready for entrepreneurs. Give the club a chance and we [will] strengthen Super League.'

All of which from a club that could last be called champions in 1977, Cup winners in 1983 and who, by their own admission, would most likely attract less than 5,000 fans, sounds like the flip side of the RFL's own self-delusion. And maybe it is. But at least if Rovers realised their dream on the back of what they actually achieved on the pitch, it would be by natural sporting selection and lack the blatant artificiality of what is still, at its professional level, an essentially regional sport governed by big fish in a very small pond.

Hey ho, t'was ever thus, and no doubt will always be, at least until the RFU come back, top hats in hand - or vice versa with flat caps - offering to let bygones be bygones.

Fat chance. On Mothering Sunday, March 2013, it's hard to envisage such an outcome. This is rugby league land, pure and simple; they'd have to wrestle it from their cold dead hands. Here it is very definitely about them and us.

To drive south towards what is nowadays the Rapid Solicitors Stadium is to traverse a cityscape that bears less and less resemblance to the 'Merrie City' of the 1960s. Mostly that is down to a road system overhauled and re-routed to allow for one of those shopping centres that are seemingly intent on turning every British city or town centre into a scene from George A Romero's *Dawn of the Dead*. Soon, though, Trinity Walk is in your rear view mirror and floodlights installed as long ago as 1967 emerge on the skyline ahead.

People stroll up to Belle Vue past Wakefield cemetery just as they have since 1895. Prior to that, the club had played at a variety of locations since its birth in 1873, formed by a group of young men from the local Holy Trinity Church.

Trinity won the Yorkshire Cup four times in nine

years back then, but in these days of spring and summer rugby, silverware has been harder to come by. Their last trophy of note came with a controversial 24-22 win over Featherstone in the inaugural Division One (ie second tier) Grand Final that earned them their ticket to Super League in 1998. Had that result gone the other way, the boot might well now be on the other foot.

The venue, too, has seen better days. A stadium that in the pre-Wembley days of 1992-23 played host to a Leeds-Hull Challenge Cup final watched by a crowd of 29,335, is downright dilapidated in parts. It certainly has the worst press facilities of any top-flight sporting club in Britain - an elongated garden shed essentially - although Castleford's Wheldon Road runs it close.

And yet as is so often the case with old sports grounds and theatres, there is also something romantic in the air. You don't need much of an imagination to conjure up ghosts of heroes long gone from the field - Brian Lockwood, say, or David Topliss, Jonty Parkin or Derek 'Rocky' Turner - indeed Neil Fox and others still turn up to watch every week.

This after all, was the setting for Lindsay Anderson's 1963 film adaptation of David Storey's novel *This Sporting Life*. And among the extras in that last of the kitchen sinkers were members of the club's playing and coaching staff and a fair proportion of the crowd that is still standing or seated here today, or certainly their dads and granddads. Action sequences were shot during a third-round Cup tie with Wigan.

For many of these former extras, such as homegrown former Labour MP David Hinchliffe, now retired from politics but a regular on the Belle Vue benches still, mere mention of that film throws opens the nostalgia floodgates.

'I was 13 at the time,' he says. 'My mates and I proudly saw our home city being portrayed to the country and the world. Seeing it today is a reminder of how so many iconic features have gone, often unnoticed. I only missed Westgate Station's former clock tower when I spotted it in the film. What happened to the Mecca Locarno ballroom that had such a special place in our hearts? Where did Trinity's wonderful West Stand go? And who pinched the cooling towers that provided the background for some of the blood and guts on-field action?'

He goes on: 'As MPs, Glenda Jackson and I used to talk about her movie debut at the piano in Wakefield's famous Dolphin pub - now the Wakey Arms - but my accounts of visits there were always somewhat partial. The landlord turned a blind eye to us sinking Beverley's Bitter and keeping tabs on the strippers. And I can claim during my playing days to have once been sent off by the film's referee. Albert Rayner, who took charge of local amateur games for many years, threatened me with dismissal during one match for dissent. Albert had a squint and after one particular fracas gave me the hard word for ignoring him. He had called me over for a rollocking, but I had genuinely thought he was pointing at somebody else.'

Nowadays, Belle Vue holds more like 12,000 people, though seldom is that capacity tested as the club continues its tortuous journey to the nirvana of the M62, junction 30, three miles north of the city centre. As I write, the Wildcats say they hope to move into a stadium owned by the Wakefield & District Community Trust as anchor tenants come the beginning of season 2015.

Today, all of that seems as distant as ever. Pulling off the A638 Doncaster Road on which Belle Vue sits is to enter a warren of redbrick terrace houses, some pebble-dashed or with other unsightly textured surface coatings, tatty shops and side streets. This, though, is where the vehicle must stay, the stadium's official car park having room enough to cope with nothing bigger than a vicarage tea party.

It's early March, not quite spring, sunny but bitterly cold with the odd flicker of snow. Folk get out of their cars and wrap up in scarves and coats, as familiar a routine as nipping out for a Sunday morning paper or walking the dog.

The visitors are Salford City Reds. A 'roses battle' then, but those don't seem to carry much weight anymore, not at this level anyway. Here it's mainly about ... well, since the end of promotion and relegation, not even survival. Building for the future, maybe, or some other such clipboard concept designed to excuse mediocrity in the here and now and, with nothing much at stake, strip any contest of intrinsic sporting drama, a nebulous philosophy of never-never.

Still, this being rugby league, there's enough action on the field to stir the passions for eighty minutes at least, even as the bigger picture refuses to clarify. A not bad at all crowd of 6,986 has turned up and, although skill-wise the game is of poor quality, a thrilling finish sees Paul Sykes kick a drop-goal to nick Wakey a point in a 23-23 draw, ninety seconds before time.

For their part, Salford are an equally unglamorous club who, since moving from their own ramshackle Willows in *Coronation Street*-land to a purpose-built venue alongside the M60, hope to leave this sort of carry-on behind. Their new owner is millionaire horse racing tycoon Dr Marwan Koukash - Dr Cashcow, as he has already been tagged - who sacked incumbent coach Phil Veivers only last week. He is promising big and, despite the Super League salary cap, intent on spending big. New to rugby league, what he makes of rundown Belle Vue is anyone's guess, though his eyes in the corridor to the dressing rooms suggest not much. This is a place where those hacks still employed by the dwindling number of national papers that continue to cover thirteen-a-side rugby drink their pre-match plastic cup of coffee right next door to the lads who are about to do battle. Cramped.

It's a place where Sean Long, former Great Britain international half-back and current assistant coach at Salford, and by season's end football manager at Featherstone, might borrow a pen from the reporter from *The Sun*. Resolutely unglamorous then and none the worse for that, with a whiff of wintergreen for added authenticity. And, as ever with rugby league, there is a distinctive family atmosphere too.

Along with nicknames like Wildcats and many a dream gone sour, the cheerleaders introduced by the Super League revolution are accompanied in their dance moves here by a gang of five-year-olds. Watched by proud parents, their tinsel pompoms in Wakefield blue and red glint in the afternoon light, one further note of incongruity in the gap between what Super League was sold as a couple of decades ago and what it has actually turned out to be.

Teams of youngsters play in a mini-tournament, too, before the kick-off proper.

'Who's your favourite player,' one boy is asked.

'Lee Smith,' he replies, Wakefield's left-centre.

'And why is Lee your favourite player?'

'Because he's my dad.'

There is also no better place than Belle Vue to observe, close up, the behaviour of the Yorkshire male of a certain age. 'What a set of shite,' says one chap, as Wakefield go in at the break 18-14 behind. These are men eternally hard done by, who complain about everything and everyone. They don't so much have a chip on their shoulder when it comes to authority as a branch of Harry Ramsden's.

After forty minutes of hurling insults at teenage touch judges for phantom forward passes, these wise guys old enough to know better turn incandescent when a penalty goal by Salford full-back Marc Sneyd is given the thumbs up from French referee Thierry Alibert. This despite the fact that one touch judge's flag behind the goal goes up to indicate success, while comically the other stays down.

And when the Sneyd drop-goal that nudges the Reds 23-22 ahead late on sails over after appearing to hit a Wakefield defender's hand, they look destined for a fortnight in Pinderfields. Once again, later video evidence confirms that monsieur Alibert is one hundred per cent correct, but where is the fun in that?

***

JOGGING has been known to make me come over all metaphysical. An example: one cool fresh morning - the weather forecasts drizzle, but it isn't raining yet.

As I gallop along, a horse chestnut 'helicopter' spirals down lightly on the breeze, striking me a glancing tap on the side of the head. This leads me to contemplate the sheer unlikelihood of such a crossing of paths. Just imagine, for my head and that 'helicopter' to intersect so precisely, every step on my run had to be of exact length and delivery. The missile itself had to hang on to the very second - letting loose at just the right moment - that its slow, weaving trajectory would guide it to arrival on the all-important spot.

And more than that. Think of all the history over billions of years leading to this moment. First the universe and then our planet had to come into being. An incredible timescale. Much, much later, the seed for the tree that would go on to parent our helicopter had to be planted at exactly the right instant to allow for an, on the face of it, trivial occurrence. The sperm of lord knows how many ancestors had to win their race to the egg - unlikely enough in every individual case - and then not get themselves killed until they had procreated. I myself had to be born, and not just that but, like my progenitors, come into the world at precisely the moment that would lead to me going out on a particular run.

The levels of convergence of space and geography and time involved are truly mind-boggling.

Back home, once I've got my breath back, I share these reflections with my wife.

'Just as well the universe didn't begin three months earlier, isn't it,' she says, 'or else it would have been a conker.'

***

IF cricket is the sport most closely associated with Yorkshire as a whole, its football league clubs capture the individual quirks of its towns and cities. Let's take a whistle-stop tour.

Leeds United: Self-proclaimed 'big club' that has indeed enjoyed the odd day in the sun, yet is nowhere near as nationally pivotal as it imagines. Superiority complex.

Bradford City: Despite big city potential, a club grown used to doing it tough. Any success - such as two trips to Wembley in 2013 - is met by a patronising pat on the head, thereby explaining a resultant inferiority complex.

York City: Another big city club that has forgotten its own promise; a sense that any great days are long behind it. Coulda been a contender.

Rotherham United: Quietly gets on with it, ignored. Lacking glamour, happy with mediocrity. In marketing speak, contributes little but critical mass.

Doncaster Rovers: See Rotherham United, only with extra comedy value; curious combination of the steady-away and eccentric. Will spring the odd surprise.

Hull City: The county's only Premier League club - i.e. on its own - having been promoted again in 2013. Idiosyncratic to a fault, its supporters perpetually live in hope.

Halifax Town: The team Yorkshire forgot. A history littered with ups and downs - mainly downs - that few have even noticed. In the shadow of...

Huddersfield Town: Try and stay awake at the back! Monumentally dull team in monumentally dull stadium who once saw (marginally) less dour days.

Barnsley: Plucky little triers with a hard-headed, clog-booted reputation defined by a rough, tough environment and centre halves who chop. In the shadow of...

Sheffield Wednesday and Sheffield United: Since the professional demise of the original Bradford Park Avenue in 1974, nowadays providers of the only genuine big city derby in Yorkshire going back to 1890, when sparks fly. United - aka the Blades - have the slight edge in these steely encounters, but neither they nor Wednesday - the Owls (after the Owlerton suburb from whence they hail) - are averse to getting dirty.

In the Steel City, however, the glory days are rooted firmly in the past, and not only a relatively recent past when United (14th) and Wednesday (7th) were founder members of the Premier League in 1992. United's tenure lasted only until 1994, while Wednesday were relegated in 2000. No, right back to the start of codified football, in fact, when Sheffield FC became the world's first official club on 24 October 1857.

Yorkshire, the birthplace of a global sporting religion? Of course! It makes perfect sense. None of this roll around on the floor with a chipped fingernail nonsense back then, was there? A game played by good honest, hard-toiling working class blokes who were not averse to a bit of sweat and graft.

Of *course*, club football was born in Yorkshire.

Well, just hold on a minute. For the world's first

soccer players did not emerge from the blast furnaces and steelworks of manual industry, on the contrary. As outlined in Cameron Fleming's *Yorkshire Football - A History*, its pioneers were a couple of young gentlemen of the prosperous mercantile and skilled professional classes. Namely: the York-born wine merchant William Prest and his Sheffield solicitor friend Nathanial Creswick, part of a distinguished family of silver plate craftsmen that dated back to the Middle Ages. Both were destined to be army officers in the Hallamshire Volunteer Rifles.

The really interesting thing about football's origin, though, is the extent to which it sprang from cricket. Prest and Creswick belonged to Sheffield CC, the forerunner of Yorkshire CCC. 'In May 1857, reputedly during a walk in the countryside, the friends discussed forming a football club as a way of keeping fit during the cold winter months ... Sheffield FC thus became the first but by no means last Yorkshire football club to owe a debt of gratitude to followers of the summer game.'

Of course, football of varying degrees of violence had been played by mobs and unruly brawlers for centuries until becoming rather trendy among the toffs in public schools and universities, hence the interest of Prest and Creswick. This, though, was the first time that a formerly rowdy pastime was formalised into an organised structure of reliable matches.

As Fleming writes: 'In the absence of any other clubs to compete against, the members split into teams along the lines of Marrieds versus Singles, Professional Occupations against the Rest, and Smokers v Non-smokers. Matches were played on several local fields and parks. One butted up to [wealthy young club president, Fred] Ward's house on East Bank Road, another was on Strawberry Hall Lane, around the corner from Bramall Lane; all were situated away from the thick smoke and grime belched out by Sheffield's industrial East End.' Strictly middle class, then. No room at the club for poorly paid labourers.

Thus were born the traditions and tactics of 'Sheffield Rules', with its long fleecy knickerbockers, coloured caps and sturdy hobnailed boots. Not much in the way of passing, but lots of bravery, brute force and bone-crunching tackles with scrums of defenders and goalless draws commonplace. And with the formation of Hallam FC came a first Yorkshire derby, just after Christmas 1860, when: '...a few hundred curious frost-bitten spectators gathered at a snowbound Sandygate to watch the "old boys" of Sheffield, clad in scarlet caps, defeat the whippersnappers of Hallam, wearing blue, 2-0.'

The match was noted for being 'conducted with good temper and in a friendly spirit' but that didn't last long. Two years later came a '...thirteen-a-side yuletide encounter so disorderly it has gone down in the annals as "The Battle of Bramall Lane" - as "...the day the waistcoats came off and the fighting began."'

It also lasted three hours, ended without a goal being scored and resulted in an early exhibition of what would nowadays be called hooliganism, albeit by army majors and self-made businessmen rather than Burberry-capped 'chavs' high on lager and alcopops. Cor, who'da thunk it?

'Excited by the wild fisticuffs,' writes Fleming, 'spectators invaded the pitch and waded into the brawl ... further play was impossible until older and cooler heads prevailed.' There then followed much mudslinging in the papers, the odd resignation and a surge in popularity.

'The unsavoury incident thrust football onto Sheffield's back pages. Readers would have been dismayed but also fascinated by how such a simple game could arouse passions so feverishly. Rather than dampening enthusiasm for the sport, the "Battle of Bramall Lane" helped to stimulate its growth. Football fever gripped the town and almost overnight another dozen clubs popped up...'

Sheffields Wednesday (1867) and United (1889) - both also born of cricket clubs - came later, but the gritty, niggling and downright bloody-minded Yorkshire derby had arrived. And soon the rest of the country - and in time the world - fancied a piece of the action too.

And so, in case you haven't worked it out yet, the roots of modern-day sport, like modern-day Yorkshire itself, come to be entwined in mythology. Thus are identities formed, traditions and perceived values encouraged or ignored as pragmatism decrees, and the cause of unity championed. Yet it is also true that while most major sports have pasts murkier than a Filey horizon, their foundations do tend to be grounded in idealism and good intentions. At its best, sport rewards excellence, shines a light on teamwork and honest endeavour, offering thrills and entertainment.

Take the phenomenon that is York Races.

Any day at the world famous Knavesmire racecourse is a day worth spending. And every season there are plenty of big meetings featuring racing's top horses, jockeys and other personalities designed to attract punters.

In recent years, despite an economic recession, those numbers have climbed. In 2010, attendances broke 350,000 for the first time in a calendar that includes the Dante Stakes, Musidora Stakes and Yorkshire Cup in May. Of course, there's a Yorkshire Cup. In July, the John Smith's Cup has them clamouring through the turnstiles and, in August, the flagship Ebor Festival includes the Juddmonte International, Ebor Handicap, Yorkshire Oaks and Nunthorpe Stakes - 'York's most prestigious and richest race,' says Steve Carroll, racing writer of *The Press*, in his book, *York's Great Races*.

'No other racecourse except its natural home of Ascot has ever hosted the Royal Meeting. No other racecourse has held a modern day St Leger. York did it twice,' he writes of a ground on which horses have been raced since 1731. Back then, when '...the region's aristocracy swapped one piece of boggy, sodden land at Clifton Ings for another...' the Knavesmire as it was then hyphenated, '..was as synonymous with public executions as it was with the horses.'

And speaking of horses, hold yours! Newsflash.

Twelve people were arrested during York's Ebor meeting in 2013. Three were nabbed at the racecourse for being drunk and disorderly; two for possession of drugs; one for breaching bail and one for using a fake ticket. Five people were also apprehended in the city centre, including one chap who, when dragged from the River Ouse, became abusive and promptly leapt back in.

Fortunately, for him, come the beginning of the 19th century, it was felt that the gallows formerly responsible for hanging Dick Turpin gave a bit of a dodgy first impression of the city, so they were removed after one last hanging in 1801. I say removed. Relocated to a more discreet, if still public, area near York Castle more like. Tradition, eh?

And as the final whistle blows, it is also worth noting that one hundred and fifty years after Nathaniel Creswick and William Prest went for their mid-summer walk, the club they formed, Sheffield FC, lives and breathes yet. Today, the club plays in Evo-Stik Northern Premier League Division One South, based at the Coach and Horses ... in Derbyshire.

***

MEANWHILE, in Barnsley, sculptor Graham Ibbeson has been forced to extend the plinth beneath a statue of former

Slouching towards Blubberhouses

Test umpire Dickie Bird to a height of five feet (1.5m), in order to stop people hanging rude items from the Yorkshire icon's outstretched finger.

According to the BBC, the piece of public art in Bird's hometown had been '...a magnet for revellers, who have hung condoms and pants on it.'

The life-size statue has an index finger raised to indicate that a batsman is out. Other items hung there have included pumpkins and chip boxes.

'I do not mind people doing it at all,' Dickie tells them. 'They can take as many photographs as they like, but they're climbing on to it and they might fall off.'

Ibbeson adds: 'We are raising Dickie up where he belongs. On Friday and Saturday night, everybody who wobbles home from the town after a few sherberts seems to gravitate towards that finger, with knickers, brassieres, condoms, whatever. Dickie has been seen occasionally on a Saturday morning cleaning the debris off himself.'

9. Nowt So Funny As Folk

Yorkshire - Where the Fun Never Ends

A MAN goes to visit a friend who lives in a terraced back-to-house in Halifax.

'Eeh,' says his mate. 'Come in.'

As he steps over the threshold, the friend's daughter, a very attractive lass in her early twenties, comes into the parlour dragging a tin bath. The bloke, understandably, looks embarrassed, especially when the girl returns and starts filling it with buckets of water. And when the daughter then starts getting undressed, the visitor's anxiety gets the better of him and he runs for the door.

'Hey, come back,' yells his pal. 'Where are you going? She's a careful lass, she'll not splash you.'

***

IT is 2010 and after a lifespan of thirty-seven years, *Last of the Summer Wine*, the longest running sitcom in the world, has just completed its final run on BBC1. Strike up the viola, violins and flute. Cue sweeping shots of the Pennine hills and

Slouching towards Blubberhouses

Holme Valley. Lulled by Ronnie Hazlehurst's soporific theme tune, for one last time Britain and the rest of the TV-viewing world have huddled together in a comfort blanket of elderly naughtiness, wellies and wrinkled stockings. Or have they?

To some, *Last of the Summer Wine* is a formulaic parade of silly old men who, when not gazing mournfully into the verdant middle-distance or spouting pseudo philosophical non sequiturs, seem condemned to the eternal pursuit of a gurning tramp in a runaway tin bath. Yet its creator, Roy Clarke, clearly intended the show to be an elegy to passing time; a wistful take on humanity, community, friendship and quiet courage at the approach of the wingèd chariot.

That the programme has poetic roots is apparent in Clarke's lyrics, sung over the familiar theme tune before the 1983 Christmas special, 'Getting Sam Home':

> The colour of summer's gone,
> Of golden days when I was young,
> Of girls who came but soon moved on.
> Is in my summer wine.
> The perfumes of earth and vine,
> Of meadows when the rain has gone,
> Of women with their finery on.
> Is in my summer wine.
> The memories I can see,
> here in my cup, Of sweet short days,
> bitter days, now all drunk up.
> The taste of the life that slips,
> From day to day through fingers blind,
> The honey from the woman's lips.
> Is in my summer wine.

Later, in 2000, these lyrics were adapted to mark the funeral of the show's best-loved character, Compo, after the actor who portrayed him, Bill Owen, passed away the year before: 'Now all of his summer's gone... Those urgent days when he was young...' And in between, in 1988, Clarke also produced a prequel, *First of the Summer Wine*, in which those urgent days were brought back to life by younger actors over a couple of series. If ever a sitcom was steeped in melancholy, it is this global favourite.

***

HUMPHREY Bogart and Lauren Bacall had Rick's. Tony Soprano and crew had the Bada Bing! *Last of the Summer Wine* has Sid's Café. Substitute one of Ivy's 'world famous' scones for Louis Armstong in full growl or a doomed topless pole dancer and the job's a good 'un. Sid's Café is a meeting point for the characters and has been since the programme was first submitted to the BBC's *Comedy Playhouse* strand in 1973, only to be turned into a proper series a few months later.

In keeping with grand British sitcom tradition, the show's most obvious original theme was class. Of its trio of leads, the first, Cyril Blamire (Michael Bates), was a former Royal Signals sergeant and so took charge, naturally. When after series two Bates was diagnosed with cancer, Brian Wilde began the first of two very successful spells as the equally militaristic 'Foggy' Dewhirst. Middle class common sense, meanwhile, was provided by the longest-serving character Norman 'Cleggy' Clegg (Peter Sallis) and the working classes were represented by woolly-hatted scruff 'Compo' (Bill Owen), destined - along with his beloved Nora Batty (the formidable Kathy Staffe) - for TV immortality.

As time went by, new characters came in, old ones left (often to the great picnic spot in the sky) and knockabout pranks gained prominence, most of them brewed at Sid's.

Slouching towards Blubberhouses

On a wet Wednesday morning in June 2008, I am outside that very eaterie and there is a funeral on - a real one at that. Tucked away in a courtyard alongside the Parish Church of Holmfirth, Holy Trinity, the real Sid's Café is, appropriately enough, bang in the middle of the town, a stone's throw from the bus station and post office, just over the old bridge. Beneath the latter runs the river Holme, destined eventually to empty into the Humber but, at this stage of its journey, a rather forlorn sight as it makes its almost apologetic way past a cluster of shops, public houses and the old Picturedrome cinema. This latter building is of huge historical interest to those of us with a fascination for British comedy. It was built in 1912 to allow the entrepreneurial local visionary, James Bamforth, to display his short and innovative comic films, in which a scruffy little vagrant named 'Winky' (who winked at the end of every reel) indulged in mischief. Remind you of anyone? There's nothing new under the sun. Or drizzle.

Back on the other side of the road, squeezed between Holy Trinity and a Help The Aged charity shop, runs an alleyway leading, rather improbably, to a 'Youth Cyber Café'. Today, the Parish church has a banner for the Holmfirth Arts Festival. Funeral notwithstanding, it also has an exhibition of Medieval miniatures. And to the right is the aforementioned courtyard in which Sid's sits, framed by an Ironmongers, two black Daimlers and a hearse with its back door up, awaiting delivery. As I make my approach, three drivers clad in black suits and gloves lean on the corner, chatting.

I've been in Holmfirth less than half an hour but Sue and Sarah, the two charming ladies who staff its Tourist Information Office, have already marked my card with regard to potential delights. Sue and Sarah take great pride in being first port of call for the 50,000-plus visitors who come here annually. Their place of employment - situated on the same bustling A6024 Huddersfield Road that houses Ashley Jackson's gallery in the upper part of town - won the White Rose Award for Best Tourist Information Centre in Yorkshire in 2007; '...and we are up for it again,' adds Sue who, in September, will celebrate her twentieth year in the job.

'We get all kinds of people. Mostly, they come for *Last of the Summer Wine* but, afterwards, lots will return for a walking holiday,' she says. 'Holmfirth is a good base for the Peak District, Yorkshire Dales and so on. We get a lot of international visitors from places like America, Canada and Japan too, as they get *Last of the Summer Wine* on cable.' And if Sue's own experience is anything to go by, she tells me, the show remains as popular as ever, with all age groups. 'It's not just elderly people who like it. We get children in here pointing at pictures of Compo on the books. That's because it's a family show that everybody can sit down to watch together, from your three-year-old to your grandma and grandad. You know there's going to be nothing offensive about it, just gentle humour. Also, we get a lot of people who come here to study local history.'

Naturally enough, this latter ingredient tends to take a backseat in promoting the area's charms. Nevertheless, it soon becomes apparent that life in the Holme Valley hasn't always been a barrel of laughs. True, *Last of the Summer Wine* and, to a lesser extent, the Bamforth family's exploits in early movies and the manufacture of saucy seaside postcards grab all the glory - 'they say that if it hadn't been for the weather, Holmfirth could have been Hollywood', Sue sighs, but there has been sadness and hardship here too. Not least as a result of the periodic floods that have swept through the town and its neighbouring villages.

Among the more serious and recent of those occured

on Whit Monday 1944, when three people were killed after a major cloudburst. The most devastating was undoubtedly the great flood of 1852, when a reservoir at the top of the valley burst its banks, taking houses and eighty-one lives with it. Here, as anywhere, the world can be at its most dangerous just when it is at its most beautiful.

Freshly armed with a handful of leaflets inviting me to wallow in 'an eclectic mix of traditional and modern' in which 'speciality shops and markets, bespoke art and tasty treats' are all 'clustered around cobbled streets', I bid Sue and Sarah farewell and step out into the distinctly uncobbled A6024. My first port of call is a small independent bookshop over the road. Toll House Book Shop actually backs onto a row of terrace houses containing the fictional home of Nora Batty, complete with its famous stone steps upon which many a contretemps with Compo ensued. Cameras off, it doubles as 'The Wrinkled Stocking Tea Room'.

Despite boasting six rooms of new, secondhand and antiquarian literature, the shop is not exactly bursting with customers, so a quick chat with the woman from Manchester serving on is no problem. So what about the, quite frankly, scandalous allegation that Lancashire has the monopoly on light-hearted eccentrics while Yorkshire folk are downbeat and glum. 'I think that's fairly accurate actually,' she says, 'and don't forget the stinginess.'

Most of Holmfirth's population, she says, hails from elsewhere. 'A lot commute. They have moved in from over the border and so forth.' Is there a community atmosphere? 'To be honest, there's more in other places. There are certainly people who try to be active and get things going and there are groups, particularly around the schools.' How's business? 'Like everywhere at the moment, not good. A lot of the local people support us by coming here instead of the chains.

Tourists come in and browse, but they don't always buy. We sell history books mainly as the new stuff is just hammered by the supermarkets.' Time to inject some levity. How about *Last of the Summer Wine*? Does she enjoy that? 'They are flogging a dead horse. It was mildly amusing in the early days but I've not watched it for years. I think you'll find that a lot of locals would say that. You used to watch it to see if your house was on but it died a long time ago really.'

Suitably uplifted, it is now that I stroll down to Sid's. By coincidence, the *Summer Wine* crew has actually been in Holmfirth this morning so, given a fair wind and good luck, they may well return for more. In the meantime, I study a timetable for the rather thrilling 'Summerwine Magic Tour', a bus trip that departs from the courtyard several times a day during high season, taking fans of the show on 'a whistlestop tour of its locations and the surrounding countryside'. Along with the hearse drivers already described, a group of four or five elderly women hang around outside Sid's Café in wait.

After deciding to go on the 1.30pm bus, I strike up a conversation. Daisy Ovenden, seated alone at a table, is from Deale, in Kent. Well, I say alone. Alongside is a four-foot high model of Compo, complete with trademark hat, scarf, scruffy old coat and trousers tied up with string, used to promote the café. Daisy and walking stick have been here before. 'I have watched *Summer Wine* since the beginning,' she says. 'I even watch the repeats.' Favourite character? 'Him,' she says, indicating over her shoulder. 'He makes me laugh, although Foggy was very good too. Oh and there's Nora Batty and her stockings. I like them all. They were all good. I like the humour, you see, because it's gentle. There's no swearing or anything like that. Anybody could watch it, couldn't they? I live in Kent now but I was born in a place called Woodhouse Mill, near Sheffield. So I like to see the scenery too.'

Slouching towards Blubberhouses

Isn't it amazing, I say, how last Sunday, the twenty-ninth series began. 'Yes,' Daisy replies, 'but it's not the same without Compo and Foggy. I do still enjoy it, though. I like the antics of Marina and Howard. Poor Howard. It's a very nice programme.'

Daisy's travelling companions, Rita and Brenda from Deale, Pat from Harlow and Jean from Saffron Waldon, sit across the courtyard. They, like her, are on a coach tour. 'We've seen *Last of the Summer Wine* on television and wanted to come and see what it was like in real life,' says Pat. 'The main attraction for me is the scenery,' continues Rita. 'Roy Clarke's writing is brilliant but I do think the scenery attracts a lot of viewers, especially when they are up in the hills. Even though the characters have changed, the sense of humour has stayed the same. They've got Compo's son in now, haven't they?' 'It's just one of those programmes we enjoy,' adds Brenda. 'There's not much else on telly nowadays, is there?' 'No,' agrees Pat. 'It's all sex and violence, horrible, horrible...'

***

WHAT is needed now is a nice hot cup of tea, so it's into the 'World Famous' Sid's Café I go, with time to spare before the bus comes in. 'Open for teas and coffees and a wide selection of snacks and sandwiches, gifts and souvenirs,' reads the sign outside. 'Try Ivy's famous scones. With real fresh dairy cream and fruit. Delicious.' It's a challenge no intrepid tourist could pass up. Especially if here for the full experience.

The first thing you notice, inside, is how tiny the place is, a lay-out different to how it is on the box. 'Ah,' says Laura, who, along with sister Ailsa, has owned the place since 2006, 'that's because all the interior shots are done in a studio.' Helping her are Ailsa and friend Zoe. Furthermore, Laura reveals, the *Last of the Summer Wine* crew only visit Sid's twice a year, for exterior shots mainly. If they need to film inside or give a glimpse from the 'street', the counter directly opposite the door is shifted to the left. All but two of the café tables are removed, pictures and menus are taken down, and away they go with a wide-angle lens. By fluke, I have just missed them. They were in here only an hour so before.

While waiting for my world famous scone, I learn that Zoe was born in Manchester but could only stick it for a year and had swapped counties by her first birthday. Laura and Ailsa are Holmfirth born and bred, although both have spent time working and studying in other parts. Ailsa confesses to having worked in a hospital in Stockport and hated it. 'I couldn't believe the difference between Leeds and Manchester. Of all the people who come here on coach trips, though, it's the Scots who are most miserable. Should I say that? It's all a stereotype really, isn't it?'

With these three running the shop, there is nothing gloomy about Sid's. The atmosphere is friendly and relaxed. Apart from one hairy moment with a female pensioner - actually, not so hairy come to think of it - when I accidentally barge my way into an engaged toilet, all is sweetness and light. Not a fearsome Ivy-like figure anywhere.

Ailsa, it seems, used to have a Sunday job here. Then, a couple of years ago, while disenchanted working for the council, the café came up for sale. 'She always said that her best job was working in Sid's Café,' says her sister. 'She just loved it, wanted to buy it and I came in with her.' The person they bought it from is Colin, who now runs - and drives - the Summertime Magic bus tours, a reminder that the hands on the clock wait for no-one. So, after the girls give me a list of available souvenirs - teapot £6.50, mugs (pottery) £3.75, mugs (china) £4.75, tea bag tidy £3.75, thimbles £2.99 each, or four

for £7.99, apron £9.99, Sid's Café T-shirt £6.50 - I pose the
$64,000 question. Do they watch *Last of the Summer Wine*
themselves? 'Yes,' says Laura. A diplomatic yes? 'No, I have
always watched it. When we were at university it was nice
to see home. I'd watch it in London and my flatmates used
to say: "what are you watching that rubbish for?" But it's
really comforting. Whether we'd watch it if we weren't from
here, I don't know. It's weird, because you've grown up with
it. You don't bat an eyelid when they are here filming, it has
always been around. I still enjoy it.'

Outside, Daisy and friends are still hanging around,
having now got back from their tour - '...we had a lovely time,
highly recommended'. There is no sign of my bus, though,
so in the interests of balance I pop into Beatties Coffee Shop,
another 'Purveyor of Fine Foods', next to Sid's. Despite a
more modern image, they sell *Last of the Summer Wine* books
too. How does the show impact on their custom? 'It's fine,'
says the man behind the counter. 'It's done a lot for the
village. They have been coming to Holmfirth for thirty-odd
years. We don't sell a lot of books, most people go next door
for that sort of thing.' And the show itself? 'It's not as good
as it used to be. They must be struggling for stories.' Does he
imagine that his business will be adversely affected when *Last
of the Summer Wine* ends? 'Not for a bit, they will carry on
showing repeats. But the interest will eventually fade.'

And now, over the road by the bus station, is that film
crew, cameras, clapperboards and all. The man in charge is
veteran TV director Alan Bell, director of one of the finest
comedy half-hours ever made, 'Golden Gordon' from Terry
Jones and Michael Palin's *Ripping Yarns* in 1979. The scene
being filmed today features a police car manned by Yorkshire
character actor Ken Kitson (who had a bit-part in 'Golden
Gordon' as a fan on the terraces) and Louis Emerick (formerly

of *Brookside*), who play dozy constables Cooper and Walsh. As normal life goes on around us, the car in which the pair sit tears up the road, siren lights flashing, before coming to a screeching halt in the parking bay opposite Sid's. The idea, says Alan, is '...to give the impression of an emergency when all they are doing is buying a couple of bacon butties.' Once parked up, Kitson leaps out of the passenger door and runs towards the Café in an arse-out, comedy waddle.

The scene is over in moments, or so it seems. The director and his assistant in a crew of five communicate with a number of other folk in strategic positions - asking them to stop traffic or ensure no one wanders into shot - by walkie-talkie. Otherwise, Holmfirth proceeds unmolested, its public happy to be incidental extras. 'Hang on, there's a bus coming - go when it's safe to come out,' says the assistant. 'Who's that stopping there...' chimes in Alan, as an oblivious driver pulls into the empty bay, before being charmed into parking elsewhere. Take one was okay but they try another for luck. And then suddenly the blue lights don't work and the camera battery runs out. Once fixed, take three sees a screech of tyres and the police car - driven by Emerick - almost run into the back of a genuine dawdling motorist. The twenty seconds-worth in the can will have to do and off they trot off for lunch.

Before leaving, Alan Bell fills me in on a show he has now been directing for over twenty-seven years. 'We tell the council where we would like to film,' he says, 'and if they have any objection we go elsewhere. As long as we are not causing an obstruction, the police are generally happy. To be honest, we don't film in Holmfirth that often now because there are too many tourists. Look how busy it is today. Once, this was a quiet village, but now you can't move for cars. We do a lot of our outside filming up in the hills, but there are certain iconic locations down here which we can't ignore, like

Slouching towards Blubberhouses

Sid's Café and Nora Batty's house. If they weren't in the programme it wouldn't be quite as strong - they represent it, I think. But if we are looking for country lanes and towns, we tend to go over to Marsden or Slaithwaite. It's a shame really, but there are just too many cars in the world now.'

I mention the achievement of lasting twenty-nine series and am rewarded with a shake of the head and weary sigh. The weather during filming for this latest run was poor. 'In the show, the sun is always supposed to shine.'

***

AT last, it's time for some 'Summerwine magic'. I wander back over to the church and its cobbled alleys and stone steps, each worn to a sag in the middle, moss-claimed at the edges.

The morning's intermittent sunshine and drizzle has given way to steadier rainfall. The vehicle waiting at the bus stop is a real antique its driver, Colin, tells me. An Asquith replica converted to fit on a Ford chassis. Colin is an amiable chap, laconic in manner with a ready supply of quips honed and tested a thousand times before. The perfect guide, in fact. With white hair, waistcoat, checked shirt and an accent like he's got a mouthful of cottage cheese, he would be a fitting addition to the show. I hand over six quid and climb aboard.

It looks delicate, this bus. Yet it is as resilient as a mountain goat. There is room enough - just - for eleven of us, a cosy fit at that. Colin tried to get a bigger one once but, over the forty-five minute trip, it becomes apparent that it's just as well he didn't. The Asquith is the ideal size for steep inclines and hairpin bends, and its compactness promotes sociability in strangers. With the exception of Derek and Valerie who live not far from here in Sowerby Bridge, near Halifax, most passengers are from outside Yorkshire. Of *Last of the Summer*

Wine, Valerie says: 'We love it. A lot of it is nostalgia. There's no bad language, no sex and violence...' 'You haven't been on this tour yet, have you,' Colin pipes up from the driver's seat.

Valerie presses on. 'It's good clean fun. No smut, nothing dirty.' Who is her favourite character? 'Well, it used to be Compo. I don't know really. Peter Sallis, Cleggy, is good. They are all good, aren't they?' Does she enjoy it as much now as she ever did? 'Yes, we do. Marina's funny, isn't she? She does well for her age. Cleggy's getting on ninety now, isn't he? It'll be sad when 'owt happens to him.'

Another couple, Brenda and Rex, are en route back to Shropshire. 'We have been up to Weardale, near Durham, and decided to stop here for three days on our way home,' says Brenda. 'We just love the programme and have always said we wanted to come and see where they filmed it.' Rex: 'I must be honest, though, it's not the same since Bill Owen passed away.' Brenda carries on regardless: '...but it's just nice easy watching - no violence, sex or swearing or anything like that. It's all fun, isn't it?' 'They never get to it, do they, Howard and Marina? They never get to it,' chuckles Valerie, before Brenda adds that her daughter finds it boring. 'But then she's a different age.' 'Didn't someone in the paper shop tell you they had been filming this morning?', Rex asks his wife. 'No,' she replies. 'That was when I was buying my slippers.'

Pat and William have driven all the way from Devon, via Birmingham and Skegness. Another couple clamber on whose names I don't have time to gather as Colin is already into his spiel. Three more folk turn up and clearly someone is going to be disappointed. 'If one of you wants to go half price, you can run behind,' he says, helpfully, before politely closing the doors and, with a groan of the engine, launching us on our way. The tannoy bursts into life with a crackle.

'If you look across the road at that parade of shops,'

217

Slouching towards Blubberhouses

Colin suggests, 'on the very end shop, the butcher's, can you see that red writing on the window?' Ooh, yes we can, everyone nods, anticipating tales of intrigue and murder. 'That's where I get my pork pies from on a Monday.'

Colin then points out the Kirkwood Hospice shop, 'which used to be a laundrette. It's where Compo, Foggy and Clegg sat in the early series. If you remember, they were always looking out of the laundrette window.' I don't, actually, but, unless they are just being polite my companions do. We continue along the river and down through what used to be the main road: 'A toll road in t' hoss 'n' cart days,' says Colin. It takes us past Nora Batty's house which, like Sid's Café, owes much to clever editing. From there, we cross the lane down which the show's leading trio once walked in the opening titles and pass the bookies from which Compo was always being thrown.

Ah, Compo. Upon nosing out by Ashley Jackson's gallery, the tower of St John's Parish Church is pointed out to the right, just above a patch of trees. It is there, says Colin, in the village of Upperthong, that Bill Owen - 'in real life, quite a dapper little gentleman' - is buried. The actor, like many in the cast, was actually born down south (in London), but specifically selected the spot as his final resting place.

As our journey progresses, it becomes apparent that Colin knows *Last of the Summer Wine* inside out. Holmfirth, for example, was not the first choice of location. That it became so owed much to the intervention of the BBC's then comedy advisor, Barry Took, who had established himself on shows like *Round The Horne* and *The Army Game* with writing partner Marty Feldman in the 1960s. When Roy Clarke was commissioned to write his one-off contribution to *Comedy Playhouse*, it was Took who suggested that he should set it in Holmfirth, after having recently made a documentary about the town and its well-known postcards. 'Roy wanted to film it in his hometown Doncaster,' Colin tells us. 'Somehow, I don't think that would have been quite the same.'

Onward and upward, where the itinerary next takes us past picturesque Hinchliffe Mill which, like everywhere else in these parts, gives the impression of being carved into the hillside. This, Colin says, is the location of Wesley's garage and the cottage of his pretty-in-pink sister-in-law, Ros. The houses around here are a sight to behold. On one side they appear to be normal two-storey properties but, on the other, owing to the sudden steepness, they can be anything up to five storeys high. 'When the reservoir burst,' says Colin, 'this was the village that took the full force. The valley is narrow here and many lives were lost.' Alas, Wesley's garage has also now gone. Upon the death in 2002 of the actor who played him, Gordon Wharmby, it was taken away and scrapped.

By now, in keeping with the programme's most recent scripts, our trusty bus is labouring somewhat. Country roads, sharp bends, vertical drops and climbs, you name it, this route has it. 'Causes a bit of difficulty when the film crew comes up,' reports Colin, as we climb ever higher. 'Sometimes they can have up to thirty-five vehicles with them, including some pretty big wagons and caravans. If they didn't organise it properly, there would be chaos.' As a way around that, a base camp is set up where all the large vehicles reside. The actors are then shuttled backwards and forwards to the set. Few natural resources are wasted, including the vertical fields. Yonder is where Compo went rolling away in a barrel. Over there is the spot where the three friends went skiing with breakfast trays tied to their feet. Filming commences in May or June and continues throughout the summer. They do approximately one month at a time, go back to the studio for a month and then return, before piecing it all together.

Slouching towards Blubberhouses

Having reached one thousand feet above sea level and only one thousand eight hundred feet below the flightpath of Manchester Airport - 'which explains the tyre marks on the bus roof' - the view is impressive. Away to the right, across the valley and above a clutch of red-brick houses, is that ill-fated reservoir. Beyond that, is Saddleworth moor: 'Where Brady and Hindley, the moors murderers, buried the children.' Again, for all its apparent beauty, this area does have its sinister, stark, dangerous side.

Over to the left, overlooking Huddersfield, is Tower Hill, on which is perched a one hundred foot-tall stone tower, built to commemorate Queen Victoria's Diamond Jubilee. 'There has always been a castle or a keep on that hill,' says Colin, 'going right back to the Iron Age.' And a little further along, taking in the vast sweep, is a solitary little bench - empty now, of course - on which Compo was often to be seen peering out across a remarkable vista, lost in thought. It is a poignant spot that underlines how, with just a smidgeon more artistry, *Last of the Summer Wine* might well have been a comedy masterpiece. You have to wonder what Alan Plater, John Godber or Alan Bennett would have made of it.

Still, on we go, past the modern-day housing estate in which Holmfirth's dullest couple Barry and Glenda live, through lanes where Glenda's mother Edie crunched her car gears, dropping down into ever more steep gradients - warns Colin: '...if anyone's wearing silk underwear, hold on tight.'

Soon, we are in Scholes, birthplace of entertainer Roy Castle. Colin points out the back-to-back terraced cottage in which the versatile showman was born, and the school and Sunday school in which he developed his record-breaking musical skills. Appropriately, Roy's daughter Antonia works on the *Summer Wine* production team.

For yours truly, the rest of the tour passes in a blur of

locations and scenes unrecalled. Over there are the bushes out of which Howard and Marina leap in and out. That's the road Norman Wisdom drove down in a mini when there was a tiger on the loose. There's where Barry was carried away by a giant kite; the brow of the hill where a balloon appeared shaped like a big fat lady rose; the very spot where Auntie Wainwright's trolley-coffin ran away, nearly taking Howard and Marina with it.

'Do you see over there,' says Colin, 'in one of them fields opposite? There it is ... a Russian tank. I only noticed it the other week, myself. I was having a run-out in my little vintage car when I saw this bloody great tank in the field. Suddenly, up pops a man out of the turret. I says to him: "Who's been on ebay then?" Apparently, it cost him £15,000. I ask him if he's taking it to any shows. "Nah," he says. "I can't afford to." He has to get a special permit from the highways, you see, because of the weight of it. And he has to get a special permit from the police too, and carry it on a low-loader, because it's a gun basically, isn't it? He just rides around in the field. Whatever turns you on.'

The anecdotes are still flowing when we reach the valley bottom and a pretty little church, scene of Barry and Glenda's wedding and, in a later millennium special, the first time Thora Hird's Edie was seen in a wheelchair, as she put flowers on her mother's grave. 'On set, she had been in one for a few years,' reveals Colin. 'She was very bad on her legs, Thora. At the latter end, any time you saw her actively moving about you were looking at a double, she only did the close-ups in the studio. When driving, she was actually sat in a car, on a trailer towed by a Land Rover.'

In the 1600s, most of the inhabitants of this village were wiped out by the plague and, not so very far away, is the housing estate on which lived Peter Falconio, destined to be murdered in the Australian outback in 2001. It's being so cheerful that keeps the Holme Valley going.

Things brighten no end, however, with the sighting of the White Horse, the official *Summer Wine* pub in the village of Jackson Bridge. Tragically, there's no time to stop for a pint, but we do get to see Clegg's cottage, along with that of Howard and Pearl who, according to Colin, is played as a bit of a dragon by Juliette Kaplan but who, in real life, is 'quite nice, quite attractive with a wicked sense of humour.'

Around here, it's all weaver's cottages, three storeys high, with their closely-packed rows of narrow windows, designed to allow in maximum light whilst the handlooms get to work upstairs. And then, just when we thought our necks couldn't get any stiffer, it's back to Holmfirth via Tom Owen's allotment, where the repo man is always on his case; another little village called Wooldale in which the Luddites secretly planned their attacks; but not, unfortunately, Auntie Wainwright's shop. That, says Colin, is eight miles away in Marsden. Meanwhile, the rain pours down.

'I bet when you watch *Summer Wine* on telly, you think it's always sunny in Holmfirth,' says Colin, as we close back in on Towngate and Sid's Café. 'Well, I can assure you, when they come filming it nearly always rains. But that doesn't stop them, because rain doesn't show up on camera unless it's absolutely throwing it down. Their big arc lights brighten things up too. Next time the programme's on, just look at the floor and see how many puddles you can spot.'

And what about you, Colin, I ask, once the bus comes to a halt. What will you do with yourself when the circus leaves town as, one day soon, it surely will. You must be pleased they keep coming back? 'Course I am,' he says. 'I've got to eat, you know. I've been doing this tour for about fifteen years now. My late missus did the café and I did this.

It's in my blood. But, my own personal opinion, I think this will be the last time. The main reason is their age - they can't get insurance now for the old 'uns.' And how will that affect the tour? 'Oh, that will carry on forever. I first bought the café about eighteen years ago and right from day one people have been saying: "Oh, they don't film that anymore do they?" And yet here I am, still talking about Compo - how long has he been dead now? Nine years? He still draws them in.'

***

BONFIRE night. Well, Bonfire afternoon. I'm at Leeds Grand's Theatre Studios on a bright and blustery Thursday, for *Jake In A Box - Jake Thackray and the Idea of the North*.

As a long time admirer of the Leeds-born singer-songwriter who, in the 1970s, was once one of Britain's most popular entertainers, I am keen to learn more about a man whose presence on TV consumer show *That's Life* among much else confirmed him as one of a kind. Physically, his vaguely threatening demeanour, saturnine with hooded eagle eyes, betrayed a hidden sadness and intensity, but he could also be gut-bustingly funny, his wry little notes of hilarity delivered in a voice of roughest silk.

Those clipped tones, directed shyly at his audience but more often than not at a jealously held guitar, drawn close as though in embarrassment that he had been noticed on stage at all and was afraid of being left to face the music alone. And what of all those wondrous words? Perfectly crafted dollops of wit and exasperation unmatched by any lyricist before or since.

The Grand studios are directly under the stage above, nowadays utilitarian rehearsal rooms, in Victorian times the place where all the gizmos and gadgets were housed that were responsible for the operating of trap doors an other phantasmagorical effects.

There are around thirty of us. We are not allowed to enter immediately and so mill about in a holding space that, given the average age, feels a little like heaven's waiting room. Masques and feathers adorn eggshell walls, along with a poster for a production of *High School Musical 2* - '...starring Les Dennis'. Tea and coffee is served 'over there' and so off I toddle, giving a pound to the nice lady serving on.

'Do you want a coffee?' one aged sparrow is asked by her friend.

'I'm not bothered,' she replies. 'I've just thrown a sandwich down.'

Before long, a few baby boomers appear and a healthy turnout builds. We get an enlightening lecture, complete with slides of Jake and his mentors, Georges Brassens and Jacques Brel, and three or four video clips of his songs to illustrate 'northern Englishness at work.' Among them: 'The Kirkstall Road Girl', 'On Again! On Again!' and this writer's favourite 'The Bull': '...the bigger the bull, the bigger the balls ... the bigger the bull-shite falls...', Jake's very own *Animal Farm*.

Described by many who count as the lost genius of British songwriting, Thackray, who died in 2002, did not miss a chance to mock the la-di-dah pretensions of the so-called social elite. Religious, literate and saucy, his provocative ideas however might be disarmed by tunes instantly familiar and catchy, especially the farmyard fables that marked his output from the 1980s onwards before he retired from performing all together. Nor did Jake much care for television, believing that musicians did not belong in a 'flickering oblong box'.

A devout Catholic, his rendering of religion and the pious tended to point up the conflict between living a good life, i.e. how we're *supposed* to behave, and the ways in which our earthly urges scupper that. North country earthiness was his thing and middle England found it strangely appealing.

A folk singer then, if out of a different mould than that responsible for Ewan MacColl, Richard Thompson or Fairport Convention, say. Nor was Thackray part of the regional folkie set for whom he blazed a trail on TV - Mike Harding, Max Boyce, Billy Connolly, Jasper Carrott and Co - only to see his reputation suffer at the hands of the 1970s alternative comedy movement for whom they themselves laid the ground, as a more blatantly political set of comedians sought to obliterate the casual sexism that many still claim to find in his songs.

To which one is bound to reply that while Jake's songs may have indeed flirted with sexism on occasion - more often an idealised view of women through masculine eyes being more like it - what they were most certainly not is casual.

The composition of Thackray's lyrics, for good or ill, are traditionally northern and observational. Direct, yet sardonic. Self-deprecating, yet elevating. Down to earth, yet soulful. Distrustful of hypocrisy, yet forgiving of it in 'ordinary folk' - '...think of all the bright-eyed children who will have to learn your name.' Biting, yet sweet. Simple, yet complex. Provincial, yet universal. Above all, oppositional.

His Gallic influences are blatant. Thackray sang the odd ditty in fluent French. Inward, so very very inward. Yet outward, always outward too.

The illumination over, it's out into an afternoon sunk now in autumnal Gothic grey. Buses swish through puddles, the city centre gears up for its latest evening rush hour.

Heading back up a sodden Aire Valley line, the harsh interior light of the carriage casts reflections on windows framed in darkness. Rain weeps at right angles on reinforced glass, through which dim visions of sheep and seagulls jostle for attention in flooded fields-turned-lakes beneath a sign:

Slouching towards Blubberhouses

'Emergency Exit'. That and our own blank faces. Mournful in the moment like beasts in a cattle truck, but then cheered by thoughts of home, we are on again, on again...

***

SIR Bernard Ingham, one time cantankerous watchdog of Margaret Thatcher, has a book out, *Yorkshire Greats*, in which he chooses the county's fifty greatest public figures.

'It's the most dangerous book I'll ever write,' he tells the *Guardian*'s north of England reporter, Martin Wainwright, in 2005, before declaring grit, persistence and bloody-mindedness as essential criteria. Explorer James Cook, abolitionist William Wilberforce and hero of longitude John Harrison are selected in positions one, two and three, while among the others to make Ingham's list are aviator Amy Johnson, cat's eyes inventor Percy Shaw, and Prime Ministers Rockingham, Asquith and Wilson.

According to Wainwright, the author also takes '...a blunt delight in rows which surfaced before the canapés had got halfway round Sir Titus Salt's old textile mill, near Bradford. Why not Geoffrey Boycott, several guests asked. Disgraceful that Barbara Hepworth was dropped. And where was Britain's first astronaut, Helen Sharman, or W.H. Auden?'

'I told you the brickbats would fly, but we like a good argument in Yorkshire,' says Sir Bernard, whose preparation was completed on a lecture cruise to Peru, where he 'filleted 226 Tykes from the *Cambridge Dictionary of Biography*.'

'It was a necessary task for the world,' he says.

***

'ENGLAND has long been known as a melting pot of musical excellence, but it's not all Beatles and Oasis,' according to the *Guardian*'s 'Cityscapes' supplement.

'Where would British contemporary music be without Sheffield's Jarvis Cocker? Dandy, wit, the common people and wiggling his bum at Michael Jackson during the 1996 Brits, he is fast shaping up to be the pop equivalent of Alan Bennett. But Sheffy isn't just Pulp ... there is Joe Cocker (no relation), synthpop legends Human League, Def Leppard (65m albums sold, whatever you think), Heaven 17 and the Thompson Twins. To continue that Sheffield strain of ironic, astute and unpretentious music we also now have the established Arctic Monkeys, Reverend and the Makers and the Last Shadow Puppets, while the next big things are Flying Squad, Alvarez Kings (razor riffed Indie rockers) and Vegas Child (frenetic punksters)...'

Sheffield equals music in a way that Leeds, for all its clout and cultural self-congratulation in so many other areas, does not. Not that West Yorkshire's biggest city - with Kaiser Chiefs, Corinne Bailey Rae and Embrace most recently to boast of - views matters quite that way, of course.

So it was doubtless with a cheery chuckle that South Yorkshire inhabitants awoke to the opening night problems of Leeds (aka First Direct) Arena in July 2013, 'the first such venue in the UK to have a fan-shaped orientation' and a rival for Sheffield's longer established Motorpoint Arena that has been in business under one name or other since 1991.

On the evening in question, *Look North* had run one of those pointless confrontation pieces so beloved of BBC news programmes - Leeds versus Sheffield, is there room for two arenas in Yorkshire? Well, given how, as reporter Tom Ingle himself pointed out, Nottingham Arena is a similar distance away from Sheffield - around thirty miles - and that *it* seems to be doing okay, the obvious answer is yes. Folk will either choose to go or not based on who's on, won't they?

Later, come reports of a sell-out crowd for debut turn Bruce Springsteen, for whom some punters have queued for days in order to get to the front and secure the best view. Words like triumphant are used. Kaiser Chiefs will front the official opening next month and Elton John is on his way too. As for 'The Boss': 'Leeds, you've got a great venue,' he yells. 'I've really enjoyed it. A lovely place to play.'

But then, the following morning, BBC Radio Leeds reports a shock development: four articulated stage trucks belonging to Bruce and his Eeh Bah Gum Street Band were given parking tickets.

Fire-fighting City Council leader Keith Wakefield leaps into action, telling *Liz Green Live*: 'They are no longer valid. Someone was a bit stupid and over-zealous.'

But the damage to the city's reputation is done. It is twenty-eight years since Springsteen last played Leeds and this 13,500 capacity venue sold out in minutes, with ticket prices on the black market rising to as much as £1,400. Now 'a massive coup' had been turned into red faces all round.

'They were not parked illegally,' according to one tickled bystander. 'They were just down a sidestreet, waiting to be called into the Arena. People are just laughing.'

***

SEPTEMBER 2013 sees Jarvis Cocker's 50th birthday. Another musical son of Sheffield, Richard Hawley, pays tribute to his childhood pal on BBC Radio 6 Music's *Radcliffe and Maconie* show, a channel on which Cocker is also a presenter.

By now Cocker has managed thirty years in the music

industry marked by four top ten albums and an eventful career with his band Pulp, as a single performer and, most recently, a quirky entertaining broadcaster. To celebrate, the programme takes Hawley to Sheffield's Forge Dam Park, in the playground of which the pair played together as kids.

'We are actually here at Forge Dam café,' Hawley begins. 'You can probably hear the waterfall and, er, dogs barking. The first time we ever met ... I remember seeing Jarvis with a hoover. He was trying to get it repaired, but Jarvis always had that slightly mad professor-ish thing about him. We kind of imagined he might be going to build a rocket out of it for interplanetary travel, but I think he was really just dropping it off at a skip.

'I don't think either of us thought we'd make it to 30. I got a birthday card off my dad when I was 30 saying: "30? Never thought you'd make it to Thursday!" If I had to choose a song, I'd want a miserable one. And I'd also like a really happy one, because we're both a bit like that. Can I have 'My Autumn's Done Come', by Lee Hazlewood?'

***

WE are filming my contribution to a BBC documentary about legendary double act Morecambe and Wise in East Ardsley, birthplace of Ernie, near Wakefield. The production crew has driven here from London - via Blackpool - for the purpose.

What are you writing next, I am asked. A book about Yorkshireness, I reply, which brings a chuckle from the sound man. 'I've filmed in Yorkshire a lot,' he says, 'and every single time somebody will beam, throw their arms open and say: "This is my office, lad."'

He goes on to tell us a joke he's heard.

'This bloke gets lost while out walking in Lancashire,

no idea where he is. Eventually, he happens across a golden telephone box - this being the days before mobile phones - and steps inside. "I'll ring for help," he thinks.

'On picking up the receiver, though, he notices a sign - God's Phone - and the only call it will make is straight to heaven. What's more, it will cost him £5,000.

'"I can't afford that," he thinks and steps back outside.

'Around an hour later, he crosses the Yorkshire border and stumbles on exactly the same thing - a golden telephone box, only this time the call will only cost £5.

'"What's going on?" he asks a little old bloke, sitting watching on a dry stone wall.

'"Isn't it obvious, lad," the old man says. "Local call."

***

THE end, when it came for *Last of the Summer Wine*, was one year later than bus driver Colin had feared. The programme had lasted thirty-one series in all, with 295 episodes made.

But even so, in April 2013, figures revealed that an astonishing 483 repeats of a show cancelled in 2010 had been shown on British TV in the first ninety days of that year alone.

'Viewers with the full range of terrestrial and digital stations are never more than a few hours away from it,' said the British Comedy Guide website, who monitored every showing of every sitcom and panel show on every channel available to UK viewers for its site www.comedy.co.uk.

'The fact that *Last Of The Summer Wine* is still being repeated so often suggests that the BBC perhaps shouldn't have closed production down,' a spokesperson added.

Colin's tour bus, too, is still going strong.

10. There's Rubble At T' Mill

Laughing Stocks - Part Two: Bradford

BRADFORD, eh? What a joke.

If it's not race riots, it's serial killers. If it's not sporting disasters or going bust, it's sacking headmasters and book burning. And have you seen the state of the city centre lately? It's an abandoned building site. How many more renovation projects will there be that never see the light of day?

Bradford, eh? What a joke.

***

TO walk through the many and varied districts of England's fourth most populous metropolitan borough is to hear the same or similar. For Bradford is a place that, for reasons long and varied, went from being one of the most important cities in the British Empire to a bruised and battered 'dump', with no self-confidence left whatsoever.

It's not about stagnation. Stagnation would be heaven. It's about a fall into a deep dark hole from which there seems to be no route of escape. Do we lay blame for this at the door of a council who churn out 'bold new initiatives' at the same rate railway companies churn out excuses? The latest such scheme is the multi-million pound Alsop Plan, with its artistic impressions of inner-city water parks, natural green havens and futuristic consumer walkways, much of it stalled by economic recession (i.e. lack of funding). Though, as I write, plans to open the cause of that building site, the £260m Westfield shopping centre - '...to include stores Next, Marks & Spencer, River Island and Debenhams...' - are 'progressing nicely' and 'on course for opening in December 2015...'

Is immigration the issue? By which we mean a mainly South Asian community that, since making Bradford its home in the 1950s, has given the city the second-highest proportion of Muslims in England and Wales outside London? At the last count, people of South Asian origin were around a quarter of the entire population. But such critics can never quite explain why that should necessarily be a bad thing and overlook Bradford's long-established history of welcoming outsiders, whether they be Muslims, Poles, Jews or the Irish Catholic influx whose 'troublesome' ways and religious differences stirred up so much anxiety in the early nineteenth century.

Perhaps Bradford's problems are merely the result of de-industrialisation, the death of manufacturing, the blind alley of rampant, unchecked capitalism? Aren't Bradford's problems mirrored in small towns up and down the land, but writ large here on the basis of sheer geographical scale?

And if that is the case, then why hasn't a city the size of Bradford been able to rise above all of that and regenerate like those other great northern cities Liverpool, Manchester, Newcastle, Sheffield and, increasingly, Hull? In the shadow of its big West Yorkshire brother, Leeds, Bradford's inferiority complex is matched only by its small town mentality.

***

I AM a Bradfordian, this is my city.

Born in 1963, I grew up in Bradford, went to school in Bradford, worked on the local Bradford newspaper, cheered on Bradford's two major sports teams, played rugby, amateur dramatics, drank, danced (badly), the city is in my blood.

My mother and father met at the Gaumont ballroom - later the Odeon cinema - in the late 1950s; my mum going on to work in the legendary department store Busbys on Manningham Lane, first in the underwear department and then behind the record counter. It was there that my brother and me, like so many other Bradfordian youngsters, were taken to see Father Christmas every year, in our case by our maternal grandma - or nana - Dolly.

Dolly had spent her own formative years working at the world famous Listers Mill; my grandad, Leonard, worked there too at one stage. After our trips to town, Dolly would occasionally buy us a miniature Hovis loaf each from the bakers next to the hairdressers on the way back to her house up Haworth Road. Eeh, it were grand.

My dad's side of the family were Bradford born and bred too. In fact, a direct line of Bradford-based Hannans can be traced to the 1871 census, when Irish immigrant Joseph Hannan and Yorkshire-born wife Ann are listed as residing at 22 Wellington Street, in a row of back-to-back terraced houses immediately behind Bradford Cathedral. According to the document, at that stage, Joseph, a coachman - later a picture hawker - and Ann, a worsted weaver, shared their tiny dwelling with a couple of young female boarders, Mary and Catherine, a weaver and bobbin winder respectively.

Ten years on and Mary and Catherine have been

replaced by Ellen, a worsted spinner, and seven (!) Hannan children. The eldest, rather mysteriously given her earlier absence, is thirteen-year-old Mary, already employed as a spinner herself. Next is eleven-year-old scholar Sarah Ann, followed by five boys: Joseph, ten; five-year-old twins Luke and John; two-year-old Thomas and Willie, four months.

The 1891 census for the same address, meanwhile, reveals that Athlone-born Joseph and Ann now share their home with 22-year-old daughter Sarah Ann - Mary having moved on presumably - 19-year-old Joseph, 14-year-old John, 12-year-old Thomas and ten-year-old William. Sadly, of twin brother Luke there is no longer any sign. Life was tough.

Although Sarah is now a worsted spinner, her 46-year-old mother Ann is listed as a housekeeper, no longer in the mill. Fast forward another decade and 62-year-old Joseph is a widower, with only John, Thomas and Willie left for company. By putting down roots in Wellington Street in the late 1860s, Joseph could not have positioned we Hannans more centrally to Bradford's story. It was here or hereabouts that the city first took shape.

Along with the rest of the row, the Hannans' home on Wellington Street is now long gone, replaced by scruffy 1960s-style flats in need of renovation themselves. Gone too is an entire community, obliterated by the modern-day ring road that cuts through a once-lively area once known as Wapping.

The ghosts, however, remain. The roofline of the last house along the Wellington Street terrace can still be seen on the once-adjoining gable of the school at the end of the row, in Victorian times a workhouse. The Hannans and their neighbours may no longer be of this earth, but they certainly left their mark, albeit one that is fading year on year.

My attachment to Bradford, then, runs deep. But you also couldn't help noticing, growing up, that the dirty old town you knew and loved, in whose book and record shops and markets you spent so much time rummaging, had a bad reputation. The grown-ups were always moaning and if you went on holiday and told folk with funny accents where you came from, a wisecrack about 'being the wrong colour' or 'needing a holiday, living there' was seldom far behind.

Bradford had an image problem. It still does.

***

IN his 1994 travelogue, *Notes From A Small Island*, American writer Bill Bryson observed that: 'Bradford's role in life is to make every place else in the world look better by comparison, and it does this very well. Nowhere on my trip would I see a city more palpably forlorn. Bradford seemed steeped in a perilous and irreversible decline. What is one to do in Bradford with three hours to kill?'

Ouch. Well, one idea might have been to visit the public library and leaf through all the national newspaper headlines it has sparked down the years.

Seldom, if ever, is the city cast in a good light. Most famously or infamously, Bradford was home to Peter Sutcliffe, the Yorkshire Ripper, who murdered thirteen women and attacked seven others during his 1970s killing spree, now serving twenty life sentences in Broadmoor. Bradford also struggles to forget kidnapper and murderer Donald Neilson, aka the Black Panther, while in 2005 the city hit the headlines for the murder of Police Constable Sharon Beshenivsky and the twisted delusions of the self-styled 'Crossbow Cannibal'.

Similarly, the sacking of outspoken headmaster Ray Honeyford provoked a media storm in 1984, when he argued that multiculturalism was having a damaging effect in local schools. When the storm over Salman Rushdie's book, *The*

Slouching towards Blubberhouses

Satanic Verses, broke in 1989, the pictures on every news bulletin were of angry Muslims burning books and an effigy of Rushdie outside Bradford magistrates court. The Bradford City fire at Valley Parade on 11 May 1985 claimed 56 people, men, women and children, while 265 more were injured.

Who, then, could blame anyone for joining the dots and coming to the conclusion that Bradford must be an absolute terrible place in which to live, a verdict its residents have taken as their own. While Bradford's paper, the *Telegraph and Argus*, sounds notes of defiance, it's in the face of almost overwhelming antipathy and ridicule. In the pubs, clubs, offices, factories and shops that remain, the outlook is bleak.

Interesting to reflect, then, that things were ever thus - if not worse. Living conditions were hellish even at the city's height of influence. George Weerth, a German journalist writing about industrial Bradford in 1846, said that: 'Every other factory town in England is a paradise in comparison to this hole. In Manchester the air lies like lead upon you; in Birmingham it is just as if you were sitting with your nose in a stove pipe; in Leeds you have to cough with the dust and the stink as if you had swallowed a pound of cayenne pepper in one go - but you can put up with all that. In Bradford, however, you think you have been lodged with the devil incarnate. If anyone wants to feel how a poor sinner is tormented in Purgatory, let him travel to Bradford.'

***

FOR all the deprivations of its working class, Bradford was a boomtown of the Industrial Revolution. It rose to prominence in the 19th century as the 'wool capital of the world', the echoes of which resound in what's left of the city's grand Victorian architecture. But Bradford's story begins way before that, in Saxon times. The name being a derivation of 'broad ford', the stream crossing that would be known as Bradford Beck. It flowed past the present Bradford Cathedral at the foot of Church Bank, landing pad of my Irish ancestors.

Inhabited by the time of the Norman Conquest, it had its first brush with destruction in 1070, the result of an uprising against William and his troops. Recovery, though, was swift. A rebuilt Bradford is listed in the Domesday Book as 'Bradeford', by the middle ages its boundaries widened to take in what are now Ivegate, Westgate and Kirkgate.

Coming centuries saw more growth before another dip in fortunes coincided, unsurprisingly, with the Civil War. But this now sizeable town had already begun to make a name for itself in the wool trade and by the late 17th century, with the nation once again calm, it was perfectly placed to take advantage of the manufacturing revolution ahead.

In large part this was down to the development of a turnpike road and, later, a new canal that, from 1774, gave access to sea routes and colonial trade via Leeds, Manchester and Liverpool. But, as elsewhere across the North of England, it was with the turn of the 19th century that Bradford really began to muscle its way onto the world stage. From being a semi-rural market town of some 16,000 people as the 18th century came to a close, and further boosted by ready access to coal, soft water and iron ore, prosperity and industry exploded. Now, wool too began to be imported, in enormous quantities, for use in the manufacture of Bradford's speciality product, worsted cloth.

By 1850, and with the town a municipal borough, the population had risen to an incredible 182,000 - well over 1,000 per cent - as a burgeoning number of textile mills filled with hungry workers from every corner of the British Isles. Soon, the green hills, moors and dales which surrounded the town were buried beneath satanic black smog and the sulphurous billows of some 200 factory chimneys. The natural beauty of the Bradforddale valley, along which Bradford Beck - now deep beneath the city streets - continued its course from the Pennine uplands to the nearby river Aire at Shipley - was lost, apparently to eternity.

So high were the levels of pollution that Bradford had the lowest life expectancy in England - a mere eighteen years of age. Around a third of children born to textile workers died before the age of fifteen. Typhoid and cholera epidemics were the norm. Yet as the city grew in importance so, too, did civic pride. In 1853, flexing their cultural muscles, Bradford's city fathers built the neoclassical St George's Concert Hall, a small-scale imitation of the one being completed in Liverpool. In a sign of things to come, it was soon overtaken in cost and grandeur by a new Town Hall in Leeds.

Bradford's grandest building, its £100,000 Venetian gothic City Hall, opened for business in 1873. In 1867, it had been preceded by an equally gothic Wool Exchange, a blatant declaration of wealth and influence. The beautiful doomed Swan Arcade, workplace of office boy and future author and playwright J.B. Priestley, rose just across the road in 1880.

The plight of the Bradford poor improved too given time, although it was no coincidence that, in 1893, some four years before receiving its charter as a city, Bradford was the place that gave birth to the Independent Labour Party. And a need for progress had been recognised in one quarter some forty years before, when Victorian industrialist Sir Titus Salt relocated five mills to a model village along that Bradforddale valley, laying the foundations of today's World Heritage site.

Victorian Bradford was a place that bustled with popular culture. In sport, Bradford City FC were considered so crucial to the future health of the round ball code that, on being founded in 1903, they were fast-tracked without playing a match into Division Two of the national Football League. Their predecessors, Manningham FC, had already been a founder member of the breakaway Northern Union and the very first champions of rugby league.

Local music halls thrived, as did theatre, which was glamorous enough to attract the greatest actor of his age, Sir Henry Irving, to the Bradford stage. Indeed, it was at the city's Midland Hotel, in 1905, after performing at the Theatre Royal, Bradford, that Sir Henry expired of a heart attack.

Amid the noise and squalour, prosperity and sheer vitality, Bradford's appetite for innovation and toil seemed destined to go on forever. Yet in common with many another great northern town and city, as Empire's grip on world markets loosened in slow and steady decline, by the mid-20th century the future was much less certain.

Into this troubled post-industrial landscape came the city's next great wave of immigrants, this time from South Asia and, in particular, Kashmir and Pakistan.

***

THE majority of new arrivals came in search of work and a better life, both for themselves and their families, much as the Irish had before them during the potato famine of 1846-49.

Back then, the Irish had tended to group in 'quarters', taking comfort from the familiar in an otherwise unfriendly alien environment. Their ethnicity and culture was expressed through religion often, namely Catholicism. Catholic church leaders became important community figures, respected by their congregations, distrusted by the indigenous population.

At the start of the 19th century, Bradford was very much a Protestant town and so the building of self-funded

Slouching towards Blubberhouses

Catholic churches - of which there were several, St Mary's being the first in 1825 - might be viewed as a provocative act. Suspiciousness of the incomers' motives was rife, which their swelling numbers exacerbated. In short, Irish Catholics were seen as a threat to the very fabric of 'decent' English society.

As early as the 1840s, large swathes of inner Bradford had been resettled by Irish migrants, almost always the areas in the worst state of repair. Incomes were low, so rents needed to be low too, families forced to share costs and houseroom with adult lodgers. Over-crowding was commonplace; beds were even sub-let on a shift rota. With clean water scarce and little opportunity for the disposal of household and human waste, disease and deprivation were constants.

Unfortunately, so was crime, with the opportunity to live up to an Irish stereotype of drinking and fighting often taken. The Irish also had a reputation for stupidity, owing in no small part to the fact that many struggled to read, write and sometimes even speak English. They were said to carry disease. The then local paper, the *Bradford Observer*, often portrayed the Irish as sub-human vermin who were an unfair burden on Bradford's fine hard-working families.

Assimilation, therefore, was unlikely and neither side seemed to want it anyway. Today, the passage of time has smoothed matters out to the extent that a Catholic-Protestant divide in Bradford is unimaginable. Yet no one would have foreseen such a situation back then.

On the BBC's Bradford and West Yorkshire website, Katie Binns writes how the mid-years of the 19th century saw: '...almost weekly references in the *Bradford Observer* to assaults on police, common assault, brawling, drunkenness and disorderly behaviour. Newspapers regularly seized upon court cases, reporting with utmost relish any instances of immigrant brogue and naivety. As a consequence "Paddy" became the frequent butt of English humour. The *Bradford Observer* used Irish jokes as space fillers in the 1830s.'

There is no chance of an infinitely more measured *Telegraph and Argus* doing similar in the 21st century. Yet it is certainly not difficult to imagine the thoughts of one Doctor Arnold repeated in a modern context, when he referred to the tremendous influx of Irish labourers: '...tainting the whole population with a worse than barbarian element.' As Katie Binns points out: 'Cultural inferiority was taken as fact. The degradation and squalor in which [the Irish] lived (which undoubtedly contributed to the rates of drunkenness and violence) was completely ignored.'

She concludes: 'In November 1948, the *Bradford Observer* reported a serious riot between English and Irish railway workers at Cleckheaton. An equally ugly disturbance in Manchester Road in August of that same year occurred when a large body of English navvies confronted Irish reapers returning from seasonal work in Lincolnshire. Were these the original race riots?'

***

IN 1851, Bradford had the highest proportion of Irish-born inhabitants - ten per cent - in Yorkshire. By 2001, Bradford's South Asian population was 20.5 per cent, a figure projected to rise to 28 per cent by 2011.

If history is any guide, it perhaps ought not come as any great surprise that similar problems to those experienced in the 19th century trouble the city today. And again we see how the reaction of existing inhabitants - when complicated by issues like economic deprivation, bad housing, substance abuse, poor education and unemployment - can lead directly or indirectly to parallel segregated communities divided by skin colour, cultural difference, suspicion and religious intolerance.

In modern-day Bradford, a brew as noxious as any Victorian mill owner's chimney reached its nadir in the race riots of 1995 and 2001. Yet an example of how Bradfordians of every colour, faith and hue can rub along quite happily is seen every summer at the annual Mela, nowadays held in the redeveloped City Park in front of Bradford City Hall, but prior to that staged in a very 'old Bradford' Peel Park.

The park lies to the north east of the city on land purchased through the raising of public funds. It is named in memory of Sir Robert Peel, father of Britain's modern-day police force and repealer of corn laws. His statue still stands midway along a 400 metre walkway, one of the first such park promenades in England when it was built in 1865. At its end is a viewing platform, Royal Alexandra Terrace, named for the Danish princess who, two years before, had married the Prince of Wales and eventually became Queen Alexandra. After falling into disrepair, the terrace was rebuilt on a smaller scale in 2000.

Give or take the odd domed mosque, a rebuilt Valley Parade football stadium to the left and the spinning arms of Ovenden Moor windfarm on the distant horizon, however, a magnificent panoramic view across the Bradforddale valley has changed hardly a jot since Victorian times. To the right is Bradford Grammar School, first established as the Free Grammar School of Charles II in 1548. Past pupils include David Hockney, Olympic swimmer Adrian Moorhouse and former Labour MP, Secretary of State for Defence and Chancellor of the Exchequer, Denis 'eyebrows' Healey.

Across the way is Lister Park, named after the owner of Manningham Mills, Samuel Cunliffe Lister (1815-1906), a locally-born inventor and industrialist later to assume the title 1st Baron Masham. His mills are also visible, surrounded by the vista's most prominent three church spires: St Paul's Church, erected in 1848; the church at Wilma Road, capable of seating 1,000 people on its opening in 1879; and the church of St Luke, built in 1881. Other religious protusions include the spire of St Barnabas Church in Heaton (1864) and the distinctive dome of the Garden of the Jamia Masjid Hanfia mosque. Designed in Oxfordshire but built and funded by locals, it opened in 1995. A little note on the viewing platform says that such domes are more usually designed for hot countries as they help to keep the inside of the building cool.

The most eye-catching sight of all, though, is that of Lister's Mill Chimney, standing 255 feet tall, hanging on obstinately despite the death of the industry that put it there.

Competition from cheap imports and poor financial exchange rates combined to damage Bradford's textile and manufacturing base irrevocably. Lister himself did not live to see his company provide one thousand yards of velvet for the coronation of King George V; still less the switch from steam to electricity in 1934 which allowed his mill to produce 1,330 miles of parachute silk and fifty miles of khaki battledress for the Second World War effort; or even the sale of curtains to President Gerald Ford's White House in 1976. But by that latter date a period of rationalisation was already in place and the Lister's Mill complex was eventually abandoned in 1992.

By which time Bradford Mela - 'Mela' meaning 'to meet' in Sanskrit - had been around for four years. To begin with a small scale affair held on playing fields above Bradford University, it still attracted 10,000 visitors. And as the event grew in stature, so bigger venues were required. First Lister Park, then Peel Park and now City Park, its present home.

To visit Bradford Mela is to be plunged into an ocean of colour and fun, where faces of every background mingle, and stalls selling burgers and basmati rice stand next to Asian sweet shops, coffee bars and Italian ice cream vans.

In Peel Park, the Mela was a place where bejewelled statues of elephants sat next to worthies in stone, like Robert Peel himself. Bombay Stores jostled for position with a rough and ready fairground ... candyfloss ... shooting galleries ... win cash or prizes. International flags flutter in the breeze, rock meets bhangra, a partnership of east and west. Parents push children in buggies. Families spread blankets on the ground, with a picnic maybe or just watching the bands warming up for evening concerts. Everyone smiling.

And Peel Park had seen its like before. The first gala there was held in 1853, a way of raising funds to secure the earlier purchase of that land for public use. Over three days in June, it boasted six bands, archery displays, ballooning and various booths in which such technological delights as camera obscura, telescopes and microscopes were displayed.

Compared to today, its attractions were rather sedate and informed by the belief that Victoria's masses ought to be elevated rather than entertained. As the years passed, its treats reflected social change and technological advances. With the advent of steam power, exciting rides came in and visiting numbers rocketed. Times changed then just as they do now, as the visionary now watching over Lister Park predicted.

A long-time benefactor of the fine arts, upon the opening of Cartwright Memorial Hall there in 1904, Joseph Lister, the very model of a Victorian philanthropist, told the gathering present that he saw Cartwright Hall as '...the place where the Asiatic of the future might come in search of the inventor of the power loom. I have a very strong impression that the east will overcome the west in coming years, and that instead of our clothing the east, they will want to clothe us,' he concluded.

***

RACE, then, is just an excuse. The rot truly set in for Bradford during the 1950s and '60s, when high-profile Yorkshire-born architect and Freemason John Poulson came to the fore, a man whose many and varied contacts put him at the heart of the so-called urban renewal of many a British city.

Yet in some ways, the times were the culprit. This was an era when provisions for continuous self-regulating flows of traffic were thought more important than practical respect for the past and what such conservation might mean for the future. Self-conscious 'modernity' led the agenda.

A large part of central Bradford was redesigned at the behest of one Stanley Wardley, city engineer and surveyor for Bradford since 1946. Wardley, for example, was at least partly responsible for Forster House, a vast and faceless Poulson-designed tower block that was part of a major reconstruction of Forster Square, site of today's thus far ill-fated Broadway shopping centre project, 'underway' since 2004. It involved the creation of a new road, Petergate, a link with Leeds Road. The emphasis was on cars rather than pedestrians; green space reduced to a walled enclave in the middle of a traffic roundabout that could only be reached by increasingly smelly, dingy underground walkways.

The most keenly felt example of civic vandalism came with the destruction of Swan Arcade, a four-storey Victorian shopping centre/office block, Italianate in design, that stood opposite the Wool Exchange. Named after the White Swan Inn, which had stood previously on the site, you entered via six grand entrances complete with images of graceful swans incorporated into their iron and stonework.

Inside, four linked arcades stood beneath wrought

iron glazed roofs, with angled mirrors along the sides of the avenues. It was a highly popular and attractive city centre amenity in its heyday.

In truth, though, Swan Arcade's death warrant was signed in 1954, when the Arndale Property Trust, a company that specialised in the development of city centre shopping sites, bought the building for around a quarter of a million quid. The developers saw the site as an opportunity to get in on what was already described as Bradford's 'Broadway development'. Work had begun on the adjoining Bank Street and Broadway itself which, it was claimed, was bound to have an improving effect. Accordingly, in October 1960, the Trust announced that the arcade would have to go.

Two years later, on its final day, only two companies were left in business - one a general outfitters, whose staff moved racks of suits and coats to a branch in Leeds, often described as 'the city of arcades'. Its impressive gates were sold to a wealthy businessman. In 1964, eight-storey Arndale House opened for business, 'structurally, the most advanced building in the UK,' according to one of its architects.

One former Swan Arcade employee was J.B. Priestley who, as an office boy, had worked in a wool office there prior to World War One. Memories of it affected him profoundly and, despite having long since moved from the city, his was one of the loudest voices raised against its demolition.

Perhaps shockingly to modern sensibilities, not many contemporary Bradfordians agreed. Few raised much of a fuss when news of the demolition came through, the seeds of future apathy sown. Priestley though railed against the loss, and four years before its demise, incurred the wrath of many, including the *Telegraph and Argus*, when he made the then-infamous BBC documentary *Lost City*.

Ostensibly the sentimental journey of 'a grunting,

saurian-eyed fatty trying to be nostalgic' - as Priestley himself put it in a 1958 edition of the *Radio Times* - the programme painted a grim and grey portrait of a city that the writer already saw as being in decline, beyond hope even. From the moment his steam train puffs into a station now also long gone with Priestley puffing obligingly on his ever-present pipe, to the final scenes in a disused theatre, via endless shots of soot-blackened terraced streets and belching mill chimneys, the mood of gloom is inescapable.

Similarly prescient was architectural writer James Lees-Milne in 1964. 'There are people today amassing stupendous fortunes by systematically destroying our historic centres,' he said, referencing similar outrages elsewhere. The fate of Swan Arcade was but one example; the public of Bradford had been sold a dream in which their tatty old buildings were to be replaced by concrete visions of a shiny utilitarian future. A dream in which health, vitality and prosperity would be won by high-speed fly-overs and inner-city ring roads.

So imagine the surprise of ordinary Bradfordians when, in 1972, a Metropolitan Police investigation led to the arrest and prosection of John Poulson. The case revealed how much of this so-called 'regenerative' planning had been driven by personal greed and institutionalised corruption, complete with a money trail that went right to the top.

As a result, Poulson and numerous associates such as Newcastle's so-called 'Mouth of the Tyne' T Dan Smith and Scottish civil servant George Pottinger, were found guilty of fraud in connection with the awarding of building projects. Poulson was jailed for five years, later increased to seven. The judge called him 'an incalculably evil man'. A trio of MPs, including then-Home Secretary Reginald Maudling, were implicated. Maudling was forced to resign.

Poulson, like T Dan Smith, died in 1993, but his legacy

survives in a weeping scab at the heart of a city that deserves better; the perfect symbol for Bradford's struggle with where it has been, never mind where it might be going next.

***

IT's not all doom and gloom. Issues perceived as having held Bradford back increasingly play a role in reviving the city as a tourism hot spot. As National Media Museum director Colin Philpott has put it: 'Being in Bradford isn't a problem, it is an opportunity. We've proven that a national institution here can be a success.'

It's a Saturday morning in June, 2013. The city centre should be heaving with shoppers, but the reality is otherwise. Boarded-up furniture 'superstores', pound shops, ghastly amusement arcades ... there are, however, signs of recovery. It is a place trying to pick itself up. The hole in Forster Square is still there with not much, if anything, going on. But City Park is a success story in a place that needs those more than most.

The week-long Bradford Festival is coming to an end and there's a Curry Festival next weekend. Yet there is no doubt about the jewel in the cultural crown. Posters for the National Media Museum abound. Less positively, this trip coincides with news that, along with Manchester's Science Museum and the Railway Museum in York, the NMM is under threat of closure owing to Government funding cuts. No less a figure than Hollywood director Martin Scorsese has waded into the fray.

'In January of 1987, I gave three *Guardian* lectures, one of which took place at the National Media Museum,' he begins in an open letter echoing the support of John Hurt, David Hockney, Michael Palin, Terry Jones and a petition bearing 42,000 signatures. 'The lecture became an introduction of sorts, making me a witness to all the educational programmes and encouragement the Museum offered to the media interested public. At this infancy stage - just four years after its initial opening - the Museum housed the biggest cinema screen in Britain, possessed the first IMAX theatre in Europe, announced the Bradford Fellowship to initiate a collaboration between artists and collectors, and introduced an interactive television gallery allowing visitors hands-on instruction for camera, sound and lighting. To say the Museum was off to a running start would be an incredible understatement.

'Nearly two years ago, the world's first colour moving picture was discovered. This find, which showed images by Edward Raymond Turner, is both highly unusual and remarkable. When I heard the National Media Museum would be showing the footage, I couldn't have imagined a better venue to showcase such an important piece of cultural record. It would remind the world of the rich history living within the Museum's walls. It would confirm the Museum's magnitude. And most certainly, it would re-establish the appreciation of film as it unfortunately becomes neglected.

'Since my lecture, I have remained a dedicated supporter of the National Media Museum as it continues to inspire and preserve the future and past of film-making. Without the Museum, a mass of people will never understand the influence, power, and inspiration that media has occupied in society and in lives. I ask you to please consider the requests of the National Media Museum's supporters. It is my hope that you sense our urgency in keeping the literacy of media alive and well in Bradford.'

The Culture, Media and Sport Select Committee are scheduled to meet in London in the first week of July and reach their decision. London, incidentally, being the location of a fourth such Science Museum belonging to owners SMG.

Slouching towards Blubberhouses

That one, it doubtless goes without saying, is not in danger. Today is also the venue's 30th birthday party and a reminder that Bradford is the world's first UNESCO City of Film. Not Cannes, Venice, Mumbai or Los Angeles. Bradford. There will be cake and the delivery of the petition.

A statue of J.B. Priestley stands guard outside, coat flapping in the wind. It blows like this even when there is no wind, obviously, a visual fart joke much seized upon by schoolboys overgrown or otherwise. Behind us is Wardley House, built in 1966 with student accommodation above and the Bradford Ice Arena - in those days 'Silver Blades' - below. Across the way, the domed Alhambra Theatre sits alongside the doomed former Odeon cinema, Art Deco meeting place of my mum and dad, now virtually derelict and far removed from the days when the Beatles, Buddy Holly and the Rolling Stones played there. Directly in front is the police station - Bradford Bridewell - and to the left Bradford Library, over the road from brutalist council offices Jacob's Well. To which we always used to reply: 'I didn't know he'd been poorly.'

It's here, beneath an overhanging part of the library, that a more adventurous wanderer might spot a blue plaque: 'Jimmy - 1959-2010,' it reads. 'Toothless Smiler and Rough Sleeper. Lived in this doorway 2005-2008. Please remember the homeless people of Bradford. Simononthestreets.co.uk'

The museum itself has a glass frontage and, as befits a birthday party, there are people with yellow balloons. Just inside are the box office and a gift shop selling books about photography, film and television - in tune with the museum's original mouthful of a name. There's also a café and the Pictureville cinema alongside. Along with balloons, there are also lots of yellow T-shirts worn by people helping out. These are somewhat disconcerting, invoking a feeling that it is you who is being watched. They nearly outnumber the visitors.

I try to get into the Cubby Broccoli cinema on the first floor but it's shut. Three folk in yellow watch me try the door.

On the second floor, Bollywood Icons celebrates one hundred years of Indian cinema and there is a display by the wonderful Ireland-born photographer Tom Wood. In the Bollywood exhibition, another T-shirt walks around in circles, like a bear in a zoo. Bedecked with film posters, it is a blaze of colour, but no one is inside. A documentary projected onto a wall explains the city's symbiotic relationship with Indian cinema as described by Asian elders in flat caps and tank tops.

Floor three is television. To the right: *Experience TV*, about the business of telly. There is advertising - did you know that on average we watch fifteen minutes' worth of ads a day, four days of adverts a year and three years' worth of ads in an average lifetime? 'Persil washes whiter.' 'In't milk brilliant?' 'You know when you've had sprouts.' There are timelines of iconic moments and displays about 'quality, taste and decency' regulations, with clips of *Love Thy Neighbour* and Spike Milligan's *Curry and Chips*. Interactivity, of course. Schedule your own TV programmes in *TV Heaven*, a nostalgia section, wherein a pensioner dressed as Elvis wanders past. Children's TV artefacts from *Doctor Who*, *Play School*, *Rainbow* and *Thunderbirds*. 'Explore over 1,000 programmes over the last sixty years of TV. Choose a programme, ask for it at the counter and enter the booth...'

The giant IMAX theatre is on the ground floor, next to a picnic area. Today it is showing *To Fly* - the first film ever to be shown here in 1983. There are only sixteen of us in for the 12.15pm performance. I don't know about my fellow audience members but I'm expecting it look rather dated. Yet it really doesn't, a thirty-year gap not having made it any less dizzying or thrilling. The vast screen still packs a pretty mean wow factor and *To Fly* has a pleasing philosophical bent, with its emphasis on humankind's shift in perspective from the horizontal to the vertical, an encouragment not to take the world as we think we know it for granted. From time to time, look at things from a different angle. From hot air balloons, to space flight, via views of New York City, Death Valley and a spectacular air show, it has a certain cute humour too.

Having left the auditorium, there are seats on every other upper level. And through that glass frontage is a vision of what a fantastic city of the future Bradford really could be.

'Nice town hall here, isn't it?' says one resting OAP.

'Is *that* what it is?' says his mate, alongside.

Floor five has a games lounge, but if you've got kids in tow then the level below is a must-visit. There's not a child on earth who wouldn't enjoy the *Magic Factory*. Special effects ... optical illusions ... all done up like Willy Wonka's chocolate factory. Why not place a hand in the centre of a mirror and shake hands with yourself? For Bradford, an apt metaphor.

***

IT could have been worse. According to an October 2013 edition of *The Guardian*, London has beaten Bradford and Chipping Norton to number one spot in *Crap Towns Returns*.

Good news for previous winner Hull, though, which drops out of the top fifty having held the dubious honour for almost a decade. 'The original *Crap Towns* was a publishing sensation in 2003, born of a moaning late-night conversation between [co-founder and editor] Sam Jordison and Dan Kieran, co-editor of the list and deputy editor of *The Idler*,' the paper reports, *The Idler* having nothing whatsoever to do with Bradford's world famous Idle Working Mens Club.

York - sandwiched by Southampton and, er, Gibraltar - came fifth.

11. The Born Identity

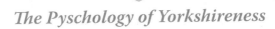

The Pyschology of Yorkshireness

SO Yorkshire's split personality: individually self-deprecating, yet monumentally cocky as a county. Identity crisis central.

Is there actually such a thing as a communal ego? Or, in super-sized Yorkshire, is boastfulness just about preserving collective self-esteem; safety in numbers? What is going on in our heads? We could do with some professional help and someone who might point us in the right direction is Eric Wright, consultant forensic and criminal psychologist.

It's a nondescript Tuesday afternoon in September and we meet, suitably enough, in the Yorkshire Rose pub in Guiseley, a small town north west of Leeds, by the A65 on its way into the city centre. It's best known as the home of Harry Ramsden's chandeliered chippy, which began as a wooden shed next to a tram stop and became the world's biggest fish and chip shop, serving a million people a year.

Today, Harry Ramsden's is a chain whose franchises are more likely to be found in airport departure lounges than suburban traffic roundabouts. Its landmark Guiseley premises closed in December 2011, bought out and rebranded as the Wetherby Whaler in 2012. The old Harry Ramsden's clock does still take pride of place on the roof, mind.

Eric and I arrive at the Yorkshire Rose simultaneously, him on coffee and me tonic water; it's too early for anything stronger, on a Tuesday at least. He gives his credentials. After completing a psychology degree at Leeds University in the 1970s, he got a job as an assistant psychologist at Broadmoor, the high security psychiatric hospital in Berkshire. That won him a place on a two-year MSc course in clinical psychology, back in Leeds. After which, he became a general clinical psychologist with the Bradford Health Authority, a job that took him to Menston's then notorious 'mental hospital', just up the road from this pub. Encouragingly or incongruously, depending on how you look at it, the site of an institution that opened as the West Riding Pauper Lunatic Asylum in 1888 is now put to more pleasant use as a modern housing estate.

After a while 'drifting' career-wise, Eric began to get interested in drug and alcohol-related problems. 'At that time in Bradford,' he says, stirring memory and coffee, 'the drug and alcohol service was at the forensic unit. The powers-that-be saw anyone with a drug or alcohol issue as basically criminal, hence the funding for the service being there. It's totally different these days; the two are quite separate. But that's how I began to take an interest in the criminal side. A lot of my clients with drug and alcohol problems were falling foul of the law so, before I knew it, I was getting loads of requests from solicitors to do court reports.'

In 1992, Eric left the employ of the NHS and began to 'do his own thing' with forensics to the fore, as has been the case ever since. Here is someone who not only knows his own mind, but can get to grips with the minds of others; ideally placed, then, to explain the psychology of Yorkshireness?

'Probably not. For one thing, I was born in Lancashire. But I'll give it a go.'

First off, the Yorkshire tendency toward exaggeration - what underpins it? Why are people so fiercely proud of their county, here, to an extent not much seen anywhere else? What is so specific about Yorkshire? Or is such behaviour just an extension of a more general human condition?

'There are geographical, economic and other reasons I'm sure, but let's look at it from a purely psychological point of view,' he offers. 'I was a bit of a rebel at university and rejected a lot of the traditional theories. You had Sigmund Freud on the one hand or B.F. Skinner on the other. It was all about inner processes, consciousness and superego, that was the Freudian stance. The behaviourists put everything down to operant conditions, nothing to do with the mind at all. I rejected both - I wasn't the only one - and found this thing called personal construct theory.'

So what's that then?

'Personal construct theory is a complete rejection of inner consciousness and Pavlovian dogs salivating in cages. It sees human beings as making choices, basically. All we do is make choices - sometimes good, sometimes bad. We tend not to live in the past. We live in the present and anticipate the future. Anyway, these choices we call them constructs. Everyone has a set of core constructs that define him or her as a person. Maybe, for some people, Yorkshireness or whatever we want to call it, is a core construct.'

Can we unpack that idea a little further?

'Well, the scientist who came up with the theory was George Kelly, an American. He began as an engineer, then somehow got into psychology and produced his book *The Psychology of Personal Constructs*, a two-volume explanation published in 1955. It's heavy going. The first three chapters explain the theory, really, the rest look at applications of it, particularly through psychotherapy. But his entire theory can be explained in one sentence: "A person's processes are psychologically channelised by the way in which he anticipates events." That's what we call the core corollary of personal construct theory. Interesting that he uses the word "he", but if you can pick that apart, you're some way towards understanding the theory.'

So, if I understand correctly, our core constructs are essentially defensive? That would certainly fit with regard to the notion of Yorkshireness.

'A construct could be a catch-all that puts a barrier between you and other people so, yes, but it also gives you a strong sense of self. It serves two purposes there, doesn't it?'

And this notion of self, why as human beings do we need that?

'According to Kelly, we couldn't continue without it. We couldn't make sense of ourselves, we couldn't make sense of the people around us, unless we had these core constructs that we treasure and prize. They are developed from day one. Kelly perceives people as being born, going along a groove and then dropping off at the end. In some ways it's quite a lonely theory. You can tell he was an engineer because, if you read the theory, a lot of it is couched in mathematical terms. It's very rational.'

George Kelly was born in Kansas, but it turns out that his chief UK cheerleader was a, guess what, Yorkshireman.

'When I did my year at High Royds,' Eric continues, 'there was a psychologist from Doncaster who died about twenty years ago, Don Bannister, the only psychologist who really picked up on Kelly and popularised him in this country. Don had quite a few disciples and I was one, although I didn't let it dominate my life. A couple have taken up the cause and are still pushing his theory as the best way to understand the sort of things you are interested in.'

So okay, let's buy into it. How might we practically work out whether Yorkshireness is indeed one of a person's core constructs?

'The thing about constructs is that they are bi-polar. The classic way of working one out is to write down a list of the people closest to you on pieces of paper. Obviously, you'd include mother, father, regardless of whether they are deceased or not, sister and brother if you've got any, girlfriend, wife, spouse, son, daughter ... all of those people you'd have to put down. But then, up to a limit of around fifteen or twenty people, you're allowed to include anyone you want who is important to you. This is called repertory grid technique. Again, it's very mathematical, but a good way of understanding yourself, I think.

'I used to encourage people to include figures from history or authors or musicians they've admired. You can put who you want ... Richard III, Geoff Boycott ... whoever. Then I'd shuffle the pack, plonk one down and ask you to talk about that person. I'd then make a note of the sorts of words you use to describe them. Before too long, when you look at this list of words and start to categorise them, you'd come up with list of about ten constructs you have used to describe the people in your world. So you might say, "Uncle Frank, oh, he's dead mean him..." so I'd write "mean". Then I'd ask you the opposite of mean ... you'd say "generous" and we've got ourselves a construct. You might say an ex-girlfriend. I'd write down the words you use to describe her and we'd work out your core constructs on a graph. You can put it through a computer these days, but I used to do them by hand. A lot of people find it useful in therapy because it does give you an idea of how you see the world and who is important to you.'

Slouching towards Blubberhouses

So how does that actually relate to your own mindset?

'Well, you get little clusters of people in certain parts of the grid. People are very surprised by that. You might find your Uncle Frank is very close to your ex-girlfriend. Or you might find that your mother and father are at opposite ends of the thing. Just to talk about that was enough, sometimes, in the therapy I used to do. Just to get people to see how they view the world, their influences and so on. You could do a Yorkshire grid, that would be interesting. Write those famous names down, good and bad - you could have Peter Sutcliffe for instance - plus all the people you've known who you associate with being strong Yorkshire people, and see if there are similarities. If the core construct Yorkshireness exists, there would be. But if it is a core construct then it would have to have an opposite.'

Lancashireness?

'Ha ha! That would be great, although I'd see those two as not a million miles apart [Do I begin to detect that Eric doubts Yorkshireness as a genuine core construct?]. I would see that as the superordinate construct "northern". It gets really complicated. "Being a northerner" as a big solid construct which can then be split down into Yorkshire, Cumbria ... I don't know... What about "Britishness", which is becoming a very nebulous construct? Whereas it used to be quite a core one for many, particularly going back into history. But now, with Scotland maybe about to go independent, a Welsh parliament and so on, I'm not too sure it any longer is. You don't really have Englishness as a construct, do you? Although you do have Scottishness.'

Yes, and such people are often viewed as crackpots or extremists.

'Core constructs do tie you down,' he says. 'You are stuck with them whether you like it or not.'

And yet, as you have just suggested, the very concept of Englishness, Britishness, Yorkshireness and so on is fluid.

'A lot of the work I do now is in the Bradford area; several of my clients are Asian solicitors. Many are second, third, fourth generation Bradfordians, with parents who came over for the textile industry. I find it fascinating to see the extent to which they identify with Yorkshire. A lot of people seem to see themselves as British first. Then Asian or the country of their background, and then Yorkshire, which is quite low down the list as a core construct. Even though they were born here, raised, here, went to school here, speak with Yorkshire accents, I tend not to find that it's the main part of their identity. It's an important part, but it's not the main part. So I'm not sure how you explain all that.'

Would it be fair, too, to suggest the generational thing as a factor? Identifying strongly with Yorkshire does seem to matter more to older members of the community. Or maybe that's just the natural rebellion of youth, kicking against parents to whom who'll you bring your dirty washing later?

'Perhaps, or maybe it is changing. Yorkshireness is obviously going to be a dynamic thing anyway, isn't it? I sense it is changing, actually, becoming less of a core construct with the younger generation.'

But as you said at the start, no one can really escape the influence of their surroundings and background, can they? Human beings are just specks in an uncaring universe, and maybe 'specks' is an exaggeration. If we didn't kid ourselves that we are at the heart of the narrative, well...

'Yes, you've got to make sense of it all and we all do it in our own way, whether we like it or not. We are in our own little bubble. That doesn't mean to say we can't interact, just that we have to acknowledge other people's constructs, share our own with them and somehow make it all work.'

Slouching towards Blubberhouses

Born in red rose Southport, Eric knows of what he speaks. His wife, who died three years ago, was a Yorkshire lass. His current partner is from London.

'She lives in Doncaster and has found it quite hard to be accepted. She is from a working class background but has a southern accent and struggles quite a bit, right in the heart of South Yorkshire. She has been to college there, works there, and says how she sometimes thinks she's being ostracised. People don't bother asking about where she was brought up, she's got a southern accent so she's seen as posh.'

What about you? As a Lancastrian, did you have any preconceived ideas of what Yorkshire folk would be like before you arrived in the county? 'No, not really, other than what my dad instilled in me. He'd say: "There's only one good thing to come out of Yorkshire ... the road to Lancashire." I'd get that as a kid. It was engrained into you. So to a certain extent, your constructs - I don't like the word inherited - you must be given a set to start with and then it's about whether they work for you. That particular one didn't for me. My wife, kids and a lot of my friends are from Yorkshire.'

It's almost time to give this brain a rest, but not before asking how those other two psychological theorists might have sought to explain Yorkshireness if given the chance.

'I've no idea - I didn't understand them! No, there must be a Freudian perception of it; I presume it would go back to wish fulfillment and having your ego influenced by your parents, in a positive way, maybe. Skinner would no doubt say it's all been brought about by reward and punishment as a child. For example, you might be rewarded for certain behaviours that fit the Yorkshire stereotype and go unrewarded for those that don't. Environmental engineering.'

And finally, as a Yorkshireman, I must ask about the practical application of construct theory. What does it hope to achieve, exactly? Might it be possible, for instance, to cure someone of Yorkshireness?

'That's a very interesting question for me, because I used to apply this theory as a therapist,' Eric says. 'Someone was referred to you with a problem and you had to try and help them to solve it. I trained at the tail end of a period when homosexuality was seen as a disease, for example. There were people writing papers on curing it. If it is a core construct, once it's there, it's there and anyway you'd only want to change it if it was causing a problem for the person. If you wanted to marry someone from a different faith for example, and that was clashing with your idea of how people should be, you'd look at ways of breaking it down, trying to broaden it, not have it so rigid. It's about choice. But if you are making choices that cause problems, explore other ways around it.'

***

THERE's a great little pub in Bradford, The Fighting Cock, up Preston Street, off Thornton Road, a hearty stroll from the city centre and stopping-off point before and after the match by many a follower of Bradford City Football Club.

It's where I find myself sharing a pint and some pork scratchings with Mick Martin, playwright of these parts, who grew up a handful of streets away from me up the hill in Wibsey, though we didn't know each other back then. This despite being regulars at the Gaping Goose, a pub that used to boast - maybe still does - the smallest bar in Great Britain.

'Yorkshire writers have definitely been very aware of themselves as Yorkshire people, haven't they, writing with a Yorkshire voice, in the Yorkshire idiom,' Mick says, in a spit and sawdust saloon. 'We are quite taciturn really, but can also be quite expressive and emotional.'

261

Slouching towards Blubberhouses

As the writer of such stage hits as *Broken Time*, a story of the rugby league-union split of 1895, and *Once Upon A Time in Wigan*, '...about the misfit community that built up around northern soul clubs - they came from all over', Mick is well placed to assess the extent to which history plays a part in the forging of communal identity. 'The mainstream work I've done is all about exploring the individual,' he says, 'trying to find his own identity or explore the boundaries of what's been set for him and how to push beyond that.'

Given our respective backgrounds, I appreciate only too well how unlikely, as a kid and teenager growing up in West Yorkshire during the 1970s and '80s, the idea of actually becoming a writer - and getting paid for the privilege - was.

'Yes, an absolute pipe dream," Mick says, 'and "not for you". Your aspirations alter as you get a bit older, though, and things come within reach. I left Bradford because I thought if I was going to have an interesting life I had to go to London. I had two or three years there, when I did all sorts of work. But all I was ever going to be in London without an education and university behind me was anything I could have already been up here. Blue collar. And when I decided I wanted to work in theatre, I looked at a list of places and on seeing Bretton Hall, near Wakefield, didn't look at any other. I homed in on it like a pigeon as it was so close to Bradford. The moment I got off the train I had a sense of belonging.'

Mick discovered Bretton Hall had a long tradition of finding '...creative misfits like me', Kay Mellor and John Godber among them, though about ten years before. 'This was 1985, the lads who became The *League of Gentlemen* were right after me. Reece [Shearsmith] is from Hull, Jeremy Dyson is from Leeds, but he didn't go to Bretton Hall.

'Without question, there was a real sense in that college of generating people who would create work about their North of England. A need to express that and give it voice was absolutely running through the place. Bretton Hall encouraged you if you were arty, but there was another side that was very aware of the cultural surroundings. Northern working class drama, educational drama and community drama were absolutely at the heart of it. If you watch John Godber's work you can very easily see that.'

Lack of money dictating a sparse style of staging ... very few cast members ... not much scenery ... imaginative use of space..?

'Yes, and it was also about telling stories that had not been properly mined. Godber's play about four Wakefield nightclub bouncers - a little stroke of genius that took you into a raft of working class experience through what people get up to on a Friday night. The *League of Gentlemen* would tell you they don't much care for Godber and Jim Cartwright and all of that, but actually they have a very northern feel about them too, whether they like it or not.'

Mick Martin's first hit play was produced in 1991 and it toured with a theatre group. *The Life and Times of Young Bob Scallion* was set in Bradford and 'a sort of a riff on a Charles Dickens novel set in the 1980s. I did well with it. Lots of work in television followed, but they didn't really want to know any Yorkshire stuff at all...'

A case, perhaps, of supposed Yorkshireness being projected onto its inhabitants by people outside?

'Well, probably, but in the 1950s, when people from London or wherever arrived and saw the mills, the smoking chimneys, the terraced houses ... of course they are actually photogenic places, especially when set against hills. Add to that the cultural heritage of two or three hundred years of industrialisation ... it must have been so strikingly powerful.

'People like Lindsay Anderson who made *This Sporting*

Slouching towards Blubberhouses

Life, which depicted rugby league as a brutal hard game with no joy in it whatsoever when, actually, if you're from up here, you know it's not that grim and it's not that hard,' he laughs. 'A lot of kitchen sink cinema was based up here and whenever anyone from the south tries to do a northern accent it's still "eeh bah gum".'

And in that way, Yorkshire has come to represent the whole North of England. Another reason, perhaps, why the place gets on Lancastrian nerves.

'The thing about the Yorkshireness as well is that a certain bluntness creates characters who will get into conflict situations. If you think about it, terribly terribly nice chaps are treated terribly terribly nicely. But your Yorkshire git isn't. That's what it looks like. Kitchen sink, they picked up on the anger and taciturnity ... *Saturday Night, Sunday Morning* ... emotional repression. Angry glowering figures. I wonder to what degree a lot of that isn't projected and then lived up to, and I wonder if, by the 1980s, when we were growing up, it wasn't already a cliché that we all signed up to and the thing began to eat itself.'

Is Yorkshire drama in a healthy state?

'Yes, I'd say it was actually. There's loads of it and lots of interesting stuff. The arts world is fighting because of the cuts... the cuts... the cuts... but there is a vibrant theatre world out there. The big issue, as elsewhere, is that the average age of the audience is about 55. Our generation is already into middle age and travelling. What will be the new sense of Yorkshire identity and how will it find expression on stage?

'We are entering another era and good thing too. Yorkshireness is going to have open its doors and accommodate those who do not fit the classic image.'

***

264

'THE Power of Positive Thinking.' It's the slogan of Mosaic Yorkshire, one branch of a national organisation founded by HRH Prince Charles which, since originating in Bradford in 2007, now operates right across the county in places like Huddersfield, Keighley, Leeds, Rotherham and beyond.

Its mentoring schemes aim to '...create opportunities for young people in our most deprived communities.'

I first encountered Mosaic in the company of a friend, Ikram Butt, England's first Muslim rugby international in either code. In Mosaic's earliest days, there was a bit of a do at Mumtaz, a superb Kashmiri restaurant on Bradford's Great Horton Road, whose website has not too shabby endorsements from Prime Minister David Cameron and the Queen: 'The food was beautiful and the atmosphere was delightful,' quoth Her Majesty. George Galloway's favourite is lamb chops.

It struck me then, as it still does now, that here was a concept with legs: pragmatic no-nonsense multiculturalism. And how appropriate that it should have been piloted at Laisterdyke Secondary School in a city that stands to benefit more than most from the practical application of such a philosophy, smack in the heart of Yorkshire, where rolling up your sleeves and getting on with it is a mantra taken as read.

Yet six years on, Mosaic is no more solely confined to West Yorkshire than it is to British Asians.

'Although our beneficiaries are mainly from Muslim backgrounds, if we are working in Leeds, say, where there is a massively diverse group of migrant communities, a school like City of Leeds has hundreds of pupils from different nationalities,' says Yorkshire Regional Manager, Nabila Ayub. 'Whereas if you go to Keighley, you've got a predominant South East Asian community. And then that picture varies nationally. Our mentors are now a lot more diverse.'

Slouching towards Blubberhouses

Thanks again to an introduction from Ikram - still involved - we are at Yorkshire Mosaic's Pudsey headquarters, an unremarkable building in an unremarkable market town, full of people doing remarkable things. Midway between the centres of Bradford and Leeds, the place is most famous for lending its name to the one-eyed bear of BBC *Children In Need* charity fame. And Bradford-born Nabila is keen to explain exactly what it is that Mosaic does. So keen, your correspondent doesn't get another word in for a good ten minutes.

'We are an initiative of Business in the Community,' she begins, 'working primarily with secondary schools, which is kind of our flagship programme. We mentor young people with low aspirations to bridge that attainment gap. We also have a primary school programme, funded by Criterion Capital, after one of our board members - a young man - decided that, actually, we don't give enough support to young girls in terms of career choice. So that has been running for the last three years and recently got funding from the Qatar Foundation. In it, we work with mums and daughters, challenging some of the stereotypes and telling them about the careers that are available and accessible to them. We try to match them with mentors with a, say, fire service or police background, where there is a stigma attached, with women not wanting to be there.

'All our programmes focus on employability. In a primary school it could be what jobs can I get into? In a secondary school it could be, I'm applying for a university and need to present myself. What sorts of things will they be looking for? We also go into prisons, where it could be about making the transition back into the community. What sorts of job opportunities can we access?

'Then we have confidence building and soft efficacy, a posh phrase for self-belief, I've no idea why we use it.

Nobody knows what it means. And that's really about young people looking at something and believing that they can actually achieve it or try it out, not having a fear of failure.

'We link mentees with mentors who, historically, came from Muslim backgrounds because that's where Mosaic started, working with young Muslims because they seemed to be the group that had the aspiration-attainment gap. That's no longer exclusively the case on both counts. Our mentors don't just come from a Muslim background, they are very often professionals who come from a whole range of different places. DLA Piper, for example, a global law firm, are huge supporters. We get a lot of pro bono backing from them ... funding ... training room hire ... and a lot of mentors to support the work we do in schools. We have Ernst & Young, a global services firm. Some of their guys sit on our regional leadership group, which serves as a steering committee that slips into our national board. They do the linking between Mosaic and key influential people in the area, support us with funding, corporate engagements, general delivery, inspirational speaking ... that kind of thing.

'In the primary schools, we have a mums and daughters programme that runs over nine weeks and is very structured, focusing on things like the role of women in society, citizenship, pathways to education and role models. Mentors support that and share their own stories. They all have some form of journey they've taken to get to where they are, and it's really about persuasion through inspiration. Women from our network talk to them about their challenges and obstacles and it ends with a visit to a university, to say to mums, look, this is where your daughter could end up. Often, if no other member of the family has gone to university parents can be fearful and therefore reluctant to allow their child to go. They gain insight, meet students, look at courses and then have a graduation where they all get certificates. At Bradford, they get little baby cakes and graduation gowns. They have a photo seminar and the mums always cry.

'In secondary schools, mentors do an hour a month, spread over the academic year with pre-GCSE students. This is a smaller group setting and there's not so much structure. It's entirely up to the mentors and mentees what they'd like this mentoring session to look like. They could focus it all on confidence building, with a presentation to the rest of the class, or it could be about mock job interviews or career mapping. That programme is complemented by a world of work visit - WOW! as we call them. They attend a prominent workplace and meet trainees, senior partners, and get to ask questions about salary, how people got those positions, how different departments operate and so on. Most people will look at, say, DLA Piper and think they are just lawyers, failing to recognise that there is an IT department there too, working globally. Or Human Resources. The mentees have a quiz, get lunch, talk to people about their degree choices and come away with goodie bags as a nice treat.

'The prison offender programme has only recently been piloted. We've got a bit of a unique set-up in Yorkshire. Nationally, we have tried to engage with prisons and do mentoring with ex-offenders. Historically, it has gone through the chaplaincy service, where the mentees have to send visiting orders for the mentors to come in. It's had its highs and lows and not really been as effective. In Yorkshire, one of our members is a superintendent who leads a unique partnership with HMP Leeds, HMP Wealstun and HMP New Hall, a female only prison. Mentors do a weekend's training, an induction, do their security clearance and then they are matched to a mentee, while the custodial sentence is being served and helping them to make the transition when they are back in the community, whether by visiting probation officers, going to interviews, looking at housing needs or meeting them at the prison gates and saying we'll make the journey together.

'Uniquely in Yorkshire, our mentors have open access. They can get out their keys and go into the wings.

'Then we have an enterprise challenge, a competition that complements the secondary school programme. Business mentors come in, play an online simulation game, generate a high score, look at how to create an ethical business and sell five products on a virtual simulation game. A league table is formed and, nationally, the five top scoring teams from each region go down to London to pitch their idea to an audience of about 150. We've had the Prince of Wales in the audience, our founding chairman Her Royal Highness Princess Badiya bint El Hassan of Jordan as well, and then there are prizes at the end of it. This year, they all got Google Chrome laptops, were driven in Bentleys, got a tour around Clarence House, dinner with *The Apprentice* candidates and a whole host of other stuff. The winning school also gets some money.'

Phew! And that's just the edited version.

Who could not be impressed by such an avalanche of enthusiasm, especially backed by cold hard achievement? No doubt Mosaic's roots are idealistic, implying one colourful picture from individual tiles of varying patterns and design. But there is something admirably down to earth about them too. Dream a dream, they seem to say, but don't think it will become reality without a dose of realism and hard work.

'Absolutely,' nods Nabila. 'And no programme would work if it wasn't for our mentors. We don't pay expenses, they come out of sheer altruism. They want to do something and give up their time for free ... even in Yorkshire. No! Yorkshire people are brilliant, actually.'

Aha - Yorkshireness! I almost forgot. The reason we are here. As a young woman born in Bradford, who moved out temporarily and then came back, would she describe herself as a Yorkshirewoman?

'I would say I'm a Bradfordian, actually.'

And suddenly we are into a whole new range of identity issues. Is it true, I wonder, that as psychologist Eric Wright and playwright Mick Martin suggest, young people don't really associate themselves much with their home county anymore?

'From a personal perspective? Absolutely, yes,' Nabila says. 'Although, to be honest, when you come from a migrant background you already have an identity crisis. In my household, for example, your family is Pakistani. You have a load of traditional values and culture that goes along with that. And then you'll end up where, actually, you don't really associate with too much of it because it's not what living in Bradford is about. Although there's a huge South East Asian community there, it's really hard to be part of it and not have conflicting values because you are brought up differently, your education has been different, you've hung around with a variety of people. What happens is you sort of battle with yourself, in terms of what do I identify myself with?

'That's especially so when faced with someone who is ignorant about your background. A week ago, I checked into a hotel in London on this summit. Somebody asked me where I was from and I said: "Yorkshire." I would never have said Yorkshire if it hadn't have been for working at Mosaic, because I now know that is my region and I strongly identify with it. But before I would have said, "up north," "Bradford" or "near Leeds." Anyway, I said "Yorkshire" and she went: "Oh, you've got really good English." And I was like, "Well, that's because I'm from the UK, Yorkshire isn't on another planet." I was a bit taken aback in this day and age ... but you do experience that kind of thing a lot.

'Growing up in school, it's a kid thing I guess, where if somebody's different you pick on them. You'd get the whole thing around your background and colour of skin, which I wouldn't really say was racist, people were just quite ignorant about it at the time. And at that point you affiliate yourself with "I'm Pakistani." Then, at home and having a moral dilemma with your family, it's really hard to say that you ARE a Pakistani. A lot of people I grew up with identify themselves as a black, British Muslim and not Pakistani or from the South East Asian community. We are a BME group. We are black, minority, ethnic.'

A typical Yorkshire way of putting it, I hazard, to the point and with a modicum of pride for good measure. Nor shall I be able to resist pointing out how Mosaic began in my own home city. Does Nabila notice any so-called traditional Yorkshire characteristics in herself?

'Definitely hospitality,' she says. 'The further up north you come, the nicer we are. I totally identify with that. A lot of my colleagues from London will come up here and say, "My god, you guys are really nice." Whereas you are left to fend for yourself down there ... the Tube is nasty, people can be horrible. I think people are happier here ... smilier. I don't think we are dour and gloomy at all. Ask for directions in Bradford and someone will take the time to at least try to help you. In London, most people don't know, don't care or are too busy even to pay any attention.

'But generally I think the idea of Yorkshireness is less and less in the mindset. Most BME people would say they are from Bradford or Leeds or Huddersfield. There are very few who'd say they are from Yorkshire, very few. I shout about Yorkshire because it's my region in the work that we do.

Slouching towards Blubberhouses

When we are in our board meetings, I'll say: "Yorkshire is going to be the best region" and drill it down. When I'm with mentors, the same. There is that competitiveness, which is quite positive. But on the whole, I don't think people identify themselves in that way anymore, especially young people. I think, yeah, this Yorkshireness thing is dying.'

So, what Nabila is saying is that people have a pride in Yorkshire as a concept only when it is something they have a personal stake in?

'Absolutely. Especially with ethnic minority groups. Having been brought up in poorer backgrounds, there's a tendency to think: "We are going to do well, we are going to get a decent education and we are going to move out of here. Living in Bradford is a cliché, Leeds has a lot more going for it, but we want to move away from Bradford for definite." That happens in a lot of South East Asian families I come across. There's a tendency to want to move south. They don't necessarily take pride in where they've come from.'

This is especially true with Bradfordians, Nabila says, '...although, recently, I've encountered quite a lot of people who are coming back to reinvest and kind of think: "Oh, my family was from here, we were brought up here ... there's not really any other area that feels like home, therefore we want to do something for our community." It's a conversation I had with somebody not so long ago, a former youth worker of mine from when I was younger. He was doing a dissertation. He asked me about things like stereotypes around Bradford, why people volunteer and give up their time. He found that there were a lot more people in Bradford now who are community activists; people with the same ideals who hang around together, as opposed to those who don't volunteer or have that general sense of wanting to give back.

'This group of people seems to be connected, in one

way or another, just because they are involved in charitable causes. When I was growing up, volunteering was really about escapism. It was about getting away from other things going on in my life. And I guess for a lot of people it would be very similar. It might be a way of getting the experience required to get into university, for example. Nowadays, I do find that Bradford and Leeds are the two areas where people are just willing to help, whatever their agenda.'

That's good to hear, I say. Especially given how the City of Bradford constantly gets such a bad rap from both within and without.

'It does. Bradford has a very bad image and I think a lot of it is, from a South East Asian community point of view, about having grown up in families where they [the original migrants] never really wanted to stay here long term. So they spent a lot of time investing in families back wherever home was, or building houses for them, things like that. What's happened is we've not invested enough time on our livelihoods or been able to enjoy our lives here. So we've grown up quite torn between the two.

'I certainly wouldn't go back to Pakistan, because I don't really have much to do with anyone there. The only connection is my mother. But a lot of young people have that dilemma. Their family sees Pakistan as this amazing world where people like themselves live, with the same values and cultures, but when you go back they've moved on sixty years and we are still hanging on to those ideals that our parents brought along with them, stuck in a time warp. I think that started a lot of the stigma that was attached to Asian people not doing well, sticking to their own communities ... it's a fear of the unknown. And now young people retaliate against it. I certainly know from my younger brothers and sisters, there's nothing Pakistani about them. They don't have the traditional values that we were brought up with and seem to want to break free from it, because they don't identify themselves that way.'

I bring up that mid-19th century Irish influx, when Catholic churches were the mosques of their day. How, over time and generations, came absolute acceptance of people who gradually flowed out of their original settling points into the wider community. Who gives a damn nowadays whether a Bradfordian is a Catholic or not? Will history repeat itself?

'Absolutely. Multiculturalism, as a theory, has been exaggerated. When I was about 16, working in Ilkley with a group of really young kids, primary school age, one said: "Miss, do Pakistanis eat curry flavoured crisps?" That stayed with me, the cutest thing ever. If they aren't going to be exposed to other cultures, I guess that's what they are going to come in with. But we do need to stop talking about integration. It will just happen. I think it has happened.

'British Muslims, or South East Asian communities, *have* integrated. All the issues that come from other dilemmas are mainly social or economic problems, with people looking for someone to blame. I worked in Ravenscliffe for a bit and said to an admin worker: "There's a job here for someone in the kitchen. Could you please pass it on because I'm going on holiday and won't see them?" "Ooh," she went, "where is it?" And she looked and said: "Manningham? I'm not being funny, and don't get me wrong, but in the middle of Paki Land?" I wasn't even going to dignify that with a response. Seriously. A 50-year-old woman. There are rare incidences when people seem comfortable saying that kind of thing, but it's usually people who live in those pockets of the community where they don't get that exposure.

'Generally, I don't think it's a problem. Whenever I've worked away, and I travel a huge amount on development work, when you board that flight and know you are coming back to 150 takeaways with any cuisine you could possibly think of, and I'm not going to be hungry, because I'm starving having eaten salads for over a month, you kind of look forward to it. As much as sometimes you want to break free, ultimately this is home. It's taken me a long time, I'm nearly 30 now, to think: "Yeah, I'm actually quite proud of being from Bradford. I'm quite proud of being from Yorkshire."'

***

SOME twenty-five years after a reported 'thousand Muslim protesters' burned copies of *The Satanic Verses* on almost exactly the same spot, Bradford's scrubbed up City Park is the venue for *Bollywood Carmen*, broadcast live by the soon to be defunct youth channel BBC3 across the nation.

It's a blaze of colour, graphics, costumes, dancing, music and fountains. Lots of fountains. Oh, and sequins too. Of pink, orange, yellow, green and every shade of blue.

'And don't forget,' says continuity man, 'you can hear backstage interviews and highlights tomorrow morning with Bobby and Anushka on BBC Asian Network from six.'

Bollywood Carmen puts a contemporary spin on Bizet that is more *Hollyoaks* than high or even middlebrow opera. With a cast of Sophia the starlet, Eddie the security gaffer, Don the lover, Tannishta the fiancée, Lily P the queen bee, Kylie, Shazzy and Carmen herself of course, tossing a rose at the camera, how could it not be?

And from the opening shots, crammed with folk of all backgrounds and culture, including someone on an elephant, the enthusiasm is infectious. As dusk falls on a beautiful day, the booming beat rattles many a familiar window. And it is clear that we are glimpsing an exciting vision of the future.

Slouching towards Blubberhouses

From his sideways pose, A.D. 'King of Bollywood', played by Abhay Deol of India's legendary acting dynasty, removes his sunglasses, turns to the hovering lens and grins.

'Oh I'm dead nervous,' drawls our heroine, in this version a Bradfordian waitress played by Preeya Kalidas (*EastEnders, Bombay Dreams, Four Lions*), in the very broadest Yorkshire tones.

'Well don't be,' replies Lily P (Meera Syal). 'It has been foretold in the cards that tonight is your night.' This being *Carmen*, she is dead by the end, but we take Lily P's point.

And 'Bolero' doesn't half sound cool gone Bhangra.

***

WHEN faced with a potentially volatile street demonstration organised by far-right extremists the English Defence League, one mosque in York invited protesters in for tea and biscuits.

Around half a dozen people had nailed the flag of St George to a wooden fence in front of the place of worship, but tensions were defused over a plate of custard creams, followed by an impromptu game of football.

Unversity of York lecturer Mohammed el-Gomati said: 'There is the possibility of dialogue. Even the EDL, who were having a shouting match, started talking and we found out that we agreed that violent extremism is wrong.'

When asked for a quote, Archbishop of York Dr John Sentamu later said: 'Tea, biscuits and football are a great and typically Yorkshire combination when it comes to disarming hostile and extremist views.'

12. The Hills Have Ayes

Yorkshire's Lost Tribe

IMAGINE, for a moment, that you are lucky enough to live in Yorkshire. Then one day you wake up, wipe some dripping on your bread (brown, wi'nowt taken out) and discover that the privilege has been removed. Just like that.

Worse. Not only do you no longer live in Yorkshire, they've only gone and shifted you next door ... to Lancashire.

I know, I know, a horror story by any definition, yet that's exactly what happened to the good folk of Saddleworth back in 1974. Having for centuries nestled in the bosom of the West Riding of Yorkshire, first as a centre of wool production, then cotton spinning and weaving after the Industrial Revolution, suddenly you're a civil parish of the Metropolitan Borough of Oldham, Greater Manchester. Well, for some the indignity was just too much to take.

Forty years on, the pain is still raw.

At least it is for the Saddleworth White Rose Society, whose website is ablaze with fierce pride - or '...dripping with Yorkshire bitterness' according to one Lancastrian friend.

Slouching towards Blubberhouses

Its secretary is listed as Mr Roy Bardsley and it's with that gentleman that I try to make contact. Sadly, it turns out, Roy has passed away, so I arrange to meet another member, Brenda Cockayne, instead. The venue will be Saddleworth museum, meeting spot of the Saddleworth Historical Society, who I am told insist on having Yorkshire in their address. There's also an equally vociferous Saddleworth Civic Trust.

Already, you feel, things are starting to get a bit daft. While the past can be an enticing place to visit, it's dangerous to live there. But, what the heck. That's easy for me to say, isn't it, sitting cosily in South Craven, where no one has ever tried to conscript me into Burnley or Accrington.

So let's just go and have a look, eh?

***

THE first thing you should know about Saddleworth is that, like the county to which it claims to belong, it has personality issues, both psychologically and geographically.

I've driven here before, but always on the route west, up over the tops of the M62 past moors bleak and famously dreadful, in the face of driving rain most often, ghosts real and imagined tapping at the window.

This time, I figure, it might be best to come in from 'the other side'. So after leaving the M60 at junction 22, it's up via Oldham towards Lees and then Springhead, one of thirteen villages and hamlets of which Saddleworth was historically comprised, the others being Austerlands, Delph, Denshaw, Diggle, Dobcross, Friezland, Grasscroft, Greenfield, Gritton, Lydgate, Scouthead and Uppermill which, if nothing else, sounds like a decent rugby league team.

Saddleworth museum is in the latter of those places, Uppermill. But even on the road in you get a sense that there may be something in this 'we're Yorkshire not Lancashire' lark after all. For one thing, leave behind the red-bricked mean streets of Oldham and you might well be in Holmfirth, it's weavers' cottages, mills, viaducts and calf-tugging slopes.

'When you come over, you can tell by the buildings,' Brenda will later say, and she will have a point.

A subsequent wander up to the Civic Centre puts the number of Saddleworth villages at seven, although a patchwork quilt on the wall there manages to quibble with that total too. Identity can be so very confusing.

There is therefore no such thing as Saddleworth town centre, but if it had one it would indeed be here on Uppermill High Street. Unprepossessing from the outside, the museum turns out to be what's left of the 19th century Victoria Mill, opened in 1962 by volunteers wanting to '...preserve for the future the relics of an already changing society...' In fact, it is in one of the outbuilding plots, the rest of the mill long since flattened under a handy car park. Another former mill over the road has been converted into modern flats.

In 1980, the site was extended and an art gallery added after a public appeal. Saddleworth Museum and Art Gallery, to give it its full title, a registered charity, continues to be an independent organisation funded by entrance fees, donations, grants and support from the Parish Council.

There's also a museum shop and Tourist Information service just inside the door and it's here that I encounter Geoff Bayley. Geoff is chairman of the White Rose Society, while Brenda is on the committee. She'll be along in a moment, he is sure, but as he's only got half an hour before the school run perhaps it would be best if we got cracking.

'You're from Bradford,' he begins. 'Everybody in Bradford knows that they are Yorkshire people and that Bradford is a Yorkshire city. In Saddleworth, we have a problem. We know that we are Yorkshire people, even though we are for administrative purposes governed by the Metropolitan Borough of Oldham. We are nonetheless geographically still part of the West Riding of Yorkshire.

'Are you aware of the statement issued by Eric Pickles on the 23rd of April 2013? He spelt out quite clearly that the historic counties were never abolished, only the administrative areas were changed and that the Government's position is that people should be aware and proud of their heritage - celebrate the fact - and indeed that the traditional county boundaries should be marked.

'Now, that's been the policy of Saddleworth White Rose Society for many years. But it's only in the last three years or so that we've been able to raise the funds to mark where roads cross the county boundary. If you go around Saddleworth, including the moorland, there's something like fourteen places where vehicles could leave Yorkshire. One or two go into Cheshire. But most of them, of course, go into Lancashire.'

I'd seen one myself at Lees called County End.

'Aye, and there's a corresponding Lancashire sign going the other way.'

I'm keen, though, to know more about the Society itself. Just how representative is it of the mood in these parts? How long has it been going - presumably since that fateful day in 1974? and how many members does it have?

It turns out Roy Bardsley had been the organisation's secretary since its inception, though Geoff isn't sure exactly when that was. 'It's had about four chairmen over the years,' he says. 'I took over when the previous one, Mike Buckley, became a borough councilor and he thought there might be a conflict of interest. He's still an active member, but he stood down at that point. It was founded later than 1974, though I'm not quite sure how much later. The purpose of the society was to promote the Yorkshireness of Saddleworth - the heritage, history and culture of the people and the area. And then we got into the marking of the boundaries. We are associated with the Association of British Counties, which no doubt you are aware of. We are affiliated members of the Yorkshire Ridings Society, who launched Yorkshire Day. In Uppermill, Yorkshire Day is one of the biggest celebrations, if not *the* biggest, in the county. It is a big affair. During the course of the day, we get several thousand people through.'

And that membership figure?

'I can't give you the exact figures, but it's not very high in terms of people who are actually paid-up members. There are various affiliated groups to whom we send our newsletters etc. There is a lot more moral than paid-up support. There are a lot of people, of course, who have moved into the area since 1974. Part of our remit now is to educate them that they are in fact living in Yorkshire.'

Really? 'Yes, because most of them think they're in Lancashire. Or even Greater Manchester, perish the thought.'

The scattered population of Saddleworth - all 24,350 of them - do pay their '...rates, or council tax, or poll tax or whatever you want to call it...' to the Metropolitan Borough of Oldham, Geoff concedes, but that is part of the problem. 'We put on one or two small social events, but the main event of the year is Yorkshire Day, which is now run by a separate committee, the Yorkshire Day Group. Our White Rose Society started it, but it became a bit too big for us to handle. The Parish Council is affiliated to White Rose, also. We persuaded them to change their letterhead. It now reads: Uppermill, Saddleworth, Yorkshire.'

Does he appreciate that, to people on the outside, this does tend to have its droll side? Can Geoff see any humour in the situation or is it all treated with deadly seriousness?

'Oh, deadly serious,' he says. 'Some of them can get quite nasty about it. Letters in the press get vitriolic, saying things like: "Saddleworth was moved from Yorkshire into Lancashire? Well, I don't remember anybody putting it on a low-loader…"'

***

THE shop door opens, Brenda Cockayne bustles in clutching a copy of *Yorkshire Ridings* magazine. Once, a writer might have got away with describing her as a pocket-battleship, though maybe not to her face. A friendly, cheerful demeanour belies a steely determination to get her message across.

She says her hellos in an accent that, like that of Geoff, has a sleepy South Pennine twang of Oldham and Rochdale, with the odd Yorkshire colloquialism chucked in for good measure. Not that it puts Geoff off his stroke.

'…and then they come up with that nonsense about Greater Manchester, whatever that is,' he hurries on, arguing with himself if necessary. 'Greater Manchester doesn't even have a council now. Yes, I know that the West Riding of Yorkshire no longer has a council either, but the West Riding County Council only lasted for less than one hundred years and it was imposed as an administrative authority to administer the West Riding of Yorkshire geographically, which had existed for over one thousand years. So…'

In a bid to head any scandal off at the pass, Geoff up front admits that he was actually born sixty yards over the border '…in a bedroom in Lees, on the Lancashire side.'

Brenda, meanwhile, hails from Delph, where Geoff now also lives, a couple of miles away. 'It's on my wedding certificate: Dobcross in the West Riding of Yorkshire.'

I am about to enquire as to her reaction on that first

day in 1974, when she realised she wasn't in West Yorkshire anymore - a dangerous turn of phrase ... 'We ARE still in West Yorkshire' - when the lady running the visitor centre steps in. There isn't much room around here so she invites us to use the gallery instead. It's up a small flight of steps, with a stairlift attached to the wall should anyone need it. We manage without and it is a lot quieter up there.

'As I said,' says Geoff, immediately back in his stride, 'I was born in Lees but, in 1974, I'd been living in Gritton in Saddleworth for about five or six years and then moved back to Lees again. Having not been involved with local politics, I didn't see the significance at the time. But you get older and wiser. Roy recruited me at the Saddleworth Show, where the White Rose Society had a stand. I thought, no, I don't want to know about gardening. A long arm came out and got me.'

Brenda doesn't remember that very first day with any clarity either. 'I do know that at some point we had a "Save Saddleworth" campaign, where we marched and had meetings to try and stop it.'

'There was a referendum held at Local Government election time,' Geoff interjects, 'overwhelmingly in favour of going with Huddersfield, which became Kirklees. The next choice was Ashton-under-Lyne, which became Tameside. Incidentally, there's more of the river Tame in Saddleworth than there is in Tameside, it's part of the same river valley system. Oldham, of course, was way down the list. There was a great mistrust of it. Even having been born and brought up in Lees, we never trusted Oldham. That big lot over there.'

Brenda: 'They only wanted the land to build on. Our rates would go sky high. This was what we thought and this is what happened.'

Geoff gets conspiratorial. 'It is rumoured, although I have no evidence, that ... Saddleworth Urban District Council, as it then was, voted to go with Oldham,' he says, weighing his words carefully. 'No doubt that severely influenced the Boundaries Commission when they came to their decision.'

Brenda: 'Sold us down the river.'

Geoff: 'Yes, the Urban District Council did the dirty on the people of Saddleworth, there's absolutely no doubt about that.'

Brenda: 'The chairman wanted to be mayor of Oldham.'

Geoff: 'That is the rumour I've heard, yes. That he browbeat the members to vote Oldham on that basis. If so, that is treason as far as we are concerned.'

***

IT's by now apparent that for the good people of Saddleworth, this issue of lost identity can be neatly divided in two.

On the one hand, there are the political and practical implications; little guy versus big guy; bureaucratic bullies; big brother stomping along in his size nines, assett stripping.

But there's a less tangible aspect to this too, isn't there? Is it not also about the need to belong ... ancestral roots ... emotional ties that bind. A wistfulness of spirit.

On the road up past Springhead, white rose in its social club emblem, and the Mancunian skyline jutting out of the haze some eleven miles distant, that this is a semi-rural environment strikes you as obvious. 'I feel it is wrong that the unitary authorities, and I'm not just taking about Oldham, I'm talking about Kirklees, Calderdale ... I think it quite wrong that they should be administrative authorities for rural areas,' says Geoff Bayley. 'It's my belief that the rural areas of the South Pennines ... Saddleworth being one, Marsden, Holmfirth, Todmorden ... they should be hived off and there should be a new unity authority based on the South Pennines.

If central Government cannot or will not do that, then they should do the decent thing and make the entire South Pennines area into a national park.

'I believe these rural areas were in the original 1947 national parks discussion but weren't successful. Since then, all the others have been so. It's time the Government got its act together and extended the Peak District - part of which is in Saddleworth already - and/or the Yorkshire Dales, so that they come together. Either that or create a new national park. It would get rid of a lot of bad feeling as it would take the planning away from these big town-based unitary authorities. Neither the administration or officers have a clue when it comes to rural affairs.'

'Most of the villages have gone, they were all good villages,' sighs Brenda.

'We're down to another thing now,' says Geoff. 'In 1974, it appeared that it was the new borough council's policy to totally erase Saddleworth's history. They took all the signs down with the utmost haste. We had quite a lot of the old finger posts, you know, with the circular top, that said Yorks WR for Yorkshire West Riding, and then the name of the village across with the grid reference...'

Brenda: 'I've got the Dobcross one...'

Geoff shushes her. 'Don't quote that!'

Brenda: 'Why not? They gave it me. I didn't pinch it.'

'Anyway,' says Geoff, moving on, 'the point is that the people from Oldham came and took those down. In my opinion, they were stealing our heritage. It's as simple as that. That was just plain and common theft. Other villages around, which have been incorporated for administration purposes under Lancashire County Council, they've still got the signs up, saying Yorkshire WR. The signs are still there. The excuse by some unitary authorities was that it was government

285

policy to take them down as they were obsolete designs. That was not so. That was an excuse. It was a recommendation, not an instruction. And subsequently the recommendation was changed. The current recommendation is that where they still exist, they must be preserved. They must be repainted at least once every five years and it even gives the reference number of the shade of paint.'

'I asked him what he were doing, the chap at Dobcross,' says Brenda. 'There were two of them, with a flat lorry. I said: "What are you doing?" and he said: "We're taking the post down now because it's not Yorkshire anymore." And I said" "It still *is* Yorkshire. What are you going to do with it?" He said: "We're tipping them." I said: "Can I have it?" He said: "Yeah, you can have it," and gave it to me. He said it would cost me a cup of tea.'

'Yorkshire tea?' I ask. Nobody laughs.

'That's the next project we have in mind, the White Rose Society,' says Geoff. 'When we've got a few more road signs up, where the 'A' roads cross the county boundary, I would like to see some of these finger post signs re-erected in the villages. We might have a battle, with the Department of Transport even, but we're not putting new signs up, merely putting back what was there before.'

And what of the future? As a completely voluntary association, it's important, surely, to attract more people to the campaign? I'm guessing the demographic is, shall we say, middle age upwards? Geoff and Brenda agree.

'We need more members and we need more young members,' says the former, 'because we need to educate the young people. They are taught at school that they are in Lancashire. Saddleworth School actually teaches in geography that they are in Lancashire.'

'Yet they have a white rose on their blazer,' adds

Brenda, 'and if you ask half of them what it is, they don't know. When you go into the Civic Centre [Parish Council offices] there's a big white rose on the floor. The sign outside the school used to have a white rose on it too.'

'Still does,' says Geoff. 'And that one's the right way up. The one on the school badge is upside down.'

Brenda: 'Yes, but we are prepared to let it be upside down.'

Geoff: 'We'll accept that. But I suggest you go up to the Parish Council offices and have a look.' I will, I say.

Mention of the school is a reminder of family duties - there are grandkids to collect. But there's still time to gauge what he would consider to be a realistic target for the society in the long run. Saddleworth back in Yorkshire I venture, once again putting my foot in it.

'We still *are* in Yorkshire!' they cry.

'But you mean for administrative purposes?' Geoff adds, before conceding that he doesn't see that as a practical aim for the moment. 'However, a change to a South Pennines authority would be, and I don't care whether it straddles the boundary and is part Yorkshire, part Lancashire. As long as we get out of the clutches of the unitary authorities.'

Is that a feeling widely held?

'Well, you know, you get people coming in and putting Oldham on their things and then you talk to them and they say: "Ooh, we didn't know we were in Yorkshire, can we put Yorkshire on?" And they're dead chuffed, aren't they?' says Brenda.

'I suggest you go and talk to people in Marsden, Holmfirth, Slaithwaite ... and see if they're happy with how things have gone under Kirklees or Calderdale. You'll find that there is disquiet about how they administer the villages. Kirklees is the biggest unitary authority, I believe, in the country. And under the government specifications they are only allowed so many electoral wards. Huddersfield have the maximum amount, but more electors per ward than what they are supposed to have, so they could afford to get rid of one or two of these villages to another authority.'

It's clear that though the membership may be ageing, for now at least the Saddleworth White Rose Society has plenty of fight left yet, even without the chap who began it all some four decades ago.

'Oh, Roy,' says Brenda. 'It was his life; a lovely, lovely man.'

'There's a picture of him in our latest news sheet, which I've just proof-printed today,' smiles Geoff, before revealing the rather startling fact that Roy Bardsley too wasn't born in Yorkshire at all.

'His parents were from here, but Roy himself was born in Derby,' Geoff confirms. 'Either they were visiting or had gone for temporary work, I don't know, but not long after Roy's birth they came back to Saddleworth. He was educated in Uppermill, went to Saddleworth School and worked at Greenfield farm for a number of years. While there, he developed a lifelong interest in cattle.'

'He was going to buy my brother John's milk round,' says Brenda. 'He's a farmer at Dobcross. Then on the very week Roy was going to take over, he was diagnosed with terrible arthritis. You've never seen anyone as bad.'

Geoff continues: 'For a time he made aluminium structures for greenhouses, local authority jobs. But as he got older his sight went, he got cataracts. And there he was, poor Roy, still compiling the newsletter. It got to the stage where I persuaded him to email it to me, because there were so many wrong spellings, and I soon realised that it wasn't that Roy couldn't spell, he couldn't see the keyboard or screen. In every case where there was a word spelt wrong, it was the adjacent key. But he still kept at it.'

Old fashioned Yorkshire stubbornness?

'Absolutely. If you'd told him he lived in Lancashire or Greater Manchester, he would have told you to wash your mouth out.'

***

GEOFF departs and Brenda and I follow him outside. She is keen to show me the statue of flat-capped Ammon Wrigley, local poet and historian (1861-1946), on a patch of grass just across the car park. A garland of white roses hang around his stony grey neck, albeit a little worse for wear on this chilly October Thursday. But the museum, it turns out, is nothing to do with the society at all.

'The historical society and civic trust are very active here and nearly all the membership is common to both, but we don't use it. Our meetings are mostly at Geoff's house now,' says Brenda, before telling me about the rush-cart tradition of Saddleworth's morris men and their dance outside every pub.

'They have a man on the top who they call the jockey and send him beer up. They go cut the rushes and put them on church floors to keep them warm with the onset of winter, pulling the cart through all the villages. Years ago, every village had its own rush-cart but they'd fight, somebody got knocked out - they were all drunk - so they stopped that. Then a chap called Peter Ashworth started it up again twenty years ago and it just went from strength to strength. They come from Cornwall and all over. They all wear clogs with bells on and jackets of red, white and blue made in Delph. It's really good.'

Slouching towards Blubberhouses

We go to the Civic Centre to confirm the big white rose on the entrance floor and it's Brenda's turn to leave. As she nips off for some pet food, I stroll back down into the high street where, after popping back into the visitors' centre for a copy of *Saddleworth Monthly* I decide to conduct a straw poll.

First, a little bookshop around the corner where the owner is telling someone's fortune and therefore too busy to talk. I should have seen that one coming.

Four lads in Saddleworth School football kits walk by, these will do. Do you live in Yorkshire or Lancashire?

'Lancashire,' they say, in swift succession, looking at me as if I am daft - which I might very well be - or worse.

Next up is Oldham ageUK, a charity shop. Given the name above the door, there's little doubt which side of the debate they'll fall down on, but you never know, do you?

'Officially, we're in Oldham Metropolitan Borough, but most people would say Yorkshire,' says a woman inside, before bustling off to attend to something out the back.

In the Vintage Cupcake Kitchen, five votes from the six young women present, three of whom are serving on, go to Lancashire. The sixth says: 'I'm from Cheshire.'

A young couple behind the perfumed counter of Sweet Memories of Saddleworth, standing so close they may in fact be holding hands, do not hesitate: 'Yorkshire'.

At Arjento Jeweller's, meanwhile, where you have to buzz to get them to open the door, an immaculately attired woman says 'Lancashire'. In the RSPCA shop opposite, two customers chime 'Yorkshire', another growls 'Lancashire.'

The Rioja tapas bar is shut.

13. I Can't Believe It's Not Buttertubs

The Future of Yorkshire

'WHIPPET good ... at last, Yorkshire gets its just desserts,' reads the headline on CNN Travel. 'Yorkshire's triumph at this year's World Travel Awards could be a step toward global domination.'

It's easy to see Welcome to Yorkshire boss Gary Verity punching the air at that. The story epitomises all he has been about since arriving in the one-time Yorkshire Tourist Board hot seat - back then more of a lukewarm seat, really - in 2008.

'In picking the winner of the Leading Destination in Europe gong,' the reporter continues, 'the judges appear to have mulled pretty much every world-historical European city and glitzy locale. For this lifetime fan of the most beautiful English county, the judges' decision to rate Yorkshire above sophisticated but snooty Paris, overrated Rome and architecturally magnificent but, let's face it, bloody cold St Petersburg, is controversial in one sense only. This part of England surely deserves to be considered not only Europe's leading destination, but possibly the greatest place on Earth.'

Slouching towards Blubberhouses

He goes on: 'In Britain, certain stereotypes adhere to Yorkshire folk, just as bad driving does to Italians and indifference to daily washing does to the French. Whippets, flat caps and ale are considered three accoutrements no Yorkshireman (or Yorkshireperson, nowadays?) would ever be seen without.'

There then follows a *précis* of the county's charms, including that aforementioned real ale - ...which elsewhere in Britain [tastes of] flat, slightly sweetened dishwater...' - tea - '...even sweeter thanks to the soft water rolling off the moors and dales...' - Yorkshire pud - '...you'd be hard put to beat the taste of this unglamorous-looking but delicious treat (which could serve as a metaphor for Yorkshire folk themselves)... - ethnic diversity - '...you can also gorge on Indian, Pakistani and Bengali curries every bit as good as those on the subcontinent...' - sporting achievements and culture.'

And there's more: 'The ancient limestone landscape around Malham, in particular the hulking mass of Gordale Scar, with waterfalls hurtling down 100m high cliffs, is a recommended stop on any rural Yorkshire wander. Extensive cave networks underneath the dales suit more active types. Potholing into the depths of Gaping Gill, on the slopes of Ingleborough Hill, easily matches the adrenaline rush of a bungee jump or hike in the Grand Canyon [or] if you prefer to stay above the surface, Yorkshire's blustery beaches offer world-class surfing.'

The writer concludes: 'Yorkshire's charm lies in its sheer breadth, from its moving dales landscapes to its uncompromising curries and its people's pluck.'

Blimey, CNN. Whippet good, indeed.

The pun, of course, comes from 'Whip It', a hit in 1980 for American new wave band Devo, whose moniker is a shortened form of 'de-evolution' rather than 'devolution', though maybe there is little difference. Lauding a county to high heaven is one thing, being proud of your roots another. But just as a large lump of land still further to the north - Scotland - is readying itself to go to the polls on just that very issue, how far, I wonder, would Gary Verity, last seen in a beer tent at the Great Yorkshire Show, want to travel down that particular revolutionary track?

What does the future hold for Yorkshire?

***

IT's a grey autumnal morning, a lone blustery shower having washed away last night's first frost of the season. Yorkshire's tallest building, the Bridgewater Place tower, prods 367 feet into the sky, giving the world the finger.

We are in Leeds, an important city, it says.

Welcome to Yorkshire's offices are down here, a brisk walk south of the railway station, in the Holbeck Urban Village redevelopment, not far from Granary Wharf. The Leeds-Liverpool Canal runs by it - as does the River Aire - a couple of clues among several as to the area's heavy industrial past.

Look down to your right on Water Lane and see the stuff that gave the street its name lapping over oily cobbled stones into the culvert that runs beneath the main road.

One or two very good pubs still dot the area, like The Grove - home to 'the world's longest running folk club' - resolutely untouched by the corporate mentality, even though the customers who pop in nowadays on their way home from work are more likely to be wearing office suits than boiler suits.

Welcome to Yorkshire live in a courtyard behind one such tavern, the evocatively named and more self-consciously trendy Midnight Bell. The address reads Dry Sand Foundry, Foundry Square, the building's former use up front and centre. Inside, it's a modern, open-plan environment, all high ceilings, wooden beams and brick walls, a partnership of past, present and, if the people peering busily into computer screens have their way, future.

I'm met at reception by Sarah, Gary's PA, who leads me up the stairs to meet her boss. And, upon turning a corner, there he is, smiling and relaxed, open-necked just as he was in Harrogate in July, in an only partially screened off area, next to a couple of comfy settees and a coffee table.

As we chat and make our introductions, I wonder when or if he is going to invite me into his office. But it soon becomes apparent that we are in it already. There is no desk because he doesn't like them. No doors to close because, presumably, he feels he has nothing to hide. In some ways, it already feels a bit *Twenty Twelve*, the wickedly accurate BBC comedy with Hugh Bonneville in the leadership role, charged with delivering the 2012 London Olympics, aka 'the biggest show on earth'.

The talk is of brands, perception and legacy. Yet to press such a comparison too far would be unfair. *Twenty Twelve* and its follow-up *W1A* take much of their humour from PR industry waffle and incompetence. No one, however, could deny how far Welcome to Yorkshire has succeeded in transforming the image of a county once known as much for its miserablism as the beauty of its landscape. And it was an achievement topped off in stunning fashion by the capture of the start of the 2014 Tour de France.

Not that there's any hint of arrogance - well, nothing above and beyond the usual Yorkshire trumpeting anyway.

'Yes, it's a fine line, isn't it?' says our leader. 'That's one thing that can wind people up. We try and ram our Yorkshireness down their throats too much and they can resent that a bit. We've picked that up around the country, the stereotypical Yorkshire cricketer who is always banging on about himself.'

Before Verity's arrival just over five years ago, it's fair to say that Yorkshire tourism, such as it was, relied for publicity on the free advertising of Sunday night veterinary TV shows and little else. But when the Yorkshire Tourist Board, around since 1972, suddenly found itself with a new boss, its name wasn't the only thing to change.

'My background is re-energising businesses that could do better, to be polite,' Gary says. 'The Yorkshire Tourist Board was definitely in that category. In Yorkshire, I obviously had a strong brand. There are very few other counties, certainly in the UK, that have the identity we have. You wouldn't call yourself a Kentish man or a Rutland man. If you go to a football or rugby match here, you'll often get the crowd chanting "Yorkshire, Yorkshire". You rarely get them chanting "Leicestershire, Leicestershire..." or whatever. We have that identity and pride.'

To an almost nationalistic degree, I venture.

'Yeah, you are kind of verging on that with Yorkshire, aren't you? Maybe Scotland would vie with us in terms of identity. One question I've been asked a lot is: "Would you get behind a devolution campaign for independence for Yorkshire?" And I've shied away from that because it's taking us to a slightly dangerous place. But I do feel we should have more autonomy from London. The way Yorkshire is treated at the moment isn't great. Not necessarily in Government, but certainly in Whitehall, they'd like to airbrush us out.'

He is referring to that public spat over ownership of the Tour de France event, whose opening stages - Le Grand Départ - are due to begin on the Headrow, in the shadow of Leeds Town Hall, in July 2014. For a while there, as seen in chapter three, matters got rather acrimonious.

Slouching towards Blubberhouses

'Ministers have come under fire over revelations that Whitehall officials are engaged in a plot to undermine the region's role in hosting the start of next year's Tour de France,' began an account of the row in the *Halifax Courier*, before going on to reveal that a blatant re-branding exercise was underway in London's corridors of power.

'The Department for Culture, Media and Sport [have] decided to market the event as the "England" Grand Départ in a snub to the region's tourism chiefs who last year beat the Government's own Scottish-based bid to secure the landmark event. Heavily-censored documents reveal UK Sport advised the Government not to give public money to the event secured by tourism agency Welcome to Yorkshire owing to concerns over the "financial and logistical viability of the plans". It expressed "limited confidence in Welcome to Yorkshire's leadership". Both the department and UK Sport even tried to bypass Yorkshire altogether via the national tourism agency VisitEngland.'

Shadow Culture Minister and Barnsley Central MP Dan Jarvis also went on the front foot. 'Given so many people felt that London was the main recipient from the 2012 Olympics, I am saddened that the Government seem determined to undermine Yorkshire's ability to use this as a unique marketing experience to showcase Yorkshire as an amazing tourist destination,' Jarvis said.

'The Tour de France is a global sporting event that will be watched by millions of people around the world. This fantastic opportunity was brilliantly secured by Welcome to Yorkshire in order to maximise the benefits for Yorkshire people and Yorkshire businesses. Let's be clear, the Tour de France is coming to Yorkshire because of the efforts of Welcome to Yorkshire and Leeds City Council. This is the Yorkshire Grand Départ not the England Grand Départ.'

It was a reaction that echoed the mood of the county. This is our party, ta very much. Hands off.

'Very much so,' says Gary Verity. 'We had a real battle on our hands. There were 170,000 people who signed a petition to back the bid to bring the Tour de France to Yorkshire and we knew that it would enthuse cycling purists. What we didn't realise, so far away from the event, was that the general populace were right behind this too and very excited and enthusiastic; people who've never been on a bike since they were a kid.

'I think they can see that this is our moment to unify behind a common cause. It will be an amazing thing and hopefully help that resurgent pride which is coming through in many different areas. We've won a whole series of awards ... global awards (he gestures towards an array of such trophies on a heaving shelf opposite) ... to put Yorkshire on the map. Last week we got the award from the *Lonely Planet* as the third best place in the world.'

They did too. Just behind Sikkim, India, in first and The Kimberley, Australia, second. Those left chewing dust included Hokuriku in Japan, Victoria Falls in Zimbabwe and Zambia, New Zealand's West Coast and even Texas, USA. Bet *they* couldn't eat a Barnsley chop.

'Amazing, really. Those things would never have been possible under the old Yorkshire Tourist Board, which is why I was very keen to do a number of important things.'

Most obviously, that meant a name change. After all, you can't sell something until your customers know what it is they are supposed to be buying, can you? And for Gary, attention to detail is crucial in painting the bigger picture. His business card, for example, is printed in English and French.

'But it's more than just changing a name, clearly. It is about changing the whole culture of the organisation and, in so doing, helping to do our bit for the county, to help invigorate the economy here. Tourism, which is how we started out, is the third biggest part of the Yorkshire economy. A quarter of a million people rely on it for their jobs and there are a lot of small businesses, as well, that create wealth.

'I think one of the greatest things you can do for your fellow man or woman is to give them a job. It gives them self-esteem, helps them to feed their family and many other good things. Thousands of small businesses employ one, two, three, four or five people. By and large, that's the lifeblood of the sector. There are some very big and successful businesses as well, mind you, but by and large the bedrock of the Yorkshire economy is involved in this. And of course that helps other businesses, because if Yorkshire has a positive image and a feelgood factor and sense of pride about itself...

'It was always said that when Leeds United were winning, productivity in the city on the Monday after the victory was a lot higher than it would have been if they'd lost. Take that back to Yorkshire scale through something like the Tour de France, and hopefully you'll find that the whole county will up its game and perform better on the back of it.'

***

LET's saddle up the specifics. Thirty-seven people currently work for Welcome to Yorkshire: '...doing everything from PR, marketing, social media ... we have an in-house design capacity ... 5,000 different tourism businesses are members of Welcome to Yorkshire ... all of those different functions including finance and the others you'd expect happen here,' Gary Verity points out. 'This is my office. The best thing I ever did four years ago was to get rid of my desk. I should have done it years before. Nowadays, you just use an iPad or a laptop anyway.'

And all of it targetted towards getting that balancing act right - avoiding stereotypical clichés while promoting the county's charms in an outward looking and modern way. The word 'welcome' being smartly chosen.

'We said that we would promote the county on ten themes,' Gary says. 'One is heritage. Another is the great outdoors, our Yorkshire landscape. The Gods were very kind to us, we have this tremendous variation in topography ... gritty Pennines ... limestone country in the Dales ... the Vale of York ... Wolds ... moors and over to the coast, a personal favourite, all the way up from the Humber to Flamborough, Bridlington, Filey, Scarborough, Whitby, Staithes, Robin Hood's Bay and so forth. Stunning.

'I had a meeting with someone doing some marketing around "Yorkshire's east coast" And I said: "Where's the west coast of Yorkshire? And the north coast?" There isn't one. But you can compare the east coast of the country to the west coast, which is quite flat. One of Scarborough's attractions is the cliff, the castle on top there. Go to Blackpool and look inland. It just goes on and on...

'We've got other themes ... take food and drink. It's because of our topography that we can provide the food we do. What we catch in the sea, grow and rear on the land is down to where we are geographically. If we were in the middle of the Sahara, we wouldn't be able to do all that stuff. That's why you've got the heritage of our food and more good quality restaurants in Yorkshire than anywhere else in the UK. If you looked as a visitor at how the food offering has come on in the last thirty, forty, fifty years... it's unbelievable. Now, you'll eat as well in Yorkshire as anywhere in the world. That was never the case before. Holidays in Yorkshire meant chicken in a basket or chicken in a basket. You try and find somewhere nowadays that does chicken in a basket.'

Slouching towards Blubberhouses

Born in Leeds, Gary Verity was educated in the city also, before spending eighteen years working for Royal Insurance, in the UK and overseas. After having opened a Hong Kong office for that company, he became 'a career chief executive'. One day, he took a phone call from a headhunter.

'They explained that they had this great job for me in Yorkshire. I already had a great job but "...with a wife who's dying of terminal cancer you need to get back to Yorkshire to look after your family and everything," they said, which was true. That was what really swung it for me.'

Was such a high-profile role the culmination of some lifelong ambition?

'No, no, not at all. If you'd said to me twenty years ago "what about running the Yorkshire Tourist Board?" it would not have been in my mind. But life is a series of serendipitous happenings often, isn't it? It was as a result of circumstances that I found myself here. But as a proud Yorkshireman it was no hardship to take on.'

His mission: To come into the company, identify what was wrong with it and put it right.

'Exactly. That's what I've done in the past and what I'll continue to do in the future, in whatever capacity I'm doing it. You work out what the problems are, find the solutions to those problems and then, obviously, the tricky bit is the execution of the solutions.'

Was there any stubborn Yorkshire resistance?

'A small amount, but we've probably won most people over by now. You'd have to be a member of the flat earth society to say we'd like to go back to the way we were.'

If foregrounding Yorkshire's supposedly welcoming nature is deliberate policy, then so is the campaign's quirky sense of humour, all the better to counter possible allegations of parochialism. One example being Welcome to Yorkshire's presence at the 2013 Chelsea Flower Show with its 'Le Jardin de Yorkshire': '...a garden that celebrates the landscapes of our glorious county.'

'Very much so,' says Gary. 'With the name Welcome to Yorkshire, we spent a lot of time thinking about that. My chair, Clare Morrow, and I spent a lot of time on the phone, virtually daily, bouncing ideas. Would this work? Would that work? How does this one sound? And we kept coming back to it, after testing ideas out on people, unbeknown to them. Yorkshireness *does* have a welcoming nature. It's in our DNA. Just park to one side the whole idea of tourists and businesses and think about that in a general context. If you look back through history, one of our things is a sense of fairness. Integrity. There is that expression - straight as a die. Wilberforce and his moral crusade ... the good philanthropic work that people from Yorkshire have done, and still do.

'Look at the migrant populations who have settled here for hundreds of years, going right back. We've always welcomed and accepted people wherever they are from into our Yorkshire family, if you want to call it that. I'm sure that's always been the case with visitors too. When people come to Yorkshire we are friendly and welcoming. We'll quite happily talk to strangers, exchanging the time of day and enquiring as to each other's wellbeing. You get strange looks in London if you say "good morning" to a neighbour. Welcome to Yorkshire sits well here. If you tried it in other parts of the UK it might work, but to a lesser degree.'

***

THE clock ticks ever faster. The countdown is on. In just over six months the waiting will be over. Le Tour will be in town and for two glorious days at least, the eyes of the sporting world will be upon us. As one among many who live pretty much directly on the day two route, it's a prospect viewed as much in trepidation as excitement. Who knows what to expect?

Will there be Frenchmen laiking boules on the Stray? Will Pontefract be awash with Parisians, Gargrave with hopping grenouilles? Is Bridlington about to be overtaken by Bretons? Will St Joan slouch towards Blubberhouses as the brass bands of Barnsley are drowned out by 'La Marseillaise'?

Will baguettes forever replace Hovis?

Will we be able to park in front of our house?

What on earth gave Gary Verity such a left-field idea in the first place?

'We came up with a lot of those,' he says. 'The Chelsea Flower Show was another. We had some cracking ideas that would have been quite awesome, but unfortunately they sometimes don't come off. The Tour de France idea came about while I was chair of the Olympics for Yorkshire. I was thinking about the effect the Games would have on London. What could *we* have? We were doing some sporting events under Yorkshire Forward - a major events contract that got novated to Welcome to Yorkshire - but they weren't anything major like the Olympics or on that kind of scale. It was clear to me that we needed a game-changer.

'I was aware of the Tour de France, having done some work around it in a previous life. And it just became so blatantly obvious that if we could get Le Tour to Yorkshire, it would be amazing. I was aware it had been to London in 2007, but cycling is much bigger now than it was back then. So I got in touch with the people in Paris and said: "How about bringing your race to Yorkshire?"

'We had an exchange of emails, but the upshot quite quickly was "come to Paris, let's have a chat and a bit of lunch." So I kind of thought, that means either one of two things. Either they are keen or interested; or they are short of people to take for lunch.'

Which, in Paris, is unlikely.

'Well, quite. And it was actually three years ago yesterday that the first meeting took place.'

Two weeks ago, anyone switching on *Look North* in the Yorkshire region would have seen Gary Verity on stage in the Palais des Congrès during the official Presentation of the 2014 route, sharing the virtues of his home county in the local tongue. 'Someone told me I sound more Yorkshire in French than I do in English,' he chuckles. 'Five thousand journalists there ... live on Eurosport ... 120 different television channels ... it was good. We had one opportunity to change perceptions and give them a glimpse of our Yorkshireness.'

Was that the moment when it all became real?

'Not really, it has been real for a while, to be fair. This year's tour [2013] has been critical in that. We've had the most incredible journey. Twelve months ago, we didn't know we'd got it. We thought we were in with a very strong chance but, if you go back eighteen months to May 2012, when the French first visited us here to look at Yorkshire and see if there was a possibility, we were outsiders in the race. There were plenty ahead of us. But a number of things had happened before - and subsequently - that would work in our favour.

'The time they came here gave us forty-eight hours in which to show off our Yorkshireness, our passion, not just for the county but for the Tour de France and for putting the two together. So we did it in a true Yorkshire way and made sure that they fully understood what we were capable of, what the art of the possible was, and used all of the Yorkshire resources at our disposal to make sure that it was clear that we were not just going to be a bridesmaid and some sort of bit-part player. We had the potential to pull this off.'

Slouching towards Blubberhouses

The subsequent heroics of Bradley Wiggins and team on two wheels, not least in Le Tour itself and the Olympics, together with the impact of London 2012 as a whole, meant that the campaign became '...pretty unstoppable. Others around Europe then tried to derail it and get it to their place, as they would do. But though there was strong competition, it was clear we were in a pretty reasonable place for it.'

The victory, when announced, came on Friday 14 December 2012, via a simple press release stating that a press conference would be held on January 17 in Paris and Leeds. The interest, not unexpectedly, was huge. On both dates.

What was the atmosphere like in this building?

'Buzzing. You've never seen anything like it. I mean, 14 December was the date of my daughter's carol service at school. The service began at exactly the time they put out the release in Paris. Well, you can imagine. I got back here at midnight, by which point you've never seen as many satellite trucks, journalists and TV crews. The BBC were camped out, Sky, ITV, CNN ... so that was completely bonkers. And then of course we had it all again in January.'

And now, with the finishing line in sight, things are gathering pace. Special road signs are going up, the potholes filled in. Just about the only thing, you suspect, that could rain on Yorkshire's parade is the good old British weather.

Not 'Yorkshire weather', mind, I said 'British weather' ... unless there's a week of glorious sunshine, naturally.

'If you remember,' says Gary, 'the summer of 2012 was very wet, but we did have two glorious days. In fact, I think the only two consecutive sunny days were on that visit.' Did he take them to a beer garden? Not quite. Well, not unless you see Yorkshire as the nation's beer garden, anyway.

'They arrived on Eurostar into St Pancras. We then brought them across London to Battersea Heliport, having borrowed a helicopter from a very wealthy and successful Yorkshire businessman. This flew them up to my sheep farm in the Dales. I had personally mown a giant letter 'Y' on the front field for it to land on. We held the meeting at the farm, on sofas just like this one, rather than somewhere more formal. We gave them a letter signed by every Yorkshire MP, bar three. A very good Yorkshire chef cooked lunch. They were blown away by the quality of food and have been every time since. We took them around the Dales in a car and put them in the helicopter again, flying them out to the coast. We then went to a dinner at Harewood House, where we had the head of CBI, head of the TUC, head of IoD, head of the Chamber of Commerce, Chief Constable of Police, council leaders, some of the captains of top Yorkshire businesses and so on, to show "Team Yorkshire" was behind the bid.

'Next day we showed them some of the hotels we would use for the teams and the facilities of Leeds, where they met the chief executive of the Council. We took them to York and showed them the Minster, then walked them back from there to the station, where we put them on the train to London. I think they realised then that we weren't just hicks from the sticks.'

Indeed not. But however the hosting of Le Tour itself turns out - and if you're reading this afterwards in a newly independent Glorious People's Republic of Yorkshire, you'll already know - surely none of it could have been delivered to the county - and country - without huge personal pressure.

My original interview with Gary, scheduled for some four weeks earlier, had been postponed as a result of him feeling 'off-colour'. Subsequently, it was reported that he had undergone hospital treatment for 'heart problems'. How is he shaping up now?

'Yeah, I'm good. How do I look?'

Very relaxed, I reply, because he does.

'Lost a bit of weight, so that's no bad thing.'

It would have to be stressful, though, delivering an enormous event like this?

'Yeah, but it's good though, isn't it? If you were a sports person, what would you rather do? Play in a Challenge Cup final at Wembley or a kick-about on a muddy field?'

And how about when the circus has left? When those colourful jerseys have zipped past in the blink of an eye, leaving us alone to tend our rhubarb? What then, when the world packs up its cameras, kitbags and puncture repair kits?

'I'll have a holiday.'

In Filey or on the French Riviera, I don't like to ask.

***

OUTSIDE it's a coat colder, but the clouds are clearing and blue skies begin to peep through.

Driving home along the Wharfe Valley past the Otley Chevin ridge, with a stunning vista ahead under a whisp of muslin, the thought is inescapable. The world's riders and cycling fans are really going to love it here, aren't they?

Oh, and one more thing.

The first Briton actually to win the Tour de France was Brian Robinson, a Yorkshireman, in 1955. He was also the first to win a stage - to Brest - three years later. Now aged 83, he holds a sportive of his own every April.

Yorkshireness, eh?

If you've got it, flaunt it.

I'll sithee!